CW00433550

Crime Scene Management and Evidence Recovery

Crime Scene Management and Evidence Recovery

Second Edition

Deborah Beaufort-Moore

Consultant Editor:
Tony Cook

OXFORD
UNIVERSITY PRESS

Great Clarendon Street, Oxford, OX2 6DP,
United Kingdom

Oxford University Press is a department of the University of Oxford.
It furthers the University's objective of excellence in research, scholarship,
and education by publishing worldwide. Oxford is a registered trade mark of
Oxford University Press in the UK and in certain other countries

First Edition published in 2009
Second Edition published in 2015

Published in the United States of America by Oxford University Press
198 Madison Avenue, New York, NY 10016, United States of America

British Library Cataloguing in Publication Data
Data available

ISBN 978–0–19–872437–7

Preface

It is a fantastic role, the investigation of crime, no matter what part each individual plays. There is nothing better than solving a crime and giving those that have suffered from it some justice.

Professional integrity—doing the right thing even when no one is watching—is the greatest asset to the investigative process. I hope this book will be an asset to your understanding of the forensic and crime scene processes and potentials.

This book was developed with the role of the operational police officer, police staff and other Law Enforcement Agency (LEA) investigators in mind. There are many books on forensic science that offer guidance to crime scene investigators (CSIs) or those studying or working in forensic science disciplines. However, many of these do not consider in depth the crucial role of the initial responders regarding the preservation and recovery of potential forensic evidence.

The actions of the initial responders are fundamental in the success or otherwise of a forensic examination and the investigation process. Police officers are generally the first officials to arrive at the scene of an incident, and the actions taken at this time can have a huge impact on the outcome of the investigation.

The CSI or forensic scientists are entirely dependent on the initial responders to ensure the potential forensic evidence is maximised. This book has been written for initial responders and non-CSI investigators, with the aim of offering guidance and underpinning knowledge on types of forensic evidence and how to preserve and recover such material to ensure the evidential potential is maximised.

In addition to practical examples for the recovery, packaging and storage of forensic material, there are chapters which provide a basic overview of the different types of forensic evidence that are commonly encountered, the evidential potentials and the limitations of the different analysis of such material.

The information in this book is not intended (nor appropriate) for investigators to undertake the role of a CSI, but to provide an awareness of the potentials available for the forensic examination of crime scenes and the techniques available to a CSI for the recovery of potential forensic evidence. It is important for investigators to be aware of what is available to them in order to consider the best course of action to recover evidence.

The role of the CSI is to support the police investigation by gathering all the relevant material at a crime scene.

Forensic science has provided investigators with great benefits regarding the evidence potentially available to identify persons and link crime scenes; however a key disadvantage to the technological advances is that it can lead to investigators becoming overly reliant on forensic evidence. Whilst forensic science undoubtedly offers huge benefits, investigators must not neglect other aspects of the criminal investigation.

There can be numerous defences regarding the presence of forensic material and it is imperative that an investigator is aware of potential defences and ensures a thorough and robust investigation is undertaken in order to put any forensic evidence into context. Forensic analysis alone does not solve crimes—thorough, professional investigations, using all the tools available to the modern investigator, can.

Deborah Beaufort-Moore
April 2015

Acknowledgements

Sincere thanks must go to the following who have offered support, guidance and advice during the construction of this book, not least to Tony Cook (National Crime Agency), my 'guru' and consultant editor. Grateful thanks go also to Gayle Cranfield, John Veale (Head of the Forensic Training Unit, Specialist Crime Academy, Trinidad and Tobago Police Service), Rob Cleary (CSI and forensic archeologist, of Wiltshire Police), Stephen Bleay (CAST), Andrew Postlethwaite (Virtual Reconstructions) and everyone else in the policing and forensic world who wish to remain nameless.

Grateful thanks also to the anonymous reviewers (you know who you are) whose wisdom, comments and guidance during the writing process have been gratefully received, as has the support and guidance offered by Lucy Alexander of Oxford University Press.

Contents

Contents

Contents

List of Figures and Tables

Figures

Tables

Glossary

Accelerant A flammable material usually in liquid form that is used to promote the ignition and/or spread of fire.

Adipocere The post-mortem presentation whereby body fats become waxy (Saponification) due to the presence of moisture.

Association of Chief Police Officers (ACPO) Former title of The National Police Chiefs' Council (NPCC).

Blood Pattern Analysis (BPA) The analysis of blood stains that may determine impact types, and points of impact to aid in reconstruction of events.

Common Approach Path (CAP) A route established from the cordon to the main scene, to be used by all entering/leaving the scene.

Contemporaneous Notes Notes made at the time or as soon as practicable after an incident. Typically these are written in notepads with numbered pages, such as a police pocket notebook (PNB) or similar. All contemporaneous notes must be kept and are subject to disclosure rules.

Continuity (of evidence) The audit trail which details the movements of an exhibit from the point of recovery to presentation in court.

Cordon A physical barrier to restrict access to a crime scene.

Crime Scene Co-ordinator (CSC) The person with overall responsibility for managing the scientific support functions in serious incidents.

Crime Scene Investigator (CSI) A person trained to identify, record and gather forensic material to support the officers in the investigation of incidents. The title of CSI is not used by all police forces, other titles such as CSE (Crime Scene Examiner) or SOCO (Scenes of Crime Officer) for example may be used to denote the same role.

Crime Scene Manager (CSM) A CSI who will have responsibility for the processing of a particular crime scene.

Diatoms Aquatic micro-organisms. They display individual characteristics that can enable the source of water they originated from to be determined.

ESDA Electrostatic document apparatus used to recover indented impressions on paper.

ESLA Electrostatic lifting apparatus used to recover footwear marks in dust.

Exhibit Any item or material recovered from a crime scene to be used as evidence in an investigation.

Family Liaison Officer (FLO) A person who acts as a point of contact between a victim or victim's family and the police investigation.

Firearm Discharge Residue (FDR) The residues of the propellant and primer produced as a cloud particles following the discharge of a firearm.

Forensic Science Regulator (FSR) Home Office sponsored regulator for all forensic science services provided to police and LEAs.

Forensic Service Provider (FSP) The supplier of forensic analytical techniques.

HOLMES The Home Office Linked Major Enquiry System, computer system for the storage and cross-referencing of information from the investigation of serious incidents.

Ident1 The national system used to compare fingerprints. Formerly known as NAFIS.

Integrity (of evidence) The principle which must be demonstrated to show that the evidence is as it was when recovered and that no unaccountable interference has occurred to it from the crime scene, throughout any examination to the ultimate destination of the court room. The honesty and accountability of evidence.

Latent Not visible to the naked eye.

LEA Law Enforcement Agency

Livescan A system which enables the electronic scanning of fingerprints.

Livor mortis The post-mortem process whereby blood settles into the lowermost areas of a body to present as discolouration.

Locard's 'Principle of Exchange' The principle on which forensic examination is based, which states that there will be a two-way transfer of material when there is contact.

Low Template DNA (LtDNA) A very sensitive technique for recovering DNA from minute samples.

Match probability The likelihood of two randomly selected individuals having an identical DNA profile.

Mitochondrial DNA (MtDNA) Present in cells, it is passed down via the maternal line.

Mummification A post-mortem process that occurs in warm, dry conditions.

National Ballistics Intelligence System (NABIS) A national database holding information on recovered firearms and ballistic material.

National Police Chiefs' Council (NPCC) Formerly ACPO.

NDNAD National DNA database holding DNA profiles from crime scenes and persons.

Nuclear DNA The DNA material present in the nucleus of cells.

Officer in Charge (OIC) The police officer in charge of the overall investigation of volume crime incidents.

Petechiae Pin-prick haemorrhages that can appear in the eyes and skin.

Post-mortem The period following death.

Post-mortem Examination An examination to determine cause of death.

Post-mortem Interval (PMI) The period of time elapsed between death and the discovery of a body.

Presumptive test Tests that can be undertaken to ascertain the presence of certain substances. Positive test results require further analysis for confirmation.

Ricochet The deviation from the original trajectory of a missile, following impact with a surface.

Rigor mortis The post-mortem stiffening of the body.

Senior Investigating Officer (SIO) A senior officer with overall responsibility for the investigation of serious and complex cases.

Ten prints A set of fingerprints taken from persons in order to be checked against crime scene marks.

1

Roles and Responsibilities in Crime Scene Investigations

1.1 **Introduction**

With the increased awareness of forensic potentials to 'solve' crimes, everyone involved in the investigative process should have a good underpinning knowledge of the techniques available to them. It must be said that forensic evidence alone will never 'solve' a crime; any forensic material must always form part of a thorough and robust investigation to put any forensic evidence into context. There are numerous defences to the presence of forensic evidence, due mainly to the minute quantities and transferability of it. With the exception of fingerprints, most forensic evidence can be transferred into and out of crime scenes in many ways.

There are many aspects to an investigation of which forensic examination is but one part. The College of Policing Authorised Professional Practice (APP) provides the underpinning knowledge requirements of policing and investigation via an online site which is in the public domain. It is recommended that non-police personnel offering services to the police familiarise themselves with the investigative process as a whole in order to put their particular role into the wider investigative context.

This book aims to develop the knowledge of the typical forensic evidence types, offering practical guidance on the correct recording, recovery and storage of potential forensic evidence, to initial police responders and to non-police investigators of other law enforcement agencies (LEAs) such as the National Crime Agency, Environmental Health and Border and Immigration agencies, for example, that are required to gather and present forensic evidence as part of their role.

The provision of forensic services to the UK criminal justice system is regulated by the Home Office sponsored Forensic Science Regulator (FSR). The FSR ensures that all forensic services provided to the criminal justice system meet a regime of scientific quality standards. In-force laboratories, crime scene investigators (CSI), pathologists, for example, and external forensic service providers (FSPs) must meet the universal standards and adhere to a set of common policies and practices which are seeking to standardise and professionalise the provision of forensic science services nationally.

The investigation of crimes will generally include some aspect of forensic examination. The level of resources utilised will be dependent on the nature of the incident under investigation. Many police forces will have a forensic/scientific support department that provides a range of forensic examination capabilities. A number of smaller forces are now combining their resources to create larger regional 'hubs' where the majority of forensic examination and analysis will be undertaken. In addition to the in-force crime scene/forensic units, there are a number of privately run FSPs that offer a wide range of forensic examination and analytical services to the police and other investigative agencies.

Each of the units within police crime scene investigation departments has a specific role to support the investigator. The overall responsibility for an investigation, however, will always be that of a police officer where a criminal offence has taken place, as it is they who will be presenting the case to a court.

Where an investigator feels that a particular aspect of forensic examination could be beneficial to the investigation, they should not hesitate to make such requests to a CSI. It can often be the case that a CSI will not be aware of all the information regarding the incident. In order to maximise the potential forensic recovery, officers should give a full and comprehensive account of the incident, outlining the points to prove and key aspects of the investigation to the CSI. It is also important to update the CSI on any new information that comes to light as this may have implications for the scene examination and any subsequent forensic analysis.

There may be valid reasons why a certain process will not be undertaken and a CSI should explain their rationales as to their examination decisions. Every person involved in the investigation is accountable for their actions (or otherwise) and the decisions made should be recorded by the investigator and the CSI.

Following initial police or other LEA attendance at a crime scene, the involvement of different personnel undertaking specific roles will be dependent on the circumstances of the incident. For volume crime incidents, the responsibility for carrying out the overall investigation will fall to a police officer or designated support staff investigator, who may be the designated officer in charge (OIC) of the overall investigation.

For more serious or complex cases a detective will be designated as the OIC. In cases of murder, manslaughter or infanticide, or complex serious/major incidents, a senior investigating officer (SIO) will take overall responsibility for all aspects of the investigation including strategic and budgetary responsibilities.

Forensic examination of crime scenes will generally be at the direction of the OIC or SIO, depending on the incident and in line with national and individual force policies. Initially, the examination of crime scenes for potential forensic material will typically be undertaken by the appropriate units within the CSI department. Depending on the nature of the case, specialist personnel such as forensic scientists may be invited to attend the scenes.

1.1.1 Crime scene investigation roles in the police service

The composition of crime scene investigation departments may vary between forces and regions in the structure, role titles and responsibilities. This chapter will offer a general indication of the typical departmental structure found in the UK, although role titles and departmental structures may differ slightly.

In 1988 a Home Office directive to chief constables identified the aspects of policing duties that could be undertaken by police staff. Crime scene investigation functions were one area of the investigative process identified as appropriate for non-police officers (police staff) to undertake. In some forces, support roles such as CSIs are undertaken entirely by police staff, others have police staff working alongside warranted police officer CSIs.

1.1.2 **Crime scene investigation departmental structure**

A departmental head will have overall responsibility for the crime scene investigation units and any in-force forensic specialist units, which will generally contain a crime scene investigation unit, a fingerprint unit, a photographic/video unit and a fingerprint development/forensic examination laboratory. Each of these units may have a dedicated departmental manager who reports to the head of the department.

1.2 **Roles and Responsibilities within Crime Scene Investigation Departments**

1.2.1 **Crime scene investigation units**

The role title may vary across forces/regions and can include titles such as scenes of crime officers (SOCO), crime scene examiners (CSE) and volume crime scene examiners (VCSE). For clarity, the title of CSI will be used throughout this book to denote this role.

A CSI has a number of key responsibilities, including:

- photographic and/or video recording of crime scenes, victims and property;
- locating and recovering potential physical evidence;
- locating and recovery of finger and palm marks at crime scenes;
- packaging and storage of potential physical evidence to prevent contamination;
- recording and sharing of intelligence on modus operandi (MO);
- offering advice on scientific matters; and
- preparation of statements and giving evidence in court.

The main function of CSIs is to *record, gather* and *preserve* all available potential physical evidence to support the investigating officer in their enquiry. In addition to physical evidence, CSIs should bring to the attention of an investigator any intelligence aspects of the crime scene that are observed during the examination of the scene. *The National Crime Scene Investigation Manual (2007)* (Association of Chief Police Officers (ACPO)/National Policing Agency (NPIA)) states that: 'The CSI should take all reasonable steps to collect fingerprints, forensic and/or photographic evidence from the scene, as appropriate. In all cases as evidence is collected, it must be correctly packaged, sealed and identified, using either a label or indelible marker.'

CSIs can be an invaluable asset in the gathering of intelligence. They are in a position to identify links between crime scenes such as a series of burglaries that have the same MO and/or the presence of similar footwear or glove marks, for example.

CSIs attend court to give evidence on their role in an investigation where required. It is important to be mindful that a CSI can give statements of fact rather than opinion. They can state what they did and how, but CSIs are not generally deemed to be 'expert witnesses' in the sense of being able to give an interpretation of what the evidence may mean.

The types of scenes a CSI will attend are to some extent, dependent on force policies. Although all serious and major investigations will be attended, where volume crime scenes are concerned, the attendance criteria of the force will dictate the CSI response.

1.2.2 **Key roles within CSI**

The role of a CSI requires that training in the identification, recording, recovery and storage of forensic evidence is undertaken. This is provided by the College of Policing forensic training facility where new CSIs will gain the knowledge and practical skills required for the role, with a range of training in specialist forensic areas including fire investigation or footwear analysis, for example, available for career development. A VCSE will not have the training in the skills required to undertake the examination of scenes of serious/complex incidents.

Crime scene manager (CSM)

Depending on the nature of the incident, a CSM may be allocated to oversee examination of a particular scene (see Figure 1.1). The CSM is generally an experienced CSI who has undertaken training in the role of a CSM. The CSM is responsible for the CSIs examining a particular scene where several potential scenes may be identified. They will undertake the necessary risk assessments and ensure the welfare of the examining team in addition to the prioritisation

Figure 1.1 A typical CSI management structure at serious incidents

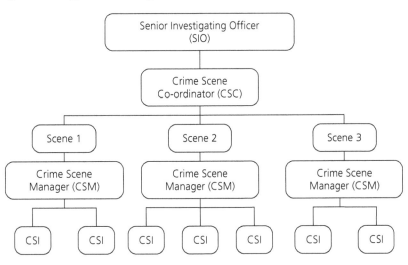

and co-ordination of the examination strategy, in consultation with the investigating officer and crime scene co-ordinator (CSC) where appropriate.

Crime scene co-ordinator (CSC)

A CSC is required where there are multiple scenes and for serious/complex cases and will be responsible for the CSMs and their teams, advising the SIO on appropriate scientific matters and generate forensic strategies in consultation with the SIO, to detail the priorities and processes required from the examination of the scene. It is the role of the CSC, where multiple scenes exist, to ensure staffing resources are met to avoid any contamination or transfer of material by CSIs attending more than one related scene.

The crime scene is a key part of the investigation and as such is ultimately the responsibility of the investigating officer who is in charge of the overall investigation. CSIs are trained to identify, record and gather all potential evidence in order to corroborate or refute allegations that may arise during the investigation and to offer advice and guidance to the investigating officers regarding forensic issues.

It is important to consider that due to civilianisation of the role, a CSI may not have the training in law or the investigative training and experience of a police officer. It can be difficult for CSIs to make an accurate assessment of the forensic potentials at a crime scene if they are not aware of the circumstances that are being investigated. It is important investigators update the CSI where further circumstances come to light which can impact on the scene examination.

Caution must be exercised in deciding the relevance or otherwise of potential evidential material to an investigation. The role of an investigator is to gather *all the available appropriate material.*

It can be easy to dismiss something as irrelevant only to find out later from a suspect or witness account that it was, in fact, very relevant to the investigation. Be mindful that the first opportunity to gather potential evidence can often be the last opportunity. Think of the initial scene investigation as a 'gift'—and **G**et **I**t **F**irst **T**ime.

In the early stages of an investigation, it is impossible to know what may or may not be relevant, so all material must be gathered unless it clearly has no bearing on the incident in question.

An example of where the potential to gather evidential material may be missed is where a defence of legitimate or public access is possible. The term 'legitimate access' is often used to describe circumstances where potential forensic evidence can be expected to be recovered due to lawful reasons. For example, fingerprints on items at a burglary where the householder suspects a previous occupant as being the offender can often lead the investigator to feel there is no benefit in having the scene forensically examined.

In such circumstances, it is important to gather any potential evidence that can later support or refute this assertion. Keep an open mind, rule nothing in and rule nothing out. The home owner may be wrong in their belief that they know the offender; conversely they may be correct. An investigator cannot know what the outcome will be at the time of the scene examination.

It is the role of an investigator to examine *all the available evidence* and allow the court to draw conclusions on the validity or otherwise of any material gathered.

Case study—Legitimate access

A male was reported for photographing females in the adjoining cubicles at a public swimming pool. A decision was made by CSI not to examine the scene as the cubicle was accessible to the public. The CSI rationalised that the suspect could claim 'legitimate access' therefore any potential evidence found would not 'prove the case' and refused to attend the scene.

'Legitimate' access does not in any way reduce the need for a forensic examination. The suspect may deny being at the location in interview, forensic evidence may show otherwise.

If the suspect's fingerprints were recovered from the cubicle, from the top edge between the two cubicles in question, that would lead to deeper questioning of the suspect, as legitimate access would not usually involve such contact. The *location* of evidence is an important factor in corroborating or refuting any allegations.

Where the potential defence of legitimate or public access is anticipated, investigators should aim to gather as much available evidential material as possible. It is ultimately the decision of the court as to what weight they feel can be placed on such potential evidence.

Legitimate or public access situations warrant a more thorough examination rather than being a reason not to undertake examination of a scene.

Any forensic material gathered may not identify a suspect, nor 'prove' or 'disprove' the offence but could provide intelligence information and perhaps be linked to other cases or scenes.

Without a thorough forensic examination it is not possible to know what will be recovered from such scenes.

An investigator should not be afraid to question CSIs regarding the scene examination to clarify what has been done and the rationales employed. If an investigator does not fully understand the processes and the possible value of any potential material gathered, others may not be able to do so either.

1.2.3 The fingerprint unit

The comparison and identification of fingerprints is undertaken by fingerprint experts whose key role is the search for, and comparison of finger and palm prints from a crime scene, with those of persons on the national database 'Ident 1', for the identification of deceased persons where identity is unknown or uncertain and in the comparison of fingerprints for elimination purposes, where a householder, for example, has given their fingerprints to be compared with those recovered from a burglary at their home.

Fingerprint experts may attend crime scenes to assess the quality of marks found and direct the CSI to recover the marks they identify as viable for searching on the national database.

The fingerprint identification officers will give evidence in court and are deemed as holding 'expert witness' status, in that they can offer statements of opinion and interpretation of the fingerprint evidence where applicable.

1.2.4 The in-force forensic laboratory

Force laboratories differ in their titles, partly due to the fact that they can offer a range of applications for evidential recovery in addition to the traditional chemical enhancement processes to develop fingerprints. Many in-force laboratories undertake techniques to recover finger/palm and footwear marks utilising chemical processes and alternative light sources to search for, enhance and record marks on items that are not able to be recovered by a CSI at the scene, including fingermarks, footwear marks, indented writing, fibres and searching items for blood or semen, for example.

Many forces also have the capacity for laboratory technicians to attend crime scenes to utilise the specialist techniques available.

1.2.5 The imaging department

Photographic and video units give additional specialist support to the CSI for digital video recording of the crime scene and are generally responsible for the printing of scene photographs and the production of photographic albums for court and evidential purposes and may, if applicable, undertake and provide aerial photographs of scenes.

The video unit will generally undertake the editing and enhancement of video footage from CCTV, audio enhancements, the conversions of various media formats (old tapes/computer discs for instance), produce photographic stills from video footage and record crime scenes with video. The collation and editing of material from crime scenes to produce presentations and briefings which can be shown in court may also be undertaken.

1.2.6 Forensic submissions department

Potential forensic evidence from a crime scene(s) may require submitting to an external FSP for examination by forensic scientists. There are a number of FSPs offering a range of analytical processes including, for example, analysis of biological fluids for DNA profiling and comparison, the analysis of glass, paint, fibres, soils and drugs. The particular FSP used will differ according to force policies and the nature of the analysis required.

There is a question based approach for submission(s) to a FSP. This aids the decision-making process regarding the level of exhibit submission and the analysis that will be required. It is essentially a two-part process and forensic submission requests are made using the MGFSP/MG21 and MGFSP/MG21A forms. The initial submission process will deal with crime scene material for the recovery of a potential DNA profile which can then be loaded onto, and searched against, the national DNA database (NDNAD) and is the *pre-charge* part of the submission process. This method is for the purpose of the *identification* of persons that may have been involved in an incident. Any material that yields a DNA profile of sufficient quality will be loaded onto and searched against the NDNAD.

The second aspect to the submissions process is the *post-charge* (evidential - EV) route. This requires completion of the MGFSP/MG21A form where evidence is required to secure a conviction or where a suspect has been charged with an offence. It cannot be used to submit evidence where a suspect has not yet been charged or identified, depending on the incident and analysis of exhibits required. (View guidelines on the use of these forms at <http://www.cps.gov.uk>). It is important to complete forms fully as a scientist will only carry out the work that is required to answer the key areas of the offence that have been requested.

The forensic submissions department in-force ensures that relevant documentation is completed accurately and will authorise the submission of the material to the appropriate service provider where appropriate. Key considerations for submissions to be authorised include the value of the potential evidence to the investigation, the likelihood of obtaining a useable result and budgetary (cost vs benefit) considerations.

If material is incapable of having an impact on the case, it is unlikely it will be authorised for submission for forensic analysis.

When completing the documentation for a laboratory submission, it is important to be clear and concise as to the required outcomes, for example:

> To compare a pair of bolt croppers found on person 'A' with cut padlocks recovered from crime scenes X, Y and Z to establish whether they were the same instrument used in these cases.

Ensure that there are sufficient details regarding the case; be mindful that the forensic submissions team and subsequently, the forensic scientist, will not have any prior knowledge or information on the case other than what is supplied on the documentation. If this is vague and does not put the request for analysis into context, the material may not be authorised for submission.

1.2.7 Role of the forensic scientist

Forensic science is the application of scientific analytical principles for the purposes of providing potential evidence in criminal investigations. The provision of such services is overseen by the FSR, and each provider must be accredited and demonstrate that their systems and processes meet the standards required. The FSR issues 'Codes of Practice' for all FSPs covering a range of forensic examination processes and can be viewed online.

The role of the forensic scientist is to examine and analyse any material submitted to them from the crime scene in an impartial, robust and transparent manner.

Forensic scientists are qualified and experienced in a particular scientific discipline. The reporting officer is the person who has the overall responsibility for a particular analytical discipline and will be the person to submit reports and provide any evidence in court.

Forensic scientists are deemed as having 'expert witness' status and can offer statements of opinion and interpretation of the evidence.

There may be the requirement for more than one reporting scientist to examine a particular item, for example where DNA and fibre evidence are present on an item. The specialist nature of the differing disciplines within forensic science means that scientists will develop their expertise in one particular area. They may have a good knowledge of other forensic disciplines but would not typically report or give evidence in court on such.

The forensic analysis of material is generally undertaken by external FSPs. The analysis can take a number of forms, depending on the case requirements and the material submitted. For instance, a scientist may be able to establish links between materials on a suspect with material from a crime scene, confirm the identity of a substance, identify and interpret a sequence of events and compare material gathered from different sources.

Forensic scientists can also offer expert advice and guidance at crime scenes and may be able to offer additional forensic recovery techniques that are not available within the internal police departments. FSPs are available to discuss any queries an investigator may have and will offer advice and guidance on maximising forensic potentials.

Following any forensic examination, the scientist will provide a report of their findings and give expert testimony regarding their analysis and the results in court.

Many providers will refuse to examine items that are improperly packaged where the continuity and integrity of the material may be compromised.

1.3 Key Roles in the Investigation of Serious or Complex Cases

1.3.1 Exhibits officers

An exhibits officer is responsible for the collation and recording of *all* the exhibited material gathered in a major or serious investigation. The exhibits officer is a single point of contact for the SIO regarding any material gathered and will provide the SIO with accurate reports on the status of any material that has been submitted for forensic analysis.

It is a key role of the exhibits officer to ensure the secure storage and accurate documentation of the movements of exhibits and ensure that the continuity and integrity of all the items recovered is maintained. During the course of the investigation any material gathered must be recorded and, where applicable, stored by the exhibits officer.

1.3.2 Disclosure officers

A disclosure officer will review *all* evidence and material in a case in preparation for court. They will make decisions, with the SIO, on what to reveal to the defence under the disclosure rules. Disclosure rules can be complex. Simply put, evidence is to be disclosed where:

- it assists the defence; or
- it undermines the prosecution.

Unless it is a serious offence or major incident, the disclosure may be undertaken by the investigating officer when preparing the case file for court. In some forces police staff undertake the role of a disclosure officer.

Both the exhibits officer and disclosure officer may form part of a larger team with distinct roles known as a HOLMES team (Home Office large major enquiry system), a computerised system to collate and cross-reference *all* the material gathered in major incidents or as part of a disaster victim identification process where it is known as a 'Casualty Bureau'.

1.3.3 Family liaison officers (FLOs)

FLOs undergo specialist training for their role and are generally deployed in cases involving fatalities but can also be utilised in cases where there has been no fatality, for victims of hate crime, for example. The FLO is the point of contact between the victim and/or the victim's family (where the victim is deceased) and the police investigation.

It is the role of the FLO to ensure that the information required for the investigation is obtained with as little impact on the victim or the victim's family as possible, and to provide them with information on the progress of the case and offer explanations into the investigative procedures. The information given to victims and/or victims' families regarding the investigation must be authorised by the SIO in order that the investigation is not compromised.

The FLO will be instrumental in ensuring support mechanisms are put in place as appropriate, such as referral to support services.

1.3.4 Coroners

The role of the coroner is to confirm the identity of the deceased and establish the medical cause of death which will be recorded on a death certificate. In addition a coroner will establish the manner of death, for example whether death occurred through natural causes, accident or suicide.

Where a doctor is satisfied that death is due to natural causes they can issue a death certificate and give authorisation for the body to be released for funeral arrangements to be made. However, where cremation is planned a second medical examination is required prior to the issue of a death certificate.

There are certain cases that, although deemed to be 'natural causes', must always be reported to the coroner. These include the following circumstances:

- where death occurs in legal custody, even where such death may occur in a hospital during the serving of a custodial sentence;
- where food poisoning is suspected;
- where an individual has undergone a surgical procedure in the three months preceding death;
- where the deceased has not been seen by a doctor in the two weeks preceding death;
- where industrial diseases are suspected; and
- where the individual is known to be an alcoholic.

In all cases where the death is regarded as unnatural, unexpected or suspicious in any aspect, the doctor cannot issue a death certificate. The death will be reported directly to the coroner for investigation. The coroner typically receives notification of such deaths from doctors, hospitals and the police.

If the coroner decides that the death is due to natural causes, the police investigation will not continue. If the coroner deems that the death requires further investigation, they may request a pathologist carries out a post-mortem examination. Where the post-mortem demonstrates that the death was due to natural causes, the coroner is not legally required to hold an inquest and the body can be released for a funeral.

An inquest will be held where the coroner is not satisfied that the death was due to natural causes. An inquest is held to establish the facts surrounding the death, which include the identification of the deceased, the medical cause of death and when, where and how the death occurred. It is not for a coroner's inquest to apportion blame or culpability; that is the remit of the criminal courts. Where a body has been released for burial and the police feel that the case requires further investigation the coroner can order an exhumation of the body for further examination.

1.3.5 Coroners' officers

This role can be fulfilled by a police officer or police staff to provide a point of contact between the coroner, pathologist, the police investigators, FLO and the family of the deceased, the defence teams and any other interested party, for example the Health and Safety Executive (HSE).

The coroners' officer will undertake the organisation and collation of material surrounding the identification of the deceased and the circumstances surrounding the death, and will gather as much information and potential evidence as required to support the coroner in the investigation of case.

1.3.6 **Forensic pathologists**

A forensic pathologist will examine the body, known as the post-mortem (PM). This will typically involve an examination of the exterior of the body and where necessary an internal examination, depending on the circumstances of the case. There are two categories of PM: the clinical and the medico-legal post-mortem.

POINT TO NOTE—CLINICAL AND MEDICO-LEGAL POST-MORTEMS

A *clinical post-mortem* involves examination of a body where the deceased has been treated for an illness prior to death and the cause of death is believed to be as a result of the illness. The clinical post-mortem is undertaken to verify the diagnosis of the illness and can only be undertaken with the consent of the next of kin.

The *medico-legal post-mortem* is undertaken where death has occurred unexpectedly and/or the circumstances surrounding the death are regarded as suspicious or unlawful. Such an examination can only be undertaken by Home Office registered forensic pathologists.

Forensic pathologist examinations are generally attended by CSIs who photographically record the examination and recover any material such as clothing and forensic samples under direction of the pathologist.

A forensic scientist or appropriate specialist may be present on the invitation of an SIO depending on the nature of the case. The forensic pathologists can attend crime scenes to examine a body *in situ* if requested by the SIO. Where circumstances of the death are suspicious, the attendance of a forensic pathologist at the scene can be beneficial.

Identification of the body should be made by two independent people where possible prior to a post-mortem, but this may not be possible due to the condition of the body, or where such persons may be involved in the death. In such cases other techniques such as fingerprints or DNA analysis may be required.

The pathologist will examine the body externally first, making notes and requesting photography of any observations. Any clothing will be carefully removed from the body and examined for any potential evidential features, such as cuts from a knife, for example. Forensic samples may be taken from under fingernails or from hair, for example, before the body is opened up in order to examine internal organs. Samples of body fluids such as blood and urine are taken along with, where appropriate, stomach and intestinal contents, and samples of organs such as the liver, heart and lungs may be recovered depending on the circumstances.

Such examinations do not require the consent of the next of kin and need to be dealt with sensitively, explaining that the reason for the examination is in order to find out what happened and to bring the offenders to justice.

Be aware that some cultures have very stringent rules regarding the body of a deceased, burial or cremation processes and it is important to be mindful of such and—where possible—accommodate the needs of the family.

A number of post-mortem examinations may be required on behalf of the defence team, as each defendant can direct an independent post-mortem to be carried out with the permission of the coroner. The undertaking of independent post-mortem examinations should not unduly delay the release of the body as this can cause further distress to the family.

Where a person has died whilst hospitalised following an assault, for example, and a post-mortem examination is potentially required, organ donation must not be allowed to occur without the consent of the coroner and where applicable, the defence team where a person has been charged.

The SIO, coroner and pathologist will consider all the implications any organ donation would have on the post-mortem examination before reaching a decision on such matters.

1.4 **Health and Safety at Crime Scenes**

One aspect of crime scene examination that is the responsibility of all police personnel is to ensure the health and safety of all persons present at the scene and those who will be handling any materials subsequently recovered.

In addition to the general hazards which will be covered by operational generic risk assessment of injuries being sustained from slips, trips and falls, the crime scene can contain specific hazards which require dynamic risk assessments to be undertaken. Crime scenes can include a variety of hazards, including those arising from biological fluids or tissue, chemicals, toxins and bites from insects.

The hazards potentially present at crime scenes are numerous. The following list is by no means exhaustive.

1.4.1 **Blood borne infections**

The hepatitis B virus is present in body fluids such as blood, saliva, semen and vaginal fluid. It can be passed via an open wound, or needle stick injury. A vaccine is available for those at risk of becoming exposed to potentially infected body fluids—contact the occupational health unit (OHU) in-force for guidance regarding obtaining a vaccination.

Hepatitis C is also a blood borne viral infection, although it can, very rarely, be transmitted through other body fluids. It is a commonly encountered disease amongst intravenous drug users. It can be transmitted when infected blood enters the blood stream, such as needle stick injuries. HIV is a virus spread through bodily fluids such as blood, semen and vaginal fluids. The virus can also be spread through sharing needles. It can be passed from infected body fluids via an open wound, or needle stick injury.

The risk of infection from body fluids can be high and protective clothing must be worn when handling material contaminated with body fluids or tissue. Be mindful that dried blood can be as hazardous as wet blood with regard to the transmission of infections. As blood dries small particles can become airborne and subsequently be inhaled or ingested.

All operational investigators required to attend incidents where such contact is a risk should ensure hepatitis B and tetanus inoculations are up to date.

Wounds such as cuts or animal bites can become infected with bacteria, especially if the wound is deep or if it gets contaminated with soil or manure, but even small wounds can allow enough bacteria to get into your body to cause tetanus.

All personnel exposed to the risk of cuts from items that are dirty with soil or manure must ensure that their tetanus inoculation is up to date.

1.4.2 **Chemical burns**

Hydrofluoric acid is extremely corrosive and can cause chemical burns to the skin.

Burned out vehicles present the risk of contact with hydrofluoric acid as the material used for many gasket rings and seals, when heated to around 400°C, will decompose on contact with water to form a charred or black sticky mass.

Touching such areas with bare skin must be avoided at all costs. If it is required to check the vehicle for identifying marks or serial numbers this should be done wearing safety goggles and sturdy impervious gloves, ensuring that bare skin is not exposed.

If contact with bare skin occurs, the area should be rinsed in clean water and calcium gluconate solution or gel should be applied to the area as soon as possible. Medical treatment must be sought following any contact with hydrofluoric acid. Gloves or clothing that may contain hydrofluoric acid must be destroyed in line with force policies regarding contaminated items.

Illicit drug laboratories and cannabis growing facilities may contain chemicals that cause harm on inhalation, ingestion or via skin absorption so care must be taken at such scenes and personal protective equipment (PPE) worn at all times when searching such locations.

1.4.3 **Weil's disease**

This can be transmitted via the urine of rats, cattle, foxes and other wild animals. The urine may be present in soil or water. The disease can enter the body via exposed cuts or through the nose, mouth and other mucus membranes such as the eyes.

Although Weil's disease is relatively rare, be mindful of the potential for the risk of this and other infections when searching areas that may be contaminated by the urine of animals.

1.4.4 **Lyme's disease**

This can be contracted from ticks which are generally found on sheep, deer, hedgehogs and other wild animals. When searching areas of woodland, grassland or similar overgrown areas where ticks could be present, protective oversuits tucked into boots and gloves should be worn, which prevent ticks from gaining access to bare skin.

1.4.5 **Legionnaire's disease**

This can be caused by inhalation of water droplets containing high levels of the Legionella bacteria. The bacteria are extremely hardy and can develop and survive in streams, lakes, moist soil, mud and on inner surfaces of moisture bearing pipes containing a layer of slime.

The bacteria normally tends not to cause infections in the natural environment, but can develop to harmful numbers in man-made water systems such as in air-conditioning and cooling systems, spas and other warm-water baths, water reservoirs in humidifiers or indoor irrigation systems.

Be aware of the risk of infection when dealing with hydroponic systems such as those used in cannabis cultivation. As the bacterium is infectious by inhalation of water droplets, a mask covering the nose and mouth is required in addition to gloves.

1.4.6 **Personal welfare**

Dealing with scenes involving death and violence can have adverse effects on the mental health of those investigating such incidents on a regular basis. The impact of such cases can manifest itself in many ways, sometimes the symptoms are quite subtle and can include increased use of alcohol or other drugs, sleep disturbances, anxiety and irritability. There are many symptoms of stress and post-traumatic stress disorder (PTSD) is recognised as affecting police and other emergency personnel who deal with scenes of death and violence regularly. Complex PTSD (C-PTSD) relates to the effects of long term exposure to distressing incidents—it is not necessarily the most gruesome scenes that can cause problems; the cumulative effect of regular exposure to incidents of heightened stress can be as harmful to health. It is important to be aware of signs of stress and to take action if you feel yourself or a colleague may be displaying behaviours that could indicate they are experiencing symptoms of stress. OHUs, doctors and charities for PTSD and stress can all give guidance and support on such matters. There may also be environmental factors in the location of the scene that can cause heightened stress levels, such as where gang violence and anti-police/hostile sentiments are prevalent in the community. It is important that this is included in risk assessments. The impact of lone working in such environments is to be considered during risk assessments and steps should be taken to ensure the personal safety of investigating personnel from hostile members of the public.

1.5 **Chapter Summary**

Responsibility for the overall investigation into a criminal incident lies with a police officer. However, depending on the nature of the incident, it could be non-police personnel such as a member of the Independent Police Complaints Commission or the HSE, for example, who may take responsibility for employing the different specialisms available for forensic examination of a scene.

CSIs are trained to identify and recover appropriate material in consultation with the OIC/SIO. For volume crime incidents the CSI will generally make the appropriate submissions in line with force policy to the applicable specialist unit, for example the fingerprint bureau, fingerprint development laboratory or external FSP.

Where fatalities occur, the criminal investigations department (CID), the coroner, a coroner's officer, possibly a family liaison officer (FLO) and a forensic pathologist may become involved.

The role of the CSI and the specialist forensic examination units is to support the police investigator in the investigation of a crime.

KNOWLEDGE CHECK—ROLES AND RESPONSIBILITIES IN THE INVESTIGATION OF CRIME SCENES

1. What is the role of the CSI CSM?

   A CSM is responsible for the CSIs examining a particular scene, particularly where several potential scenes are identified. They will undertake the necessary risk assessments and ensure the welfare of the examining team, prioritise and co-ordinate the examination strategy of the scene, in consultation with the investigating officer and CSC where appropriate.

2. Name the units that typically make up the Crime Scene Investigation department.

   CSI, fingerprint unit, photographic/video unit, forensic submissions unit, specialist laboratory for development of marks and searching of exhibits with light sources.

---

3. State the purpose of a coroner's inquest.

   A coroner's inquest is a public enquiry which seeks to establish the medical cause and the manner of death (eg, suicide, accidental or natural causes). It is not the remit of the coroner's inquest to establish any blame or culpability.

4. What is the role of a Home Office forensic pathologist?

   To undertake a forensic medical examination (post-mortem) of the deceased to identify, record and recover any potential evidential material in cases of unexplained or suspicious or unlawful deaths.

5. What circumstances surround who can issue a certificate of death?

   A doctor can issue a certificate of death and give authority to release the body to the family where there are no suspicious or unexplained circumstances, and the doctor believes death is as a result of natural causes.

   Where cremation is planned a second medical examination is required prior to the issue of a death certificate.

   A certificate of death cannot be issued without referral to the coroner where death occurs in legal custody, even where such death may occur in a hospital during the serving of a custodial sentence.

   Other circumstances which must be referred to the coroner include where:

   1. food poisoning is suspected,

   2. an individual has undergone a surgical procedure in the three months preceding death,

   3. the deceased has not been seen by a doctor in the two weeks preceding death,

   4. industrial diseases are suspected,

   5. or if the individual is known to be alcoholic.

   In all cases where the death is regarded as unnatural, unexpected or suspicious in any aspect, the doctor cannot issue a death certificate.

Recommended Reading

Crime Investigators' Handbook (2013) Cook, T, Hill, M and Hibbitt, S.

Family Liaison Officer Guidance (2008) ACPO.

Forensic Science Regulator website: <http://www.gov.uk/government/organisations/forensic-science-regulator>.

Guidance on DNA Charging <http://www.cps.gov.uk/legal/assets/uploads/files/pdf_000328%20-%20%20DNA%20Charging%20Guidance.pdf>.

Investigating Burglary: A Guide to Investigative Options and Good Practice (2011) ACPO.

Investigation—APP <http://www.app.college.police.uk/app-content/investigations/?s=>.

Investigation of Volume Crime Manual <http://www.acpo.police.uk/asp/policies/ Data/volume_crime_manual.doc>.

National Crime Scene Investigation Manual (2007) ACPO/Centrex.

Post Mortem Examinations and the Early Release of Bodies Home Office Circular No. 30/1999.

Practice Advice Core Investigative Doctrine (2005) ACPO.

Crime Scene Preservation and Management

2.1 **Introduction**

Rapid technological advances within forensic science mean that the police and other Law Enforcement Agency (LEA) investigators need to be aware of the implications of the two crucial issues of *contamination* and *transfer* of evidence and take steps to minimise such. Failure to do so can render any potential evidence unfit for analysis or inadmissible in a court of law. The success of the crime scene investigator (CSI) or forensic examiner to recover material that can be used as evidence in court is dependent, to a large extent, on the actions of the initial responders. Police officers are usually the first officials to arrive at the scene of an incident and have a number of responsibilities to undertake—some of which may conflict with the need to preserve the scene. It may not always be possible to keep a crime scene in a sterile condition; however the actions of the initial responders can have a huge impact on the subsequent investigation.

POINT TO NOTE—TERMS

The term 'investigator' as used within this book encompasses the roles of police officers, police community support officers (PCSOs), other designated police investigations staff and other LEAs. The term 'initial responder' relates solely to police officers.

This chapter outlines the actions and procedures which should be employed by initial responders to preserve the crime scene, minimise the destruction or loss of material and to maximise the forensic evidential potentials within a scene. The importance of the responsibility required of initial responding officers cannot be overstated in achieving a successful forensic examination.

The Association of Chief Police Officers (ACPO)/National Policing Improvement Agency (NPIA) manual, *Investigating Burglary: A Guide to Investigative Options and Best Practice* (2011) states this principle succinctly:

> Gathering evidence as expediently and accurately as possible is essential to the success of a burglary investigation. The most significant contributing factor is the first investigators report and the quality of the actions taken at the scene.

This is true of any crime scene, not just burglary. The role of the initial responders is to preserve and protect the scene in order to maximise the evidential recovery opportunities for the CSI and the investigation team as a whole.

It is important that initial responders deal calmly in taking steps to preserve a crime scene. There is no doubt that some scenes will be distressing and may create heightened emotions, but once any preservation of life steps have been taken where appropriate, taking slow, considered actions, as outlined here and in the College of Policing Authorised Professional Practice (APP) online training material, ensures that the scene is preserved in a professional and forensically sound manner that will ensure the best evidence possible can be obtained and such actions will withstand scrutiny in court.

2.1.1 What is a crime scene?

A crime scene is generally regarded as being the location where an offence occurred; however, there will always be 'satellite' scenes. These are other related aspects of the incident, such as offenders, victims and possibly witnesses who may have had contact with the suspect or victim, any vehicles used, other related premises and deposition sites where weapons, bodies or other relevant items may have been deposited.

Each is a separate and distinct 'crime scene' in its own right and should be approached with a view to preserving any available forensic material.

Consider that each offence always has a minimum of two 'scenes'. For example, a dwelling burglary where the homeowner was not present has essentially a minimum of two scenes, the offender and the location—if these two aspects can be forensically linked, it can strengthen the case against the offender.

The number of scenes would increase where vehicles are used or the homeowner was present and had contact with the offender, for example. Locard's 'Principle of Exchange' illustrates the two-way transfer principle; *every contact will leave a trace*, making it possible to link scenes together. The term 'forensic' is used generically to describe the range of scientific analysis of material that is available to investigators to enable them to establish/confirm the identity of persons and to ascertain the existence of any links between scenes and offenders.

Locard's Principle of Exchange

> Any action of an individual, and obviously the violent action constituting a crime, cannot occur without leaving a trace.

Put simply, when *A* comes into contact with *B*, traces of *A* will be left on *B*, and vice versa. Every contact will leave a trace, whether that be fingerprints, DNA, fires, soil, etc. With increasingly sensitive analytical science techniques, more can be gleaned from decreasing amounts of material.

All those attending crime scenes *must* be aware that they too can both introduce and remove minute traces of material.

There will *always* be a transfer of material between a person and items that they come into contact with. This means that investigators and others attending a scene must be aware of where they walk and what they touch. Material can be brought into and taken out of a crime scene by initial responders and others attending the scene.

Treating offenders, victims, witnesses (where appropriate) and associated locations (eg, vehicles, weapons or premises) each as a separate and distinct 'scene' means that the issues of transfer and contamination are brought to the fore. Investigators must be aware of such issues and take steps to reduce the risks. An investigator who deals with the crime scene should avoid dealing with a suspect or victim or any other associated 'scene(s)'.

Scenario 1—Potential forensic links

A homeowner returns home to find a person attempting to gain entry via a broken window. The victim tries to detain the person, a brief struggle ensues and the offender runs off. The homeowner runs after the offender and sees a vehicle making off at speed down the road. The homeowner reports that a window was smashed by the offender and that no entry was believed to have been gained. A plastic holdall and a metal bar have been left at the scene by the offender.

How many 'scenes' are there?

There are potentially four—the location and items left behind, the homeowner, the offender and the vehicle. There may also be material that can be forensically linked to other crime scenes.

What potential evidence may be available at this scene?

The metal bar and bag may have fingerprints and/or DNA material available as they were brought to the scene by the offender. There will be footwear marks present which could be used if of sufficient quality. Tyre marks may be present which could be useful if of sufficient quality, to compare with suspect vehicle tyres. Glass fragments from the window can be compared with any glass on a suspect's clothing. Fibre evidence may be available on the window from the suspect. Fibres from the suspect may be on the victim's clothing and vice versa, due to the struggle.

The CSI should ideally attend and examine the scene and recover the bag, the metal bar, and a footwear mark beneath the window, glass samples, fibres and glove marks from the window frame and items of homeowner's clothing.

Figure 2.1 illustrates the potential evidence available and the links that may potentially be made forensically. A summary explanation of the evidential links is given in the following checklist.

Checklist—Summary of forensic links

Fibres

- Between victim and suspect. Fibres from the victim may be on the offender and vice versa due to the struggle.

- Fibres from the victim may also be found in the suspect's vehicle.

- The victim's clothing should be seized where there has been bodily contact with an offender.

Plastic holdall

- Between scene and suspect, may also link to other scenes due to material including fibres or glass recovered in or on the bag.

- Possibility of fingerprints being chemically developed on bag.

- Potential for DNA recovery on handles.

- May link to suspect's vehicle through fibres or similar from the vehicle being on the bag.

- Impressions left in a surface by a tool can be photographed and a cast made of the impressed mark. If a tool is used to break a window, there may be glass present on the tool.

- Consider whether the bag may have been stolen from previous incidents or a similar bag being described by witnesses at other scenes.

Metal bar

- Between suspect, scene, other scenes and possibly suspect vehicle.

- Fingerprints and DNA recovery may be possible depending on the condition of the bar.

Footwear mark

- Can be linked to the footwear that made the mark.

- Footwear marks will be present at every crime scene; the mark can be recorded and recovered to compare with suspect's footwear. It may be possible for the make and model of the footwear to be identified.

Tyre mark

- Tyre marks can be compared to the tyres that made the mark. It may be possible for the make and model of the tyre to be identified. A partial tyre mark with no distinct pattern will not enable investigators to identify the make and model of the tyre.

Glove marks

- May provide links between other scenes, the suspect and the suspect's vehicle.
- Glove marks can provide evidence of links between different scenes.
- The glove marks may also be in the suspect's vehicle, premises or indeed on the suspect's person.
- The gloves may contain glass from the scenes.

Glass

- Links may be made between the suspect, the location and the suspect's vehicle.
- Glass fragments may be recovered on the suspect or suspect's clothing and in the suspect's vehicle. Links with glass recovered from other scenes may also be established.

Figure 2.1 Potential forensic links

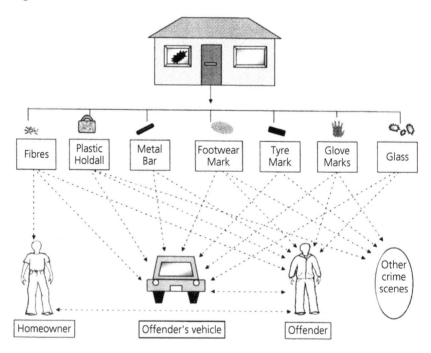

It is important to remember that potential forensic evidence can be present in microscopic amounts. Such material is therefore vulnerable to loss, damage, destruction, contamination and cross-transfer if preservation of the scene is not undertaken properly.

Cross-transfer of material such as glass, fibres and body fluids can occur in police vehicles. For example, fibres from a victim transported in a police vehicle can transfer to the vehicle seat.

If a suspect is later arrested and transported in the same vehicle, it can be argued that any fibre evidence linking the victim and suspect was gained through both parties sitting on the same seat. For this reason, recording the vehicle details in contemporaneous notes (pocket notebook (PNB) or similar) is advisable.

In cases where evidence of contact is required, when transporting persons, placing a disposable paper sheet on the seat and backrests acts as a barrier to reduce the transfer of material. This sheet should then be carefully retained to ensure any material stays on the paper sheet and exhibited.

2.1.2 **Purpose of crime scene preservation**

It is vital that crime scenes are preserved in order to maximise the potential for gathering any material which can corroborate or refute allegations or versions of events. Much of the material gathered in the initial stages of the investigation may not be used in court, but this does not mean it should not be gathered, recorded and stored correctly. It is impossible at the outset of an investigation to know what material will or will not be utilised as evidence.

Definition—Material

Material is defined in accordance with the Criminal Procedure and Investigations Act 1996 Code of Practice under Part II of the Act:

Material is material of any kind, including information and objects, which is obtained in the course of a criminal investigation and which may be relevant to the investigation; Material may be relevant to an investigation if it appears to an investigator, or to the officer in charge of an investigation, or to the disclosure officer, that it has some bearing on the offence under investigation or any person being investigated, or on the surrounding circumstances of the case, unless it is incapable of having any impact on the case.

Material can be used as evidence, intelligence or information or a combination of these.

The first opportunity to gather the material is often the last and it is much better to collect something that is not used, than to leave something behind that could be important.

Irrespective of the time elapsed between the incident and the attendance of investigators, failure to protect and preserve the scene at the earliest opportunity can lead to potential evidence being lost or destroyed.

At the outset of any investigation, information on the incident is usually limited, so it is vital to be open minded. The ABC principle sets out the approach that all investigators should adopt when dealing with any incident:

Assume nothing
Believe nothing/no-one
Challenge everything

In addition, the 'C' could include 'clarify, consider and check' everything. Investigators should never accept at face value what is presented to them and should always consider other possible explanations for the presence or absence of material. Investigators should never hesitate to question the CSI or forensic scientists about any material they recover. If investigators do not understand the material, it may be difficult to explain it to others.

It is not uncommon for the CSI at the scene to have a limited knowledge of the event under investigation, so communication with the scene examiners is vital to ensure potential evidence is maximised.

The purpose of preserving a crime scene is to maximise the recovery of material by the CSI, which may then provide evidence to identify and link offenders, victims and locations and serve to indicate the sequence of events. In order for the recovered material to be admissible as evidence, it is vital that the integrity of the scene can be demonstrated and that no unaccountable interference or contamination could have occurred, either accidentally or deliberately.

The principles of crime scene preservation are essentially the same for a dwelling burglary or a murder: to protect the potential evidence. The scale and procedures employed will differ greatly according to the specific offence. For example, a volume crime incident such as criminal damage to a vehicle will not warrant the closing of roads and the instigation of a scene log, but the principles of preserving the evidence remain as valid for volume crime as for serious incidents.

2.2 Roles of the Initial Responder

The actions taken by the initial responders at the scene can have a huge impact on the investigation. Destruction, contamination and transfer of material are most likely at the time of the initial response. When an investigator is tasked to an incident, there may be several demands competing for attention such as violent confrontations, public disorder, injuries, distressed victims or witnesses.

Whilst the simplest rule is to stay out of crime scenes and touch nothing, this is not always appropriate.

There may be occasions where initial responders have no alternative but to enter a crime scene prior to the forensic examination in order to fulfil the key role of a police officer—to preserve life. When this function has been fulfilled however, initial responders must then concentrate on securing and preserving the scene until the CSI arrives.

Any actions undertaken at a crime scene must be recorded, rationalised and undertaken with as much care as possible in order to minimise any loss, destruction or contamination or transfer of evidence. It is important to be open and honest about your actions within a crime scene as these can be taken into account by the CSI.

Failure to report your actions within a crime scene accurately can lead to unnecessary and costly analysis being undertaken, not to mention the damage that will be done if something you do not declare initially is revealed in court.

Be mindful that the media and members of the public at scenes may record your actions, as highlighted in the Omagh bombing appeal where it was reported that investigators stated they wore protective suits at the scene, however media images showed that they did not. The implications of such exposure are huge, casting doubt on the honesty, integrity and professionalism of the investigators and the police service.

2.3 **The Five Building Blocks Principle**

The five building blocks principle is an excellent framework for approaching an investigation. With regard to the crime scene preservation, the framework can be applied with the following considerations.

2.3.1 **To preserve life**

The preservation of life is a fundamental responsibility of police officers; however this can sometimes be in conflict with the principles of scene preservation. Preservation of life will *always* take precedence over forensic issues. There are steps that can be taken to reduce the impact of officers' and paramedics' initial actions to administer first aid or check for vital signs of life. In such situations:

- Record what has been done. If items have been moved, note the original position and final position.
- Make sketch plans and concise notes showing the layout of the scene.
- Establish a single route into and out of the scene, known as common approach paths (CAP), which should be recorded on any sketch plan.
- Be prepared to hand over your footwear and clothing to the CSI if requested.
- Inform the officer in charge (OIC)/senior investigating officer (SIO) and the CSI of your actions.
- Any materials used by medical teams should remain *in situ*, at the location and on the person in the case of fatalities.

- Ensure contact details of any medical crew attending are obtained—*do not however delay them in their duties to attend to a casualty to get such information.*
- Request the medical crew retain any clothing that they may cut from the victim during transport to and/or at hospital if applicable. It is helpful if you can supply them with appropriate packaging if an officer will not be escorting the casualty.
- If injuries are life threatening, request that a pre-transfusion blood sample is taken.
- Ask the medical team for their prognosis on the condition of the victim to update the OIC/SIO.
- Investigators who have dealt with the victim within the scene have the potential to transfer material to other aspects of the scene. Avoid direct contact with the CSI or other investigators who may be required to arrest suspects or examine related locations.
- Investigators and CSI should record the fleet number of the vehicle travelled in after the event.

....

Case study—Initial observations

A police officer arrived at an address to undertake a welfare check. This proved to be the scene of a murder. The officer secured the premises and waited outside the address for support to arrive. The officer noted a dry area the size of a vehicle on the road by the kerb outside the address. It had been raining heavily for some time, ceasing approximately 30 minutes before the officer arrived. By the time other officers arrived it had started to rain again and the dry area was disappearing.

The observation of this officer, which was noted on a sketch diagram, indicated the possible presence of a vehicle during a specific timeframe, enabling investigators to factor this in during questioning of neighbours. It transpired that the absent vehicle belonged to the victim and had been stolen by the offender within the thirty minutes prior to the officer's arrival. This kind of information was incredibly useful to the investigation.

....

2.3.2 **Preserve scenes**

Potential forensic evidence can be microscopic. Destruction, loss, transference and contamination of such material are very real risks. In order to maximise the recovery of material, the scene needs to be preserved.

In order to preserve crime scenes for forensic examination it is important to first 'identify' the scene(s). In some cases the scene may be fairly obvious, for example, a burglary scene may be the premises and the immediate vicinity such as garden area. In some cases the extent of the scene may not be obvious, look for entry and exit routes that may have been used by the offenders or victims and consider the possibility of other linked scenes, such as vehicles used.

Scenario 1—Cordons

A female victim awoke to find a male in her bedroom searching through her belongings. The offender made threats to shoot the female with the firearm he was holding if she screamed. The offender then raped the female.

The initial responders secured the bedroom where the alleged offence occurred by closing the door and stopping anyone going into the room.

The problem here is that no consideration was given to entry and exit points of the offender, who must have entered via the ground floor front door and traversed through the kitchen, and up the stairs (there was neither rear door access nor other viable routes to the bedroom).

The potential for the loss and destruction of any potential evidence in this situation is huge as further investigators arrived and walked around the ground floor.

What potential evidence may have been available from the entry/exit points?

Footwear marks, fingerprints, tool marks/glass (if door was forced) fibres or hair at point of entry and on stairway, other particulates (soil or paint flakes) and DNA-bearing material such as body fluids on the stair wall, banister rail, door handles/frames, etc.

Where would you put the cordon in this instance?

A more appropriate initial cordon would be to cordon off the premises at the front gate and allow access only to scene examiners initially.

Once a potential scene has been identified it needs to be secured if forensic examination of the scene is required. Securing a scene means preventing access to the area by anyone other than authorised personnel (CSI, Home Office pathologist and those authorised by the SIO).

Indoor scenes are relatively easy to secure by the closing of doors and restricting entry into the premises, initially by the presence of investigators at entrance and exit points.

Restricting access at outdoor scenes can be achieved by the use of physical barriers or cordons. Methods for cordoning an area include the use of police cordon tape and vehicles to block entrances and police or designated police staff positioned at key areas of potential entry can be utilised to set a cordon. Natural boundaries such as hedges and fences can form part of cordon, bearing in mind the potential for offenders to have discarded items such as weapons or stolen property over such boundaries.

The general rule for cordons is 'bigger is better'. It is less problematic to reduce a crime scene cordon than it is to increase it. However, a cordon that is not controlled to restrict access is of little use. Cordons should be manageable, and whilst bigger is better, it is not always appropriate or practical on initial arrival. The CSI and SIO will review cordon parameters on their arrival and make any adjustments as necessary and at any time during the examination should further information come to light.

For serious cases, two cordons may be set. A smaller inner cordon to protect the immediate area of the incident usually sited around the body or attack site. The size of an inner cordon ideally should enable room for CSI to undertake examinations and for a team to remove a body (where applicable). A larger outer cordon should be set with wider parameters to allow a search of areas that may contain potential evidence and to stop public access to the area. This can often include closing off potential routes into and out of the area of the incident as offender(s) may discard items when they leave the scene, for example.

If the main area of interest is, for example, a first floor room in a detached house, the house itself would constitute the inner cordon with the garden perimeter (at least, depending on nature of incident) being the outer cordon. The CSI or crime scene manager would be responsible for the activities within the inner cordon and investigators will be responsible for controlling the outer cordon.

Where circumstances dictate, once an initial cordon has been established by the initial responders, the possible extent of the scene should be identified and colleagues directed to areas to set a wider outer cordon. It is neither necessary nor helpful for all investigators to attend the main inner scene. Areas where additional resources, such as CSIs and other relevant personnel can meet, referred to as a rendezvous point (RV) should be identified as soon as possible.

The RV point should essentially have easy access for police and other relevant vehicles, enable access to the crime scene and, where possible, be away from public gaze. In circumstances such as terrorist incidents, the RV point should be searched prior to being used to ensure there are no secondary devices or hazards.

....

Case study—Cordons

Two patrol officers were tasked to respond to reports of a fight between youths in a local park. On arrival the officers were faced with a hostile group of about twenty people. A male lay seriously injured on the floor. Most of the group made off on arrival of the police but a few remained and were very agitated. As one officer undertook first aid on the male on the ground, the second officer attempted to move the agitated group away.

The initial cordon, maintained by the physical presence of the officers, was therefore only about two square metres in size.

The male's condition was declared life threatening by paramedics. When further officers arrived, approximately ten minutes later, the cordoned area was immediately increased.

The weapon used (a fencing post) was recovered within the boundaries of the second cordon.

....

....

The initial cordon in such circumstances will be smaller than appropriate initially, but as soon as additional resources arrive the cordon should be extended. There is no advantage to setting a large cordon area if there are insufficient resources to ensure it is secure and cannot be breached. The cordons will be reviewed by the CSI/SIO if necessary.

....

Scene logs

A scene log should be instigated at the earliest opportunity where the incident is serious. All who enter the scene of serious incidents should be wearing protective clothing (scene suit, gloves, boot covers as a minimum).

Persons should not leave the outer boundaries of the scene wearing the protective clothing and then subsequently re-enter without changing their protective clothing. This is especially important in serious cases where the media may record such activities which could then lead to suggestions of contamination and transfer.

POINT TO NOTE—SCENE LOGS

Scene logs can be pre-printed booklets or written on a piece of notepaper or in contemporaneous notebooks. Pre-printed scene log forms differ across forces, but are the ideal way in which to record the activity at the scene. Whatever the manner of recording (printed forms, PNB, notepad, etc), it is vital that a scene log is instigated as soon as a cordon is set in place.

The scene log becomes the exhibit of the person who instigates it, with those subsequently taking possession of it signing the exhibit label continuity. The log is an official document and subject to disclosure to the defence teams. Minimum details to be included in a scene log are:

- the details (name, rank, personal ID number) of all those entering or leaving the scene;
- the time of arrival and departure of such personnel;
- the purpose or role at the scene;
- telephone contact details; and
- the person's signature.

It is important all information is clear and legible

It is advisable to request some form of identification of those entering the scene if you do not know the person. Accuracy is of paramount importance—ensure the correct spelling of names to avoid later confusion.

It may be beneficial to also record details or descriptions of persons showing inappropriate levels of interest. Do not give any details out regarding the incident to anyone other than those known to be part of the investigation team. Persons asking a lot of questions could potentially be the offenders, media reporters or related in some way to the victim.

Common Approach Paths (CAP)

A common approach path should be established at the earliest opportunity. The CAP should be the route into and out of the crime scene for all those subsequently attending the scene.

On initial arrival at a scene where the preservation of life is required, it is likely that the most direct route to the victims will have been taken by initial responders and medical teams in order to administer first aid or check for signs of life. Where possible, this route should be used to exit the area, unless it becomes clear that the offenders have used that route (eg, footwear marks or other potential evidence are noticed).

It is vital that the details of those initially attending are recorded and CSIs are informed of the route taken into and out of the scene. This can be achieved by a sketch plan, detailing the routes taken and positions of items of interest.

Ideally the CAP should be established on a route least likely to have been used by offenders or victims and it needs to be wide enough to enable CSIs to carry in equipment and for the removal of any bodies where applicable. In cases of a serious nature, where there is only one route in, movement on this route must be restricted to the actions required for the preservation of life until scene examiners arrive.

> *Tip*: At outdoor scenes use hardstanding or compacted path areas as much as possible to establish a common approach path as such surfaces are easier to search than grassland.

At serious incidents, the initial responders will soon have support available to them which can enable a review and possible relocation of cordons and common approach paths.

At a dwelling burglary however, the initial responder or CSI may be the only ones to visit the scene. Here, it is just as important to establish a CAP, avoiding the route most likely used by offenders. If it is reported that offenders entered and exited by the front door, investigators should go to the back door (if available).

Case study—Common approach paths

An elderly person was subjected to a distraction burglary whereby offenders had gained entry through the front door. It was reported that there was one male who went into the kitchen with the victim on the pretence of checking the water.

The initial responder went to the rear door of the property to speak to the victim, who wanted to walk around showing what had been done. The investigator declined to do this and suggested they go next door to a neighbour's home to talk. When the CSI arrived, because the scene had been kept intact, a lot of footwear evidence was recovered which indicated three offenders and also indicated which rooms they had entered, which was more than the elderly victim was initially aware of.

The actions of this officer ensured that potential evidence was maximised and intelligence gained on the number of offenders.

2.3.3 **Secure evidence**

The securing of a scene is perhaps the most important action to be taken in order to establish the chain of continuity and the integrity of any material subsequently recovered.

The securing of the scene can ensure that the contamination, transfer, destruction or loss of potential evidence is minimised. It is important to be aware of factors that can result in loss or destruction of potential evidence.

Ideally, any material should always be left *in situ* for recording and recovery by a CSI. However, if there is a risk that the material will be lost or damaged steps should be taken to protect it. Any steps taken to protect potential evidence must be undertaken carefully and only when absolutely necessary.

Scenario 2—Preserving the potential evidence

Figure 2.2 illustrates the scene of an assault in the street. During the assault the window got smashed when the attacker hit it with their elbow, the attacker then used a piece of broken glass from the window to stab the victim. The victim has been taken to hospital. It has just started to rain.

How may the potential evidence be preserved for the CSI examination?

Figure 2.2 **Example of an assault scene**

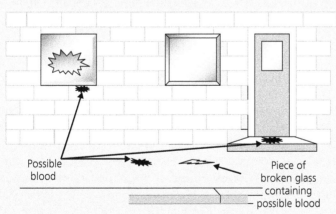

Possible blood

Piece of broken glass containing possible blood

- Set up a cordon to stop anyone walking or driving through the scene.
- The possible blood needs to be protected from the rain. The stains and glass (which may contain the attacker's fingerprints) on the floor can be covered with something that does not come into contact with the stain, a

35

police 'stop' sign, a plastic bollard or a box lid, for example, may be used. These are not ideal but in the absence of anything else it is better than losing the potential evidence. Be mindful however that rain water can run under such coverings and wash away any potential evidence. It may be appropriate (where CSI may be delayed in attending) to carefully collect the broken glass and exhibit it. It is important to ensure the location of any item removed in such circumstances is recorded by making a sketch plan of the scene. It may be appropriate to take a photograph of the material *in situ* on a personal data assistant (PDA) or police issue camera equipment.

- A *clean* plastic sheet or dustbin liner can be taped onto the wall to cover the window and preserve any evidence. The edges of the plastic should be secured onto the wall and not onto the window frame as there may be potential evidence such as fibres, hairs, possible blood and fingerprints around the frame and on the window. Be mindful that there may also be fibre or possible blood evidence on the wall, so ensure any tape used to secure the plastic sheet is away from likely areas of contact.
- The victim's clothing needs to be recovered. An investigator, who ideally has not attended the scene, should attend the hospital with appropriate packaging material for the purpose of seizing the victim's clothing at the earliest opportunity.
- Be aware of the risk of damaging any evidence on the floor whilst securing the window area.
- Only undertake such preservation techniques if absolutely necessary and only if the potential evidence will be lost, damaged or destroyed if left exposed.
- Ensure you document your actions and inform the CSI and OIC of what has been done.

The weather can be problematic at outdoor scenes; evidence may be blown away or soaked with rain. Where items cannot reasonably be covered to protect them then they should be seized and exhibited if possible, noting the original position. If covering items to protect them, ensure the cover does not come into contact with the item and avoid using items of clothing or hats to cover items due to the risk of contaminating the item with DNA.

There may be rare occasions where the scenes need to be searched prior to the forensic examination. A risk assessment needs to be undertaken to consider the benefits of a search against the risks of contamination or destruction of material.

Factors that may warrant the search of the scene prior to a forensic examination include:

- the need to preserve life;
- an immediate threat to life;
- the immediate pursuit of a suspect;

- the likelihood of destruction, damage or disposal of material caused by weather or outside interference with the material; and
- the likelihood that recovering the material will lead to a rapid arrest of a suspect.

The potential risk of contaminating the scene is increased with such searches and unless circumstances dictate, the general rule is that the forensic examination *must take priority* unless one or more of the critical factors above exists.

Any search must be properly risk assessed, rationalised, documented and undertaken with due regard to minimising any potential damage, contamination or transfer of material. Where possible, the advice of a CSI should be sought on the most appropriate methods to employ.

Where it is clear that the incident is serious and there is no threat to life or risk of interference or damage to potential evidence, the initial responders attending should seek to secure the scene, inform a supervisor and await the arrival of additional resources.

POINT TO NOTE—LEGISLATION REGARDING CORDONS AT CRIME SCENES

Generally speaking, cordoning off a crime scene is not problematic. However, consideration should be given to *DPP v Clive Winston Morrison* (2003) which highlights that the only authority in English law for the setting up of a cordon to restrict access is the Terrorism Act 2000, s 33 which is not generally applicable in most cases requiring a crime scene search.

In summary, police attended a mall where reports of a fight between two groups of males had been reported. Within the mall, items believed to be weapons were observed. The area was cordoned off as a crime scene pending examination by CSIs. A person attempted to proceed through the cordon and was stopped. This person challenged the right of the police to stop him entering the cordoned off area. The cordoned off area was privately owned, no consent had been sought from the landowner and no warrant had been obtained.

It was held in this case that although police officers do not have an unfettered right to restrict access on private land, they could rightly assume consent to act in setting up a cordon in such circumstances.

Providing the police do not go beyond what is reasonable and necessary to preserve evidence of the crime, the owner's consent can be assured for routine scenes of crime searches without warrant. Should consent be withdrawn, consideration to obtaining a warrant applicable to the needs of the investigation will be required.

2.3.4 **Identify victims**

Consider the victim as a crime scene where the circumstances of the offence so dictate. In cases of serious or fatal injuries being caused to a victim, it can be beneficial to ascertain their identity as soon as possible as this can lead to the early identification of possible suspects or lines of enquiry.

The identification of an unknown/unidentified deceased victim can be undertaken initially by checking for any identification such as bank cards, etc. The search for such items must ideally only be undertaken by a CSI due to the potential risk of damage to forensic material if suspicious circumstances exist. There are other methods to establish and confirm identity forensically such as fingerprints, DNA and dentition but these can take time to undertake and delay identification. Investigators who deal with victims should not subsequently deal with any potential suspects during the same shift, in order to avoid the potential for contamination and cross transfer of evidence.

....

Case note—Contamination and cross-transfer

Two investigators attend a reported fight occurring in the street. On arrival first aid is administered by both investigators. It comes to light that members of the public are holding on to the alleged offender who is struggling violently, just around the corner. One of the investigators leaves the victim to arrest the suspect.

What potential problems can occur as a result of this action?

Material from the victim can be transferred onto the alleged offender via the investigator.

What actions should the investigator now take?

Inform the OIC/SIO and CSI of this factor; arrange transport in a separate vehicle from their colleague who has continued to deal with the victim; document any visible material (eg, blood) that may be upon their person; exhibit their clothing for forensic examination at the earliest opportunity; do not deal with seizing any clothing or samples from the alleged offender.

There was no other appropriate course of action available at the time. Contamination and transfer of potential evidential material could not have been avoided in this situation. By recognising this and taking the appropriate steps, the impact on the case can be reduced.

The recording of the potential contamination or transfer issues and the seizing of the officer's clothing can enable the forensic scientist to assess whether any fibres or blood staining on the alleged offender may have been as a result of transfer from contact with the officer or as a result of the assault.

....

The consideration of any victims or witnesses (where appropriate) as crime scenes in their own right ensures that the potential forensic evidence can be maximised.

2.3.5 Identify suspects

The main feature of an investigation is to identify the offenders. It is possible to forensically link offenders to scenes and other associated persons based on

Locard's 'Principle of Exchange'. There are generally at least two elements of a crime: the offenders and the location of the incident. This increases where victims are involved.

The suspects may be identified by forensic evidence such as DNA or fingerprints or by linking other evidence such as fibres, footwear marks, or glass for example, but the forensic evidence alone is rarely enough to present before a court, it must form part of a thorough investigation.

2.4 **Chapter Summary**

The purpose of protecting a crime scene is to maximise the potential evidence available for recovery by CSIs.

It is the role of an investigator to gather as much material as possible, as soon as possible, in order to corroborate or refute allegations and identify offenders.

The actions of the initial responders can have a huge impact on both the quantity and quality of the material potentially available for the investigation.

The cordoning and control of crime scenes can go a long way to preserving potential evidence. The actions of the initial responders can have a huge impact on any subsequent forensic examination and admissibility of any forensic evidence.

The responsibility of initial responders to secure and preserve a scene cannot be overstated. The control of cordons and the establishment and maintenance of scene logs is a vital role in ensuring a successful forensic examination to support the investigative process.

KNOWLEDGE CHECK—CRIME SCENE MANAGEMENT

1. State the ways scenes can be preserved to secure and protect potential evidence.

   Establish cordons to restrict access, identify common approach paths, instigate a scene log, record details of initial observations made on arrival, sketch a plan of the scene where possible.

2. What are the details required on a scene log?

   Date and location of the offence; name and contact details of all entering the scene with the times of entry and exit; record the purpose of their attendance and obtain their signature (in case of a later dispute as to their presence).

3. Is the scene log an exhibit?

   It is the exhibit of the person who starts it. Those who take it on should record on the log the time and date they take responsibility for it.

---

4. What is 'material'?

Material includes information and objects obtained in the course of a criminal investigation and which may be relevant to the investigation. Material may be relevant to an investigation if it appears to an investigation team that it has some bearing on the offence under investigation or any person being investigated, or on the surrounding circumstances of the case. Material can be used as evidence, intelligence or information, or a combination of these.

Recommended Reading

Crime Investigators' Handbook (2013) Cook, T, Hill, M and Hibbitt, S.

Investigating Burglary: A Guide to Investigative Options and Good Practice (2011) ACPO, London.

Managing Investigations College of Policing (2014) <http://www.app.college.police.uk/app-content/investigations/managing-investigations/>.

The Police and Criminal Evidence Act 1984 (2013) Zander, M.

$\boxed{3}$

Crime Scene and Evidence Recording

3.1 **Introduction**

One of the most important aspects of crime scene investigation is the detailed recording of the scene in as an uninterrupted state as possible. The best way to achieve this, in the first instance, is for initial responders to ensure scene preservation techniques are employed to reduce the disruption of the scene, and then by the subsequent photography of the scene and items/marks of potential evidence before they are moved. Photography is a complex subject, and crime scene photographers undertake extensive training to achieve the ability to record crime scenes and evidence accurately, in often difficult lighting conditions and environments. Technical photography is therefore a key skill of a crime scene investigator (CSI) or anyone who is required to gather evidence for potential criminal proceedings. The training at the College of Policing Forensic Facility ensures that the technical photography that a CSI must undertake enables them to cover the vast range of situations that they encounter.

The term CSI is used within this chapter to include all investigators, such as vehicle collision investigators, forensic scientists and other law enforcement agencies (LEAs), for example, that attend scenes where they are required to undertake photography for investigative and evidential purposes. The roles, processes and techniques undertaken by CSI and initial responders/investigators differs regarding photography—these roles are outlined in this chapter. However, although the principles of scene photography can be applied by initial responders/investigators in certain situations, they *must not* remain in a scene of a serious nature or when a CSI will be tasked to take photographs. Once preservation of life actions has been fulfilled where appropriate, initial responders must concentrate on securing and preserving the scene, and await a CSI who will undertake the necessary photography.

Ideally a CSI photographer should be available to photograph every exhibit recovered by initial responders, however there are many incidents that a CSI will not be tasked to and occasions where an initial responder or investigator must recover items of potential evidence. It is always advantageous, where practicable to do so, to photograph or create a sketch diagram to show the items, *in situ*, before moving them. However, the quality of any images taken on mobile devices (eg, personal data assistant (PDA), mobile phone or tablet) will not be of the standard required for most evidential purposes. A key difference generally between CSIs and initial responders is the quality and specification of the photographic equipment available to them.

Sketch diagrams are a good method of recording a crime scene. For initial responders, sketches provide an aide memoire for writing reports and statements and enable them to brief CSIs and other investigators as to the general layout of a scene and the relative position of key aspects of the scene. A CSI will also produce a sketch diagram of the scene during their examination, which will be much more detailed. A third type of diagram that may be produced at serious incidents is a plan drawing, this will be undertaken by a qualified technical plan drawer and will be to scale.

This chapter aims to give a basic overview of crime scene and evidence photography as undertaken by crime scene and other forensic investigators. Some of the processes for photographing exhibits can, and should, be used when initial responders have no option but to take a photograph if the potential evidence would be lost, damaged, destroyed or otherwise compromised if it was left. Sketch diagrams by initial responders can be produced once a scene has been secured. The CSI will produce a more comprehensive and detailed sketch plan at scenes of serious incidents. The CSI sketch plan will including relevant measurements, which when used in conjunction with the photographs, can provide a great method of showing the scene and exhibits in context.

The initial recording of a crime scene or road traffic incident is an important and time consuming process; an awareness of the processes involved and why they are required can be beneficial in creating an understanding of the necessity of this vital aspect of scene examinations.

The advantage of having a photographic record of the scene of an incident and related exhibits cannot be overstated, showing others involved in the investigative process the nature and extent of the scene and potential evidence which can greatly aid understanding of the nature and scope of any incident. Juries also find photographic evidence useful and in some cases, a photograph may be the only record of potential evidence, such as an image of a fingerprint in blood on the wall inside a house, for example.

Digital imaging technology has transformed the use of photographic images for crime scene recording. For example, 360° photography has become increasingly useful in capturing overviews of a crime scene and may, alongside still photography and/or video footage, be used to create a digital 3D virtual reconstruction of a crime scene that can be used as a briefing presentation and in court.

3.2 **Sketch Diagrams**

Whilst a good photographic record is a fundamental requirement for the documentation of a crime scene, it can be difficult to determine relative distances between items/areas of interest in a photograph. This can be overcome with a sketch diagram showing areas of interest that relate to the investigation, such as the relative position of exhibits and marks and stains. Sketches can be drawn in contemporaneous note books or on a separate piece of paper that can be exhibited and must be drawn in a non-erasable medium.

3.2.1 **Initial responder/investigator produced sketches**

The scene sketch created by initial responders/investigators will typically be less detailed than those of a CSI; nonetheless they serve a very useful purpose as they can indicate to the CSI and other investigators a general layout of the scene, and can serve as an aide memoire for later report/statement writing. It is not necessary to produce a level of artistic merit in sketch diagrams, nor should initial responders remain in a scene to do so where actions to secure and preserve the scene would be delayed. Whilst a scene sketch may be useful, it is not essential that initial responders produce these at serious incidents.

One format is the 'birds eye view' or floor-plan sketch where the relative positions of items within a scene can be illustrated. It is not necessary to draw the item; it is easier to use lettered or numbered squares or circles, for example, to represent various objects in the sketch. The details of these can these be placed in a 'key' or 'legend' to correlate with the relevant letters or numbers used in the diagram, in the scene, as illustrated in Figure 3.1.

Another common type of sketch illustrates the relative location of potential evidence on a vertical plane. Whilst measurements are useful, especially where potential evidence must be moved prior to a CSI attending, or for those incidents that will not require a CSI attendance, they may not be easily obtained unless the initial responder has a tape measure available. It is important not to disturb/disrupt potential evidence in order to take measurements. Never guess at measurements.

Checklist—Sketch diagrams

- *Do not* use pencil or other erasable medium to create sketch diagrams.

The following should be recorded on the sketch:

- address/location of scene;
- case/incident number;
- date of sketch creation;
- name, identification number, rank/position;
- key to identify the different objects in the sketch;
- an arrow to show the direction of north (if known) and/or arrows to show directional information such as which way a footwear mark is orientated, for example;
- annotation on sketch '*not to scale*';
- where appropriate, show locations of windows/doors and indicate if open/closed/broken, for example;
- a curved line drawn to show which way doors/windows open;
- never guess at measurements;
- initial responders *must not* remain in or move around a scene of a serious incident unnecessarily for the purposes of making a sketch. Scene security and preservation is more important.

Figure 3.1 Example of initial responder scene sketches

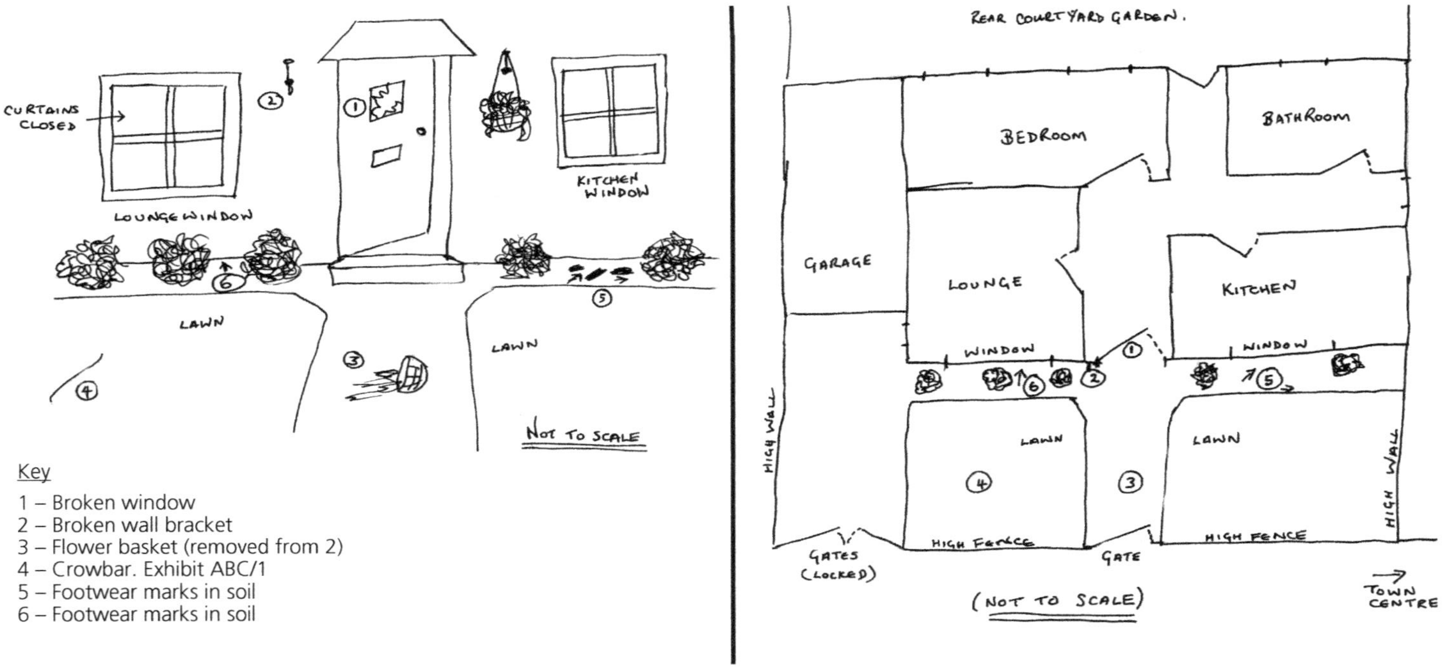

Key

1 – Broken window
2 – Broken wall bracket
3 – Flower basket (removed from 2)
4 – Crowbar. Exhibit ABC/1
5 – Footwear marks in soil
6 – Footwear marks in soil

Any sketch diagram is subject to disclosure rules and should be retained in a good condition. Sketches produced on a separate piece of paper should be exhibited (see Figure 3.2).

Figure 3.2 Example of a CSI sketch showing marks on window

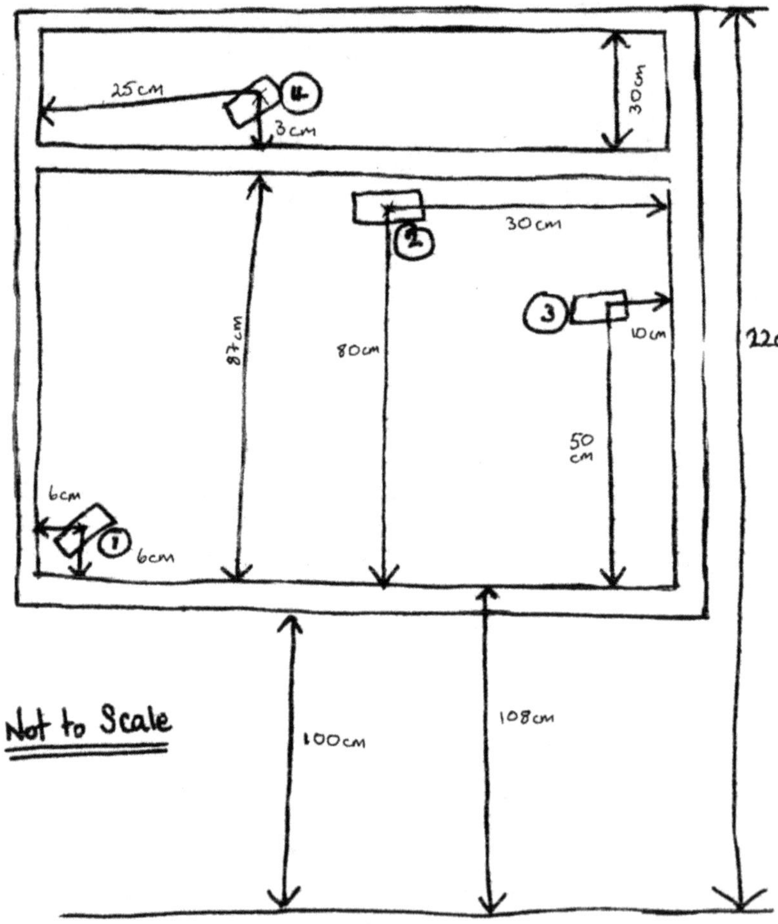

3.2.2 CSI produced sketches

These are more detailed than sketches an initial responder/investigator needs to produce, and will contain additional information and measurements of items and distances between key areas/items within the scene. These are usually produced following the initial assessment of a scene to identify key areas/items of interest. A CSI will use numbered photographic marker boards by each area/item of interest. The numbers will then be used to form the 'key' or 'legend' for the sketch and will provide reference points for subsequent photography. This ensures that when sketches and photography of the scene are undertaken, each method can be correlated with the other to provide a much fuller depiction of the scene, beneficial to all those who will subsequently be investigating the incident, and for presentation to a jury.

3.2.3 Crime scene video

The use of digital video at crime scenes takes the viewer 'real time' through the scene as seen by the investigator. Footage from bodycams is useful in the first instance; however if video recording of a crime scene is required it should be undertaken by those who are trained and experienced in the use of video equipment. Poor video footage, such as rapid switching of viewpoints, shakiness created when recording whilst walking, for example, is very frustrating and difficult for the viewer, and so may not serve any purpose to the investigation. Video recording of a scene is a skill that requires the use of specialist equipment and trained operators.

3.2.4 Virtual 3D crime scene reconstructions

In some cases video footage can be used in conjunction with 360° and still photographs to create a 'virtual reconstruction' (VR) of the crime scene (see Figure 3.3). This technique essentially 'sanitises' a crime scene for the purpose of presenting it to the court; this means juries are not subject to overly disturbing footage. Figure 3.3 shows an example of a VR of an indoor scene.

Virtual reconstructions rely on good quality recording of a scene; photographs, video footage and accurate measurements are essential. In many cases, the provider of the VR service can attend scenes to do this. The use of 360° scanning equipment enables the production of an interactive 'walk through' of a scene, whereby the user can 'move' around the scene and stop to then view a photograph of a particular exhibit or wound or even to listen to audio files, such as may be present on a telephone answering machine, for example.

Figure 3.3 Virtual reconstruction image

Source: Andrew Postlethwaite, Virtual Reconstructions

3.3 **Crime Scene Photography**

At serious incidents scene photography must only be undertaken by a CSI. However, there will be occasions where initial responders/investigators may need to take photographs, where the incident will not result in a CSI attending or where an item needs to be moved to be exhibited, for example. If in doubt as to whether a CSI will be attending, it is advisable to check with the force control room to make sure. The following principles relate to the processes undertaken by a CSI, but are worth bearing in mind for initial responders and how best to approach photographing evidence.

Typically, initial responders will not have the quality of photographic equipment available to CSI photographers and images are generally taken on mobile devices such as PDAs, mobile phones and tablets. The image quality of such devices is generally poorer than that obtained with SLR cameras (discussed later); compact digital cameras used by some investigators may have a better image quality.

The photographing of a scene or of potential evidence follows a sequential process. The three main categories of photographs required of a scene include a wide overview of the scene, mid-range views which show the relative position of each exhibit (denoted by the placement of numbered marker boards) and close-up shots of exhibits at each marker board. A photographic log or 'shot sheet' must be completed to record the image number and a description of the shot being taken.

Following a visual assessment of the scene to note key areas/items of forensic interest within the scene, plastic numbered markers are placed by such items/ areas (eg, a possible weapon, a footwear impression or a fingermark in blood) to denote the location and relative position of each item. It is beneficial to ensure the numbered markers all face the same way as they are easier to view and distinguish on the photographs. In an ideal world this process would be a single act to identify all the exhibits within a scene, however, in reality it can be an ongoing process; as the scene is examined in more detail, there may be further exhibits identified.

A key error made with digital photography is poor out of focus images, particularly when auto focus settings are being used. The auto focus settings can result in poor images as there is, with digital cameras and mobile devices, a slight delay between pressing the shutter and the image being taken. If the photographer moves the camera during this delay, this can cause an image to be blurred. The use of a tripod and patience is required. Ensure the camera is not moved during this short delay.

3.3.1 Overviews of scene

These shots are taken using what is termed the 'quartering' technique, and are taken from the perimeter of the scene with each shot having an area of overlap with the last. In serious cases, 360° photography can be utilised for overviews. This requires a camera mounted on a tripod that has a motorised head which turns slowly, synchronised with the camera. A number of shots are taken automatically as the camera is turned to capture a good photographic overview of the scene.

The 'quartering' technique may require more than the four shots the name suggests; see the checklist later in the chapter for the basic requirements for capturing overviews of commonly encountered scenes and the information required on a 'shot sheet' (photographic log). Table 3.1 shows how images can be recorded on the photographic log. (If the exhibit number is known at the time of photographs, this can also be recorded.)

Table 3.1 Example entries on photographic log
Crime/Incident reference number: XY999Z
Address: 16 Sandford Crescent
Date: 12.01.20XX

Image Number	Description
011	Overview kitchen from front door towards microwave
012	Overview kitchen from front door towards fridge
013	Overview kitchen from corner by doorway into hall towards sink
014	Overview kitchen from corner by microwave towards front door
015	Overview kitchen from corner by front door towards microwave
016	View of exterior front door
017	View of interior front door
018	Error—flash misfire
Note: Many overview and mid-range shots would be required before close-up images are taken	
090	View kitchen table and floor from front door
091	View close up of mobile phone on floor (marker 6)
092	Close-up broken glass on floor (marker 8)

Photographer: CSI Will Shire

Overview shots should include access routes into and out of scene, both looking towards and away from the scene, for example where a lane goes into a field that is the main area of interest, images must be taken of the view of the lane itself, from the lane into the field and then views from entrance to field back up the lane. Wide angle overview shots should have an area of overlap with the previous image using fixed points such as trees/lampposts/furnishings, for example, to show the totality of the scene including any numbered markers and police cordons.

In some cases a police photographer may take aerial photographs of the scene and immediate locality, from a police helicopter.

3.3.2 Mid-range photographs

These are images of areas within the scene to show the relative positions of items, such as a desk in a room and items on/around the desk, a door with a foot-wear mark on it, a broken window etc. These shots typically will show more than one item and should include the numbered markers. Where marks are on a vertical plane, a mark in possible blood on a car door, for example, the photographic marker board should be placed on the floor directly beneath the mark. If a mark is small an 'arrow' sticker is useful to highlight the area of interest.

3.3.3 **Close-up photographs**

These are taken of each item to be recovered and exhibited. It is important to 'fill the frame' with the item and numbered marker. With close ups it is vital to use a 'scale'—either a rigid ruler or printed adhesive backed paper rulers. This ensures that images can be produced 1:1 ('life size') and the size of an item established. This is especially important when photographing footwear marks.

For initial responders who may not have these items available, a coin can be placed next to the item as these are of a fixed size. The actual size of the item can then be calculated from the dimensions of the coin (see Figure 3.4).

Figure 3.4 Close up showing use of a coin for scale purposes

Marks that are on an inclined surface must be photographed at the same angle of the mark (see Figure 3.5). Use a tripod and align the camera to be parallel with the mark—if the mark is on a surface at a 45° angle, then the camera must be set at the same angle. Use a spirit level to assess the angle and set the camera to this.

Figure 3.5 Photographing marks on an incline

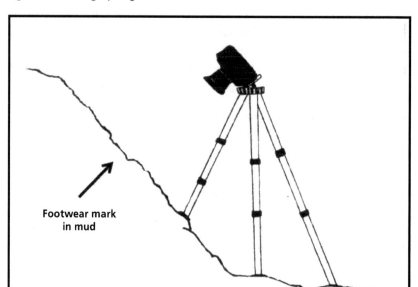

Footwear mark
in mud

Checklist—Photographs required at typical scenes

A room in a premises	*Overviews*—from each corner, or more if necessary to cover the entire room. Shots into and away from entrance/exit points.
	Mid-range shots—items/areas of interest within the room, for example a broken window and the area adjacent to it to put it into context.
	Close-up shots—ensure a scale is included. Fill the frame with the subject.
Vehicles	*Overviews*—a shot of each corner to include vehicle registration plates plus a shot of the back and front of the vehicle.
	Mid-range shots—exterior shots of marks/damage on doors,
	interior shots of vehicle taken from each door/window area.
	Do not sit on vehicle seats, they may have evidence on them and may also have sharp items (eg, used needles) hidden within them, placed to injure emergency service personnel.
	Close-up shots—include a scale and fill the frame with subject.
Outdoor scene	*Overviews*—as many shots as required to show an area of overlap with the last and to cover the entire area looking both into the scene and where necessary routes into/out of the scene. Include cordons where appropriate.
	Mid-range shots—Items/areas of interest within the scene and the area immediately adjacent to it to put it into context.
	Close-up shots—Include a scale.

Exterior of house or other premises	*Overviews*—Shots taken from the road/access into and out of house/premises to cover entrance/exit points as for outdoor scene.
	Shots of each exterior aspect of the premises including views of and road/access into and outwards from the premises and any perimeter boundaries.
	Include cordons where appropriate.
	Mid-range shots—shots of doors, windows, driveway, for example, and key areas of interest.
	Close-up shots—include a scale.
Footwear marks photographs	Use a tripod. A scale must be included on the two edges of the mark (length and width) and camera set parallel to mark.
Injury photographs	*Overviews*—where appropriate (for deceased) showing body in wider context of scene.
	Mid-range shots—head and shoulders (to ensure identity of the person relates to injuries). Show injuries in context, for example, if injury on arm, show the arm in full.
	Close-up shots—images of the injury with and without scales.
	NEVER remove dressings to photograph injuries (the injured person or a medical professional where appropriate should do this).
	Same sex photographer should be used where possible, bearing in mind the nature of the case.
	As with all kinds of forensic/scene photography, the requirements depend on the nature of the task—this is not a definitive list of considerations.

KEY POINTS—SCENE PHOTOGRAPHY

Use a tripod.

Ensure through cleaning/decontamination of tripod when scene has been photographed to avoid any transfer/contamination at subsequent scenes.

Be aware if using flash of reflective surfaces such as mirrors, windows, pictures, glass fronted cabinets, high gloss paintwork (on vehicles), for example, especially if using flash.

A polarising filter reduces reflections and can improve shots taken through windows.

Close-up and mid-range photography of marks on an inclined surface requires the camera to be set on the same plane as the item/mark to be photographed. A spirit level should be used to ensure camera is parallel to mark.

Be aware, especially when using autofocus settings of the slight delay—depress shutter partway to focus, then depress fully to take shot—keep camera still during this time.

Scene photography cannot be rushed. It is vital all images are correctly exposed and in sharp focus. It can be a time consuming process and the recovery of exhibits cannot be undertaken until this process is complete. One great advantage of digital cameras is that it is possible to review images as they are taken prior to leaving the scene to ensure they are of evidential quality. In the days of the film camera, a CSI could spend many sleepless nights waiting for the photographs to be printed to see if they had captured the scene and exhibits well enough, especially if photographs had been taken in difficult lighting or environmental conditions.

It is better to have fewer good quality images than lots of poorer quality ones— so a review of images before leaving the scene is an important task, as it will not be possible to return to the scene as exhibits will have been recovered.

Checklist—Scene photography

- It is important that no *unnecessary* CSI or police kit (eg, clipboards, cases and coats) are left in the areas to be photographed (with the exception of, eg, numbered markers and stepping plates).

- The camera must be mounted on a tripod unless unsafe/impractical to do so.

- Overviews, mid-range and close-up shots are required.

- Each image number must be recorded with a description of the photograph, including any numbered markers on a photographic log. (A digital voice recorder is ideal for situations where writing a log at the time would be difficult—poor weather, for example. This can be used to then write up the log as soon as is practicable.)

- *NEVER delete* an image—where errors have been made, denote with 'X' or 'error', for example.

- Format memory cards *before* each individual scene.

3.4 **Digital Image Storage Procedure**

Digital images of crime scenes and potential evidence are subject to the same principles of continuity and integrity as any other exhibit. The audit trail for the taking of, storage and retrieval of such images is subject to a procedure that enables the integrity and continuity to be maintained.

Digital cameras have a facility to record data which includes the date, time, camera settings, lens used and the geographical location (on GPS enabled cameras) of each image taken. It is important therefore that cameras used for such purposes have the correct time and date set. This information is recorded with every image taken, referred to as metadata or EXIF (exchangeable image file) data, and it enables an in-camera continuity record to be generated. This data can be examined to establish the integrity of an image.

Before any images are taken at a scene, the removable storage device (memory card) must be formatted; this can be done via the camera settings menu. This ensures all data from previous scenes is removed. Deleting images from a memory card does not remove all the data of previous images, and in evidential photography deleting images is strictly forbidden.

Once images have been taken, they must then be downloaded for storage onto a WORM (write once read many) storage medium such as a CD/DVD or a secure hard-drive, for example.

Where copying to a CD/DVD, the disc must be 'closed' or 'finalised' to prevent the original images being altered, and an invisible 'watermark' may be embedded into images to demonstrate the integrity. This disc is labelled as the *'Master copy'* and must be sealed and exhibited. Copies of images to other CD/DVDs are then labelled as *'Working copies'* for use by investigators to view and disseminate images in briefings, for example, or for any enhancement techniques to be utilised, to gain a sharper image, for example. Where images are of a graphic nature, a warning to this effect must be printed onto the exterior surface of the disc. Dissemination and viewing of crime scene images should be restricted to essential personnel only. Figure 3.6 shows the digital image procedure as a flowchart.

Figure 3.6 Digital image procedure flowchart

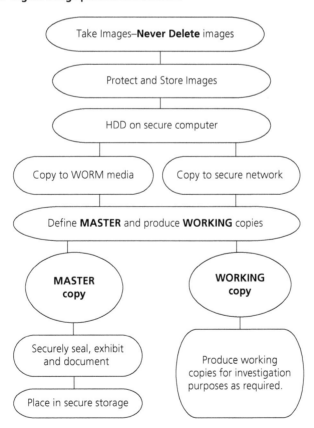

3.5 **Digital Photography—An Introduction**

It is beyond the scope of a single chapter to explain the detail regarding technical aspects of digital photography; however, the information herein will provide a basic understanding of the key aspects of digital photography and give a base level of knowledge for further learning if so required.

Digital single lens reflex (D-SLR) cameras are used by CSI as they have interchangeable lenses and a range of settings available to ensure a high quality image can be obtained in all lighting situations, giving the photographer much greater control and choices, to ensure a clearly focussed and evenly exposed image can be obtained.

All digital cameras have a sensor, on which the light is captured and converted to an image that can be viewed through the sensor or LCD screen, essentially an electronic equivalent of film. The charged coupled device (CCD) is one of the oldest digital sensor technologies and is still commonly found in budget/entry level cameras; however in newer higher specification cameras complementary metal oxide semiconductor (CMOS) sensors are replacing the CCD technology.

3.5.1 **Lenses**

The range of lenses available for the D-SLR enables the photographer to select an appropriate lens to ensure the best quality image is captured. The two main types of lenses are known as 'prime' or 'fixed' lenses and zoom/telephoto lenses. Typically a CSI scene photographer will have a number of lenses that can deal with the varied photographic tasks they may face. For example, wide angle lenses for overviews, a macro lens for close ups and a telephoto zoom lens for mid-range and possibly close-up shots. The range of lenses and focal lengths available is quite vast; however for scene work the following lenses are examples of what a scene photographer may use:

- 50mm prime lens—this best represents what can be seen by the human eye without causing any magnification or distortion. It is ideally suited for photographing injuries, people and mid-range shots of a scene and to provide the 'range of view' of drivers involved in road collisions, for example.
- 18mm—70mm lens—used for wide angle, overview shots of scenes.
- 200mm/300mm zoom lens—used for mid-range and close-up shots, for example when it is not possible to get near enough to the subject.
- Macro lens—enable close-up photography of small items/details at a ratio of 1:1 ('life-size'). A prime macro lens is typically the better option; however it must be possible to get very close to the subject with such lenses, not always possible (or pleasant) at a crime scene. A telephoto zoom lens with the facility to be switched from normal to macro mode allows close-up images to be captured from further away. For example, for photographs of maggots on a decomposing body, a prime macro lens with a shorter (eg, 60mm) focal length

would require the photographer to get within centimetres of the maggots. A longer focal (eg, 105mm) length macro lens would enable the same size image to be obtained from further back, which in such a case would be preferable to most photographers.

A sturdy tripod is an essential part of the scene photographer's kit and must be used at all times, except where space may be limited or the terrain is too difficult to set up a tripod. It is important that the tripod is thoroughly decontaminated after every scene as it can collect minute traces of material such as fibres, DNA material and body fluids. Glass may be on the feet and legs. This can cause transfer/contamination of evidence when used at multiple scenes.

In addition, a minimum of a flash gun, remote shutter release, numbered marker boards, small stickers and permanent fine tipped marker pen (for creating labels for photographs), spare charged batteries, scales (rigid and printed paper sticker type rulers) and polarising filters ensure that the CSI/police photographer has what is needed for the majority of the tasks they will encounter.

3.5.2 Exposure

The correct exposure of an image is critical in achieving a good image; if an image is too dark (under-exposed) or too light (over-exposed) then crucial detail can be lost. It is sometimes possible, by using image software, to recover some detail in under-exposed images, but if an image is over-exposed any detail cannot be recovered. It is therefore preferable that all images are correctly exposed.

The elements that combine to provide a good, even exposure ensure the correct amount of light falls on the sensor—this is achieved by the shutter speed and aperture settings, the sensitivity of the sensor to light and ISO—these three aspects are referred to as the 'exposure triangle'. The white balance (WB) settings are also an important factor in ensuring the image represents the actual scene/item/person.

It is beyond the scope of this chapter to cover technical aspects and settings required; however the following information gives a basic overview of the key areas that need to be mastered to achieve a correctly exposed image:

Shutter speed setting

The shutter is a series of very thin metal blades and the length of time these are open affects how much light reaches the sensor. Shutter speeds (the amount of time the shutter is open) are measured in seconds or fractions of a second, ranging, for example, from thirty seconds to 1/3200th of a second. The longer shutter speeds are typically used for low light photography where a tripod is a must to avoid blurring of image. There is also a 'B' setting on most D-SLRs, this refers to the 'bulb' setting that was on film cameras and allows the shutter to stay open as long as the photographer requires—up to several minutes. This is useful for photographing very dark scenes.

Aperture settings

The aperture is the opening in the lens that allows light to pass to the sensor. The incremental adjustments are referred to as *f*-stops/*f*-numbers. The lower the numeric value of the *f*-stop, the larger the aperture (opening) which will let more light through in a set time, the larger numeric value of the *f*-stop then the smaller the aperture (opening) is, letting less light through in a given time.

Another important function of the aperture is to control the depth of field (DoF). This relates to how much of the subject is in sharp focus, around a third in front of, and two thirds behind the subject. Larger apertures (small *f*-numbers) will enable a shallow depth of field to be obtained, isolating a subject from the background, and is often used in creative photography due to this effect. Smaller apertures (higher *f*-number) will give good DoF whereby everything one third in front of and two thirds behind the subject are in sharp focus, which is clearly what is required for crime scene photography. The *f*8 and *f*11 aperture settings give a good depth of field for a lot of general scene work, *f*16–*f*22 may be used where photographing the length of a road, for example, as these settings produce a good depth of field over distance.

To remember the fact that the larger *f*-numbers produce a smaller aperture (opening), consider a cake being divided—when it is cut into four pieces (*f*4) the size of each slice is relatively large. If it was cut into sixteen slices (*f*16) then each slice will be a lot smaller.

The reciprocal relationship between the shutter and aperture ensures that a balanced exposure can be obtained by adjusting the length of time, and the intensity of, light reaching the sensor.

International Standards Organisation (ISO) settings

Historically, the ISO devised a standardised numerical value to indicate the sensitivity of a particular photographic film. Film photography required the used of different ISO rated films, such as ISO100—a 'slow' film, so called as it had a reduced sensitivity to light, whereas an ISO400 film, a so called 'fast' film has an increased sensitivity to light. This required carrying a range of films with different ISO ratings to suit the different lighting conditions.

Digital camera ISO settings follow the same principles, and are altered by algorithms within the camera—the sensor itself does not physically change. 'Pushing' the ISO up to be in the higher range (more sensitive to light) enables photographers to capture images in low light without the use of flash. The main disadvantage of higher ISO settings is that there is an increase in 'digital noise' which gives a speckled, grainy effect to the final image. The particular ISO setting where such 'noise' becomes visible and detrimental to quality in the final image varies with different cameras.

As each scene and lighting conditions are different, there are no fixed rules for what settings should be used—which is why police/CSIs must undertake technical photography training.

White balance (WB)

Although not part of the 'exposure triangle', the WB setting used can have a great impact on the final image. White light, as we see it with the human eye, is made up of the different colours of the spectrum, and although we may not see anything but a neutral light due to the way our brain processes such information, the camera sensor records the light as it is, which can result in the final image having a 'colour cast' if the wrong setting is used. Photographs taken where tungsten light is the main source of illumination, for example, often have a predominant orange colour to them. The WB settings compensate by essentially filtering the light to remove predominant colour casts created by differing illumination sources and balance it to better represent what we see with the human eye. This is important in evidential photography as colour casts can cause colours in the final images to be changed from what we see. For example, a white car under a sodium street lamp can look silver, blue, beige or even pale orange/bronze on final image, for example, where incorrect WB settings have been used.

3.5.3 Using flash

As there is not always sufficient available (ambient) light to achieve the correct exposure for an image, it is often a requirement to use a flash. The 'pop-up' flash on most cameras is rarely sufficient as it has a restricted out-put and range; a dedicated flash gun is therefore carried by scene photographers. Such flash guns can be attached to the hot-shoe on the camera body or used 'off camera'. These units synchronise with the camera so that settings information from the camera are wirelessly transmitted to the flash gun, and enables the correct exposure to be achieved via 'through the lens' (TTL) light readings. One key consideration when using flash is to be aware of the shutter speed synchronisation settings—most flash guns will synchronise with the camera to speeds of 1/250th of a second.

Ring lights are useful for macro, injury, footwear and portrait photography and may also be used for general indoor scenes. These are circular shaped light sources that attach to the lens and many have the capability to use continuous light or act as a flash, and can have different settings so that one half of the ring only is active, for example.

It is important to be aware of reflective surfaces such as windows, glass fronted cabinets, pictures, mirrors and high gloss surfaces which will 'bounce' the light back and create areas of 'white-out'—intense areas of highlight that possibly mask the subject (eg, a fingermark on a mirror) when using flash.

There are several techniques that enable a photographer to control the direction and intensity of light from a flash gun, which have many variables and are beyond the scope of this chapter. The main techniques used for flash are summarised below:

- *Fill-in flash*—used to light up areas of shadow, for example when photographing a weapon that is beneath a vehicle. To use fill-in flash, the correct exposure

59

settings for the ambient light are selected on the camera, and the flash, positioned to light up shadowed area (eg, beneath the car) is set to one or two aperture (*f-stops*) below the camera reading to 'fill-in' the area that is in shadow to give an even exposure.

- *Balanced flash*—this technique is used to create a 'balanced' exposure in situations where light and dark areas are present, such as when photographing into a darker hallway of a house from outside or when shooting the exterior area from the darker hallway. This technique requires setting the shutter and aperture on the camera to give correct exposure for ambient light. The flash, used off the camera and seated on a stand or tripod, can be placed inside the darker hallway, for example, and will (if synchronised with camera), calculate the correct flash out-put to give a balanced exposure. It is also possible to manually set the flash to obtain correct, balanced exposure by reducing the aperture setting on the flash gun. When photographing inside to outside, set camera to ambient light of interior. The flash can be used on- or off-camera (depending on circumstances) to give a balanced exposure. It is important to be aware that when using flash, it can create shadows that were not originally visible; the correct positioning of flash guns will reduce this effect as will using 'bounced flash'.
- *Bounced flash*—this technique is good for photographing interiors where there are reflective surfaces, for example. The direction of the flash is set to fire at a ceiling or wall, for example, rather than at the subject. Bounced flash produces a more diffuse light as its intensity is reduced as it has further to travel before reaching the subject to be photographed. This can eliminate the problems of glare where flash is bounced directly off a reflective surface. Be mindful of the colour of the surface from which you are 'bouncing' the flash as dark colours will tend to create a colour cast in the light. It is advisable to bounce flash from white or light neutral coloured surfaces.

As this chapter is not aimed at providing in-depth details regarding the technical aspects of photography, it is advisable to research the key terms for more information and tutorial guidance.

3.6 **Chapter Summary**

Scenes can be recorded by a range of means; scene sketches, photography and digital video recording. The use of the three techniques can provide a more detailed view of a scene than using one singular method. 360° photography can also provide additional images that can, with other recorded images and measurements be used to produce a 3D 'virtual' reconstruction of a crime scene to present a sanitised visual presentation for court purposes.

Initial responders should produce a sketch or photograph of any item/mark that they need to recover as an exhibit where it will be lost, damaged or destroyed if left or at incidents where a CSI will not be tasked. Initial responders and those untrained and unequipped in the technical and procedural aspects of scene/

evidence photography *must not* remain unnecessarily in a scene of a serious incident to begin documenting it. Once any preservation of life actions have been taken, the immediate priority is to secure and preserve the scene.

A crime scene photographer is a professional technical photographer, comprehensively trained to record the scene and potential evidence. A CSI/police photographer is required to undertake the photography of scenes and exhibits in those cases that warrant it. Although an initial responder may need to take photographs on a mobile device such as a PDA, mobile phone or tablet, these will not replace the images captured by a trained CSI/police photographer. It has been reported that initial responders, when using personal mobile phones to take photographs, have had their phones siezed as evidence on occasion. Where possible it is advisable to use issued photographic equipment for such purposes.

A CSI/police photographer will be required as part of the role to record a varying manner of 'scenes', which requires a comprehensive knowledge of technical photography and lighting techniques. Often operating in difficult environments with challenging lighting conditions, it is vital that each photograph is clearly focussed and correctly exposed at the first examination of a scene. A CSI/police photographer may also be required to photograph serious/fatal road traffic incidents post-mortems, injuries, and can be required to provide photographic records for other investigative bodies including the health & safety executive, border control, social services and HM Coroners, for example.

KNOWLEDGE CHECK—CRIME SCENE AND EVIDENCE RECORDING

1. What is the procedure for the taking of and subsequent storage of digital images?

   Format memory card before each scene.
   Never delete images.
   Record each image on photographic log
   Store to a WORM media/secure hard drive.
   Designate a MASTER copy, ensure images are finalised to prevent any alterations.
   Master copy to be sealed, exhibited and stored securely.
   Designate WORKING copies for dissemination/enhancement as appropriate.

2. Describe the three main categories of scene photographs.

   Overviews—wide angle views into and out of the scene, to include cordons
      where appropriate.
   Mid-range views to show areas of interest/exhibits in context.
   Close-up views of each exhibit.

3. State a key requirement for close-up photographs.

   Close-up photographs must always have a scale in order for final image to be reproduced as 1:1 ('life size'). This can be a purpose specific ruler or a coin placed by the item/mark.

4. List the information required on a sketch diagram.

All sketches must be annotated 'Not to Scale'.
The address of scene.
Time and date created.
Details of investigator producing sketch.
Incident reference number.

Recommended Reading

Crime Scene Photography, 2nd edn (2010) Robinson, E.
Digital Imaging Procedure (2007) Cohen, N.
Virtual Reconstructions <http://www.virtualreconstructions.com>.

Exhibit Handling

4.1 **Introduction**

Generally speaking, items required for forensic examination should be left, where possible, in their original position (*in situ*) for recovery by a crime scene investigator (CSI), who is trained to identify any forensic potentials and recover items appropriately to maximise the types of analysis available and the evidential value of such.

However, if the circumstances are such that the item may be lost, destroyed or damaged if left in its original position, it must be preserved immediately. If this involves recovering and exhibiting an item, its original location must be recorded either on a sketch diagram or photograph, and the CSI informed. The movement of items requiring forensic examination must be done with care and consideration to the potential forensic material available.

With the increased use of technology, digital media investigation is becoming a key consideration in investigations. It is beyond the remit of this book to offer details into the role and techniques that a digital media investigator (DMI) will undertake. The seizure, packaging and storage of devices to recover the best digital evidence possible follows specific procedures in addition to the general exhibit handling techniques for physical evidence. There will be occasions where investigators have to recover items for forensic examination as CSIs will not be available or where the incident type does not warrant CSI attendance. This chapter covers techniques for the recovery of items in a manner that will ensure that potential evidential recovery is maximised, health and safety is protected and the continuity and integrity of the exhibit can be demonstrated.

4.2 **Principles of Exhibit Handling**

When material is seized for use as potential evidence it is imperative to ensure that two key principles of continuity and integrity are adhered to. The continuity and integrity of any material seized for evidential purposes must be demonstrated in order to show the item's provenance, its progress throughout the forensic examination process and to prevent damage, loss or degradation of potential evidence and for the material to be admissible in court.

KEY POINT—CONTINUITY

This is the term used to describe the continuous audit trail which records the movements of the material from its initial recovery, through any forensic examination processes, and to its ultimate destination of the court room. Continuity of material can be easily demonstrated by accurately recording the description of the material, its exact location when recovered, the details of the person recovering the item and those subsequently handling the material and where the material has been stored.

> **KEY POINT—INTEGRITY**
>
> It is vital to demonstrate that any material recovered can be shown to have suffered no unaccountable interference or contamination, whether caused accidentally or deliberately, from the initial point of seizure, through forensic examination processes to the courtroom.
>
> The correct packaging of material will minimise the opportunities for contamination and cross-transfer of potential evidence and ensure that investigators can be sure that the material initially recovered is in fact the same as the material presented in court.

When any physical material is recovered during an investigation, it becomes an exhibit. The handling, packaging and storage of exhibits must ensure that the items are not subject to any further damage or interference in order to facilitate the recovery of forensic evidence. The continuity and integrity of exhibits must be proved beyond reasonable doubt in a court of law and the value of the principles of continuity and integrity are only really appreciated when an exhibit is lost, damaged, destroyed or the evidence devalued through the neglect of these principles.

4.2.1 What is an exhibit?

An exhibit is any physical item that is recovered or generated in the investigation of a crime or incident. The minimum information required to begin the chain of continuity is an accurate description of the item and the date, time and location from where the item is recovered, along with the details of the person seizing the item. This information should initially be recorded on the exhibit label and in the investigator's notebook.

Initial notes made regarding any incident are referred to as contemporaneous notes—an accurate record, made at the time, or as soon after the event as practicable. These should ideally be made in notebooks with numbered pages such as the police pocket notebook (PNB) and form a record of relevant observations by the maker of the notes. Contemporaneous notes are disclosable, meaning copies can be requested for use in court proceedings.

All items seized should be recorded on a central property recording system and the details entered into any investigation reports and statements, as appropriate. It is important that the exhibit details recorded in the investigator's notebook and any subsequent investigation reports or statements are exactly the same as those on the exhibit label. A statement will be required for court purposes from the investigator recovering the item and all those who have had subsequent access to it during the course of an investigation.

4.2.2 Preservation of forensic material

Locards 'Principle of Exchange' is essentially the foundation on which forensic examination is based. The principle highlights that a two-way transfer of material can occur in the commission of any act. The transfer of such material can subsequently be used to establish links between objects or persons, for example a footwear mark at a crime scene can be linked to the shoe that made the mark, and glass fragments on a suspect's clothing can be linked to a broken window at a burglary scene. Most potential forensic evidence, however, is microscopic; there may be very small amounts of material present that cannot be readily detected by investigators handling such items.

The types of material available for transfer between suspects, locations and/ or victims is infinite, with the most common potential evidence types including DNA from biological materials, fibres, hairs, glass, soil, paint, pollen, drugs. Such types of material can be present in microscopic amounts often referred to as trace or particulate evidence. The microscopic nature of such material can render it easily transferable and therefore extremely susceptible to cross-transfer and contamination.

Definition—Cross-transfer and contamination

Cross-transfer—This is the term used to describe the manner in which material from one location can be inadvertently transferred to another. The most common situation for cross-transfer to occur is in police vehicles where a victim has been transported and then subsequently a suspect is transported in the same vehicle, for example.

Material such as fibres, for example, may transfer onto the vehicle seat from a victim. A suspect could then pick up those fibres on their clothing when they later sit in the vehicle. In such circumstances any fibre evidence could be rendered useless.

This problem can also occur when an investigator deals with a victim of crime and then subsequently deals with the suspect. Where evidence of contact is required, it is vital to ensure that it can be demonstrated that any such evidence has not occurred as a result of cross-transfer.

Contamination—This is defined in the Forensic Science Regulator's (FSR) publication *The Control and Avoidance of Contamination in Crime Scene Examination involving DNA Evidence Recovery* as:

> The introduction of DNA, or biological material containing DNA, to an exhibit at or after the point when a controlled forensic process starts

Essentially this is when something is added to the sample, accidentally or deliberately after the point official investigation has commenced. This can occur, for example, by an investigator sneezing over material that potentially bears DNA; their DNA can then contaminate the stain. As forensic analytical techniques become more sensitive and able to detect increasingly smaller amounts of material, contamination is a *very real issue*.

Cross-transfer and contamination can be avoided by ensuring that investigators deal with only one particular aspect of the investigation, avoid unnecessary movement around a scene, and be mindful of the vehicles used by themselves, victims, witnesses and potential offenders.

Gloves

The wearing of protective latex or nitrile gloves when handling items of potential forensic value is essential, both to protect the evidence and protect investigators—items may bear material that is hazardous or causes risks to the health and safety of those that handle them. Wearing gloves, however, does not make the wearer immune to the possibilities of contamination and cross-transfer of evidence. Gloves should always be changed when handling different/separate items that potentially contain body fluids, drugs, firearm or explosive residues, due to the high transferability of such material and the sensitivity of the forensic analytical processes that may be required.

Conditions of storage

Where an item is seized for the recovery of potential forensic material, it is important to ensure that it is kept in conditions which will maximise the potential for any forensic material to be recovered.

Where an investigator has seized an item for any purpose, they have a duty to ensure that the item is kept in the condition that it was found in, prior to forensic examination.

Where items are not required for forensic examination or analysis and have been recovered for safe keeping or identification purposes only, it must be borne in mind that such material may be returned to the lawful owner at some time. It should therefore be returned in the condition in which it was recovered.

....

Case study—A consequence of improper property storage

Items of clothing and personal effects were seized from a deceased person who was unidentified for some time. It was later found that no suspicious circumstances surrounded the death and the next of kin requested that the property from the deceased be returned to them. Due to improper packaging and storage, items of the deceased's clothing had developed a substantial amount of black mould upon them due to being damp when they were improperly sealed into a plastic bag.

The police force in question was liable to pay compensation for the damage caused to the property. In addition to the loss to the deceased person's family and the potential financial cost to the police service, there is the damage caused to the reputation of the service as a whole.

But the most important point here is that in the event that any forensic examination would have been required, the condition of the items could mean that certain forensic analysis techniques would not be viable.

....

4.2.3 Health and safety considerations for exhibit handling

Items recovered from crime scenes may present risks to health and safety. There may be associated risks of infection from items containing bodily fluids/bacteria and the risk of injury from items such as broken glass and knives, for example. It is vital that investigators take precautions to avoid the risk of injury or infection during the initial handling of potentially hazardous items and that any associated hazards are communicated clearly to all those who will subsequently handle the exhibit.

The wearing of disposable latex gloves to handle exhibits is the *minimum* requirement when handling exhibits, as protection from possible infections and to protect any potential forensic evidence. Disposable dust masks should be worn to protect from the inhalation of airborne materials at illicit drug laboratories and where dried blood/body fluids are present. Dried bodily fluids such as blood can become airborne as small particles when disturbed, these airborne particles can then subsequently be inhaled.

Items bearing body fluids must be labelled as 'Biohazard' in a manner that makes it clear to everyone who will subsequently handle the exhibit that there is a risk of infection from biological material. Where it is known that the donor of the body fluid has an infectious disease such as HIV or hepatitis B it is vital this information is documented and made available to those who will be undertaking any forensic analysis on the items.

'Health hazard' labelling should be used in circumstances where a risk to health exists but is not in the form of bodily fluid, for example, powdered drug residues that can be inhaled. Items that contain solvent and liquid accelerants such as petrol must be labelled as 'flammable' and stored in a cool, well-ventilated area. Exhibits that contain broken glass, knives and similar objects that can cause injury should be packaged so as to prevent injury occurring to those that subsequently handle the items.

The basic rule is that all exhibits must not only be packaged in a manner that will protect the evidence but also protect the health and safety of all those who may subsequently come into contact with them.

4.2.4 Digital evidence preservation

Digital forensics is the term given to the recovery and analysis of data from digital devices and as such is not covered within this book; however the proliferation of digital technology means that investigators will inevitably be faced with seizing devices such as computers, mobile phones, tablets, satellite navigation systems, 'wearable technology', smart watches and digital cameras/videos, for example.

There are specific considerations to be made regarding the recovery and storage of such items as incorrect handling can result in data loss and therefore evidence.

KEY POINT—THE FOUR PRINCIPLES

These are to be adhered to when seizing digital devices. In summary, investigators must consider the following four principles when seizing any digital media devices;

Principle 1:

No action taken by law enforcement agencies or their agents should change data held on a computer or storage media which may subsequently be relied upon in court.

Principle 2:

In circumstances where a person finds it necessary to access original data held on a computer or on storage media, that person must be competent to do so and be able to give evidence explaining the relevance and the implications of their actions.

Principle 3:

An audit trail or other record of all processes applied to computer-based electronic evidence should be created and preserved. An independent third party should be able to examine those processes and achieve the same result.

Principle 4:

The person in charge of the investigation (the case officer) has overall responsibility for ensuring that the law and these principles are adhered to.

If these principles cannot be shown to have been applied, this could render evidence as inadmissible.

In addition to exhibit handling protocols covered later in this chapter to preserve physical evidence, digital devices require specific procedures to recover, transport and store them where digital evidence is required. Where any doubt exists as to the correct actions for a particular case, the advice of a DMI should be sought.

Checklist—Seizing devices to preserve digital evidence

General considerations

- Handle all items with due regard to physical forensic evidence such as fingerprints, DNA and trace material such as drug residues, for example.

- If a device is on, switch it off in accordance with particular guidance below. Unintended and unwanted changes can be made to potential evidence if a device is not handled properly.

- Ensure suspects/users are prevented from accessing/interfering with the device to prevent changes/loss of data.

- Some screensavers may give the appearance that a device is off, check whether LED lights of hard drive/monitor LED are illuminated.

- Document what is on the screen, including any date/time shown on the display. This can be recorded as written notes, and/or by photographing the screen.

- If a device is off *never* switch it on. Be aware, some laptops automatically power on when lid is lifted.

- Allow any printing to finish.

- Recover any user manuals, packaging (which can contain international mobile equipment identity (IMEI)/personal identification number (PIN) and PIN unlock key (PUK) codes), any notebooks/diaries/scraps of paper that may bear passwords.

- Recover all peripheral equipment as appropriate for each case—cables, hubs, printers, cameras (eg, if case requires digital cameras containing metadata that can be used to link indecent images), media storage such as memory cards/sticks, CDs/DVDs, external hard drives, for example.

- Disconnect USB and power cables from the device and *not* the power source (eg, wall socket).

Computer specific actions

- To power off a computer, *only where appropriate to do so*, remove all cables from the machine—*NEVER* unplug power cables from an electric supply point.

- For laptops, remove the battery before removing any power cable or closing the lid—some laptops will automatically turn off or go into standby mode when lid is closed.

- Never search a computer for potential evidence, it may be overwritten, lost or otherwise compromised. Only DMIs are able to do this in a manner to preserve digital evidence.

- Record all cables, *in situ*, prior to removal as outlined earlier. This can be done with a sketch diagram or photograph.

- Trace all cables along their length, they may lead to devices in other rooms/hidden in lofts, for example.

- If a program or document is running that may contain potential evidence *do not* attempt to turn the device off. Contact a DMI for advice.

- Suspects with a high level of technical knowledge may have installed encryption software, if the device is powered off data will be lost. It is possible to remotely trigger devices to 'wipe' the hard drive to destroy evidence. If it is believed that the computer has been activated to destroy data, immediately remove power cable from the device (not the wall socket)

- Allow equipment to cool down before packaging in anti-static bags. If such bags are not available, paper evidence sacks or cardboard boxes may be used, or wrap items in paper sheets before sealing into an aerated plastic bag secured with numbered cable ties.

Mobile device specific actions

- If the device is on, record what is on the screen before switching it off—consideration needs to be given as to whether this is appropriate in each particular case. Switching it off preserves battery life but it may be password protected when switched on. If left on, then it should be examined by a DMI at the earliest opportunity.

- As guidance above but in addition mobile devices that are wireless/WIFI enabled (eg, mobile phones, tablets, personal data assistants (PDAs)) should ideally be sealed in a 'Faraday' evidence bag to prevent it receiving signals if digital evidence is required.

- Computer equipment that may have been connected to the handset for synchronization or similar should be seized where appropriate.

Transport and storage

- Keep digital devices away from magnetic fields that are produced by radio transmitters, loudspeakers, heated seats and windows in vehicles, for example.

- Ensure all items are protected from physical shock and keep computers upright.

- Store at normal room temperature, avoiding extremes of temperature and excess humidity.

To maximise the best forensic potentials it is important to discuss the requirements of the case with a CSI and DMI.

4.3 **Basic Principles for Packaging of Exhibits**

Certain principles will always apply to the packaging of exhibits to ensure that potential forensic evidence is preserved.

Exhibits must always be packaged and sealed at the time of seizure to ensure that the continuity and integrity of the item can be demonstrated.

KEY POINT—PACKAGING

Take the packaging to the exhibit and *not* the exhibit to the packaging.

It is useful to photograph an item *in situ* if possible, or document its position on a sketch diagram if potential evidence requires recovery prior to attendance of a CSI. This should only be done where absolutely necessary, to avoid loss or destruction of evidence or when the incident is one that a CSI would not be attending.

TV cameras at scenes have often recorded items being removed from a scene in unsealed bags, thus giving the defence team an argument that cross-transfer and/or contamination has occurred. This has, on occasion, resulted in evidence being rendered inadmissible. Similarly, cameras in custody units record unsealed bags being removed from cells after seizing clothing and the defence team have a right to view such footage. However, safety concerns may mean it is unadvisable to remain in a cell with a person who is violent/agitated, though the movement of items away from the cell area should be minimised and bags sealed as soon as safely practicable.

Once securely packaged and sealed at the scene, the exhibit must not be subsequently opened to be shown in an interview with a suspect, for example. This is where detailed notes, exhibit descriptions, sketches or photographs can be useful. Suggestions that any forensic material recovered from an exhibit has come from the suspect during the interview procedure can render any evidence of contact as inconclusive and possibly inadmissible in court.

Where an exhibit needs to be opened for sub-exhibiting or photography purposes, this must be done in clean secure area to avoid any cross-transfer or contamination. Covering a bench or table with a clean paper sheet is recommended, gloves should be worn to handle the item and a record of what has been done, by whom and where, and for what purpose should be made and the continuity part of the exhibit label completed. Exhibit the paper sheets if material such as fibres, glass or body fluids, for example, could potentially have been transferred onto the paper.

Where an investigator has taken the trouble to seize an item for evidential purposes, it is inexcusable to then jeopordise the potential evidence by the incorrect handling, packaging and storage of the exhibit.

Checklist—Exhibit handling

If items of potential forensic evidence are to have any value at all, it is imperative that they are handled with due care and consideration to the forensic potentials. Investigators must:

- Avoid giving support to a defence team by enabling the suggestion that the evidence lacks integrity and value.

- Demonstrate the integrity of exhibits by ensuring correct recovery, recording, package and handling is undertaken at every stage.

- Show that continuity of the item is proven by correctly completing exhibit labels and keeping notes of what has been done with the exhibit, by whom and when.

- Remain vigilant to the issues of cross-transfer and contamination of evidence.

- Be honest about movements within a scene and any handling of potential evidence. This ensures such actions can be taken into account in any subsequent forensic examination/analysis.

- Always wear gloves as a minimum when handling potential exhibits, to protect any evidence and ensure risks to health and safety are minimised/eliminated.

4.3.1 Packaging of dry items

The type of potential forensic evidence required will determine the type of packaging method used. Generally, brown paper evidence sacks or plastic bags can be used for dry items; however the following considerations need to be made if the following types of forensic analysis are required.

Indented writing or footwear

Where paper or other pliable material has been walked over by an offender there may be indented impressions of footwear present. Similarly, paper may bear indented impressions of handwriting. To preserve indented impressions on paper such items must be placed into a rigid package, either a box or between sheets of card, which is then sealed into a paper or plastic evidence bag. *Do not lean* on the packaged item to write exhibit labels, as the indentations from this can show up when the item is processed.

Fingerprints

Brown paper sacks or envelopes, cardboard boxes or plastic bags are suitable for items that may contain fingerprints. Consideration should be given to the fact that fingerprints can be removed or damaged by friction, so any movement of the item within the packaging should be restricted.

Footwear or leather items

If dry such items should be packaged in paper evidence sacks or cardboard boxes. If sealed into plastic packaging, mould can develop on the items which can degrade any potential DNA material and disrupt or destroy the potential for any other evidence such as fingerprints or fibres.

Where possible, footwear should be placed in a paper 'window' sack with the sole visible through the transparent panel. This enables the sole pattern to be viewed without having to unseal a bag.

If the item is wet, package as per the guidance given below. With footwear, package one shoe per bag, do not place both shoes in the same bag.

4.3.2 Wet or damp items

Items that are recovered in a damp or wet condition should ideally be air dried as soon as possible in a designated secure and forensically clean drying cabinet that meets the requirements set out by the FSR. One exception to this is where analysis for suspected accelerant is required. Drying cabinets or rooms are generally available within the CSI department for this purpose. The drying cabinets used should undergo decontamination cleaning prior to and following each use to ensure that no transfer or contamination is possible.

Checklist—Drying wet items

- Deal with one item at a time.

- Packaging should be opened at the opposite end to the original seal (so that the integrity of the original seal is verifiable).

- Packaging to be opened outside of, but very close to, the drying cabinet.

- Place a clean paper sheet under the item to capture any trace evidence that might fall off while it dries.

- Do not re-use hangers.

- Items from the same case should be segregated. Exhibits from different scenes, suspect(s) and victim(s) should not be handled or dried in same location. Similarly, items from any other scene should not be present during drying process.

- Dried exhibits should be re-packaged and re-sealed. The paper used beneath the item whilst it was drying must be packaged separately and kept with original item.

- Use the original packaging to re-package dried items, if this is not possible use fresh packaging and retain the original packaging (placed into a separate bag) with the exhibit for continuity purposes.

- The location of the drying cabinet, time and date of the drying should be recorded in the investigator's notebook. Exhibit details should be recorded in the drying cabinet log book.

- Packaging for items that contain bodily fluids must be clearly marked as 'biohazard', either by using biohazard tape or by writing 'biohazard' on the exterior of the packaging so that it is clearly visible.

- If items cannot be dried in a designated, secure drying cabinet, they must be frozen as soon as possible.

Paper evidence sacks are porous and it has been noted on occasions that moisture from damp or wet items has been absorbed by the paper to be visible on the outer surface of the bag. By placing the item in an *unsealed* plastic bag which is then sealed into a brown paper evidence bag any seepage can be avoided, preserving the integrity and avoiding cross-contamination and any potential risks to health and safety (see Figure 4.1).

Figure 4.1 Packaging technique for damp/wet items

Example—A shirt stained with wet possible blood. Be mindful that where the positioning of potential blood or other wet staining will be required for the forensic examination, the item needs to be kept flat or carefully folded and not crumpled up, to avoid transference of the stain to other areas of the item.

Brown paper must be inserted between folded surfaces to reduce the risk of the stain transferring to 'clean' areas. Seek the advice of a CSI if in doubt.

Place the item into a clean plastic bag. Roll the top of the plastic bag down so it remains slightly open, allowing air to circulate and stop mould forming on the item.

DO NOT SEAL THE PLASTIC BAG.
Place the unsealed plastic bag into a paper evidence sack. Securely seal the paper evidence sack.

KEY POINT—DRYING WET/DAMP ITEMS

Under no circumstances should wet items of potential evidence be dried in office areas/locker rooms, for example, as this undermines the integrity of the item, poses a risk to health and safety and enables transfer and contamination of potential evidence.

Frozen items should be air dried prior to submission for forensic analysis unless they are being taken directly to a lab and their frozen state can be maintained. It is important to check with the individual laboratory to ascertain their preferences for receiving items that have been frozen.

75

4.4 **Packaging Materials**

When an item containing potential forensic evidence is exhibited, consideration must be given as to the type of evidence that may be available and appropriate steps taken to ensure that the item is kept in a manner to get the best evidence from it.

In serious cases, most of the items required for forensic examination will be recovered by CSIs or other appropriate forensic specialists, who are trained to identify the forensic potential of items and who will have a range of purpose specific recovery methods and packaging available to them. There are occasions, however, where it is necessary for an initial responder or other investigator to recover items of potential forensic value. Advice and guidance on particular evidential recovery and packaging techniques can be sought from a CSI by way of telephone/radio communication.

There are various packaging materials available for the recovery of exhibits, and the type of packaging used should ensure that the item cannot suffer any damage, alteration, loss or destruction and that the health and safety of all those who may handle the exhibit is protected. The following materials are those that are commonly used for exhibit packaging (see also Figure 4.2).

Figure 4.2 Example of packaging materials

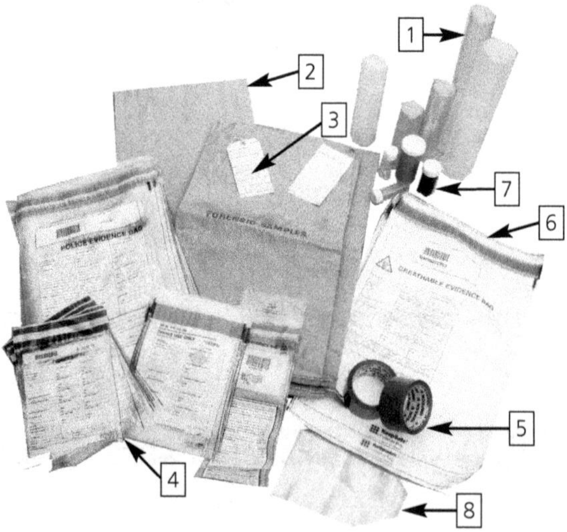

Key

1 Knife tubes

2 Paper evidence sacks

3 Exhibit labels

4 Tamper-evident bags

5 Parcel tape

6 Breathable tamper-evident bags

7 Poly pots

8 Plastic bags

4.4.1 **Paper evidence sacks**

Brown paper evidence sacks can be used for the packaging of all dry leather items, footwear (one shoe per bag) and other dry items. The technique shown in Figure 4.3 for the sealing of the brown paper evidence sacks will ensure that the integrity of the exhibit can be demonstrated.

Figure 4.3 Sealing of brown paper evidence sacks

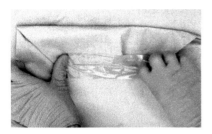

Fold over the top corners of the evidence sacks; fold over again to make a flap and tape this down, covering all the folded edges.

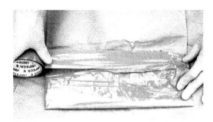

Fold the top edge over again and secure with tape ensuring the edges are covered.

Using parcel tape, seal over the stitched seal at the bottom of the bag and around the transparent 'window' edges if appropriate to prevent loss of microscopic particulate evidence and increases the integrity of the exhibit.

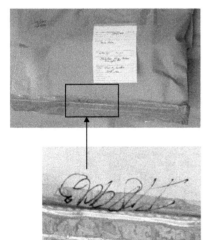

Sign and date over all the taped seals on all edges. An alternative to this is to use a signed and dated adhesive label placed over the seals. Securely attach the exhibit label by tying/taping the string securely to the exhibit. Using staples to secure labels is not advised.

It is prudent to write exhibit label details onto the bag in case exhibit label becomes detached.

Ensure any hazard warnings (eg, biohazard, health hazard) are clearly visible on outside of packaging. Store in a cool dry secure store if exhibit is dry or in a freezer if exhibit is wet/damp or contains body fluids. 'Breathable' tamper-evident evidence bags are an alternative to brown paper evidence sacks.

4.4.2 **Tamper-evident bags**

These bags are constructed from a strong plastic and have an adhesive strip seal and can be used for dry items and are particularly good for packaging items of value such as cash or drugs or DNA bearing material, as each bag has its own unique barcode and reference number making them particularly useful for continuity and integrity purposes. Record the reference number of the bag in contemporaneous notes and on investigation logs/statements.

The exhibit label is pre-printed on the bags and should be completed prior to inserting the item—with a fine tipped permanent marker or ballpoint pen (gel inks can easily be removed from the label).

4.4.3 **Boxes**

Cardboard boxes are useful for packaging items that would suffer damage if not protected by a rigid container, such as indented writing or footwear impressions on paper or pieces of glass, for example. To secure items into a box to avoid movement, boxes which have a removable inner liner containing pre-punched holes through which cable ties can be inserted to secure items are best. If these are not available, small holes can be punched in the bottom of a clean box, the item then secured with string or plastic cable ties, in a manner that will restrict movement without jeopardising potential evidence (see below). It is vital that any holes made in a box are covered securely with tape to avoid contamination or loss of material. It is best to place such boxes into a paper or plastic evidence bag to ensure that the integrity of evidence is maintained and eliminate the potential loss of microscopic evidence.

Do not use adhesive tape to secure an item into a box as this can damage potential evidence when it is removed. See Figure 4.4 for the method to secure items into a box.

Figure 4.4 Securing items into a box

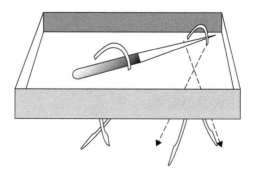

Where the box will not be sealed into a bag, the lid must be securely taped down and all visible seams of the box taped over. Sign and date across all the taped seals.

4.4.4 **Knife tubes**

These are purpose made plastic tubes in a variety of sizes for packaging sharp, bladed items including knives and screwdrivers, for example, in a manner that protects the evidence and anyone coming into contact with the exhibit.

KEY POINT—KNIFE TUBES

It is important to be aware that when the two parts of the tube are twisted together, it is possible for sharp blades to pierce the bottom of the tube if closed up too tightly, resulting in possible injury and contamination/loss of potential evidence where, for example, a blade is required for tool mark analysis, minute striations can be altered by such activity. The tube needs to be secure enough to prevent movement of the item without being overly tightened.

Knife tubes should be sealed with tape to cover the joint of the two parts. Sign and date over the taped joint with a fine tipped permanent marker pen. Place the sealed tube into a paper evidence sack or plastic bag (ideally a tamper-evident bag) and seal.

Attach exhibit label to the bag (if using tamper-evident bag, complete the label *before* inserting the item).

Where any of the contents may contain body fluids the exhibit packaging must be labelled as 'biohazard' either by using a pre-printed adhesive tape or by writing 'biohazard' clearly and visibly on outer packaging.

4.4.5 **Nylon bags**

Nylon bags *must always* be used where analysis for the presence of liquid accelerants is required. Clothing from a suspect, victim or witness believed to be involved in arson and containers or other items that are believed to have contained liquid accelerant *must* be packaged in nylon bags at the earliest opportunity to prevent loss of potential evidence through evaporation.

KEY POINT—LIQUID ACCELERANT ANALYSIS

Forensic analysis for accelerants, very simply put, involves heat being applied to the packaged exhibit and a fine probe inserted into the bag to sample the vapour inside in what is termed 'headspace analysis'. The analysis can, depending on the

---

circumstances, provide information of the chemical nature of any liquid accelerant, establish the amount of accelerant present in the sample and provide comparisons with samples from different locations to potentially link a suspect with the crime scenes. The success or otherwise of the analysis is dependent on the correct packaging of the exhibit.

Such items ideally should be recovered by a CSI; however there may be occasions where an initial responder must recover the item to secure any potential evidence.

Nylon bags should be kept in a secure area away from any potential contamination—having such packaging loose in the boot of a police vehicle, for example, is not appropriate. The batch number of the bags used should be recorded in contemporaneous notes and subsequent statements.

A control sample of the nylon bags must be submitted, to enable a scientist to determine if the bags used for packaging contain any contaminant that may have an effect on the analytical results.

It is not advisable to use adhesive tapes to seal the bags as the adhesive may 'relax' during heating, allowing any vapour to escape. There is also a small chance the adhesive may interfere with the analytical result.

Use the largest size bag available as both ends of the nylon bag need to be sealed using a 'twist and tie' swan-necking technique (see Figure 4.5), which will reduce the space available for the exhibit. Double bagging is required with both bags sealed with the swan-necked sealing technique. It is important *not* to expel all air from the bag. Where clothing or other textiles such as cloths/carpet pieces, for example, are wet or damp from suspected accelerants they *must not* be air dried prior to packaging.

Liquid accelerants or fire debris must be contained in clean glass or metal containers. It is always preferable to seek the advice of a CSI or suitable forensic expert before decanting such material from its original container.

Figure 4.5 'Twist and tie swan necked' sealing technique to preserve a suspected accelerant

1. Twist the bottom sealed end of the bag and tie a knot in the twist, about halfway along its length. Fold the twisted tail of the bag over the knot. Secure above and below the knot—with string or a cable tie, ensuring there will be enough room in the bag for the item.

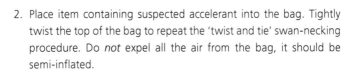

2. Place item containing suspected accelerant into the bag. Tightly twist the top of the bag to repeat the 'twist and tie' swan-necking procedure. Do *not* expel all the air from the bag, it should be semi-inflated.

3. Bend the twisted neck of the bag over on itself and secure tightly above and below the knot with a cable tie or string.

4. Take a second nylon bag and repeat the twist and swan-necking technique as per steps 1–3. Place the first sealed nylon bag containing the exhibit into the second nylon bag. Repeat the 'twist and tie' swan-necking technique to seal exhibit into second nylon bag.

5. A control sample of the nylon bag is a requirement of many analytical laboratories. Please check your local policies.

6. To submit a 'control' bag and air sample take an empty nylon bag from the same pack used for exhibit. Use the 'twist and tie' method to seal one end of bag, and in the vicinity from where exhibit was recovered, trap some air in the bag, seal other end of bag with 'twist and tie' technique. Double bag control sample in the same manner as the exhibit.

7. Place the sealed exhibit into a brown evidence sack or box to prevent the nylon bags being punctured. Attach exhibit label to bag/box and label bag as 'Flammable'. Place control air/bag sample in a separate bag/box. This should be labelled as 'control air/bag' on exhibit label.

The advantage of submitting a control bag/air sample is that if analysis recovers accelerant in the exhibit but not in the control sample then it can be ascertained that the exhibit contained the accelerant and its presence did not arise from residual levels in atmosphere.

KEY POINT—NUMBERED CABLE TIES

When using numbered cable ties, record these numbers in contemporaneous notes and any reports/statements to ensure continuity and integrity.

It is advisable to write the details from the exhibit label directly on the outside of a box or bag in case the label becomes lost or damaged. If a box is not available, a sturdy brown paper evidence sack is a good alternative. A 'flammable' warning should be attached using printed hazard warning tape/stickers or by writing clearly on the outside of the box/paper bag. Exhibits suspected of containing accelerants must be stored in a cool well-ventilated secure store away from ignition sources.

KEY POINT—ARSON EXHIBITS

Due to the seriousness of arson cases, it is preferable that a CSI recover any items for accelerant analysis as they have the appropriate packaging materials and training to recover such potential evidence.

4.5 Exhibit Labelling

Applying an exhibit label is the first stage in the continuity audit trail of an item and is used to record the details of the exhibit and its movements during the entire investigative process. The exhibit label has a key role in the demonstration of the continuity and integrity of the item. Details entered onto an exhibit label *must* be accurate and precise; any mistakes in recording information may lead to questions on the integrity of the exhibit, ruling it inadmissible as evidential material.

Exhibit labels may differ in format; however the key information required is standard.

4.5.1 Identifying reference or exhibit number

An exhibit label must contain a unique identifying reference number, which is the seizing investigator's exhibit number. A common format for an exhibit number involves the investigator's initials followed by a number—for example, ABC/1 is the first exhibit seized by Arthur Brian Chalk, subsequent exhibits seized by Mr Chalk—in the same case—would be ABC/2, ABC/3 and so on. This may then be followed by the unique case reference/incident number, for example ABC1/123456.

The numbering of exhibits will recommence at number 1 (eg, ABC/1) when the investigator deals with exhibits for different cases. Although the investigator may seize several exhibits denoted ABC/1 on the same day, the exhibit details such as the location and unique case/incident number will serve to distinguish the items and link them to the correct case/incident.

An exhibit reference should not be confused with the court exhibit number which is applied during the trial process and is for the use of the courts only. An investigator may have siezed twenty exhibits, for example, but the court may require only three of these.

Some forces use the case reference number and/or the investigator's collar/shoulder number in addition to the initials and sequential numbering in differing sequences. The individual force policy on exhibits will detail the force requirements for exhibit numbering.

4.5.2 **Item description**

The description of the item should note key identifying features; descriptions such as 'brown envelope' are not appropriate. 'Brown envelope addressed to…' is much better for continuity and integrity purposes as it distinguishes one brown envelope from the many others that may be submitted for forensic examination and individualises this particular envelope as the one that was seized.

Stating very specific details such as measurements on exhibit labels, for example, 'knife with 10cm blade', should be avoided as this can lead to questions being raised in court if the blade is subsequently found to be less, or more than 10cm in length. Terms such as 'approximately' should be avoided as this can lead to unnecessary judicial questioning—an approximation can be regarded as a 'guess', and as such is not appropriate for a profession that deals with facts. Where details such as the length of a blade are required, the item should be photographed next to a scale (ruler), ideally by a CSI and in such a manner as not to jeopardise or interfere with any further forensic analysis.

Similarly, there should be an avoidance of stating any stain is 'blood'; terms such as 'possible blood', 'apparent blood' or 'presumed blood' are more acceptable if there is a belief blood stains may be present, for example, 'Shirt containing dark staining (possible blood)'. This is because only a scientist can state that a substance is definitely blood following analysis of the stain. Describing the stain as 'possible blood' indicates that the investigator was open minded as to the origin of the stain, whilst highlighting the potential biohazard risk. The key difference between making a descriptive statement regarding the length of a blade and the nature of a stain is that it is necessary for scientific analysis to establish the identity of such a stain.

The same consideration should be observed when making any statements that aim to identify any substance; a gold ring should be described as a 'yellow metal ring', for example.

KEY POINT—EXHIBIT DESCRIPTION

Avoid stating anything on an exhibit label descriptor that you *do not know as an absolute fact.*

4.5.3 **Time and date**

This is the time and date the item was originally seized as an exhibit. It is extremely important to ensure these details are totally correct as mistakes as to time and date can prove costly at a later stage if doubt can be raised in court. The time should be taken from an accurate source and not guessed at and the same goes for the date. Any alterations can look suspicious and may need explaining under cross examination in court.

4.5.4 **Location details**

The location from which the item was seized should be similarly accurate and specific, detailing the precise location from which the item was recovered. If an item was recovered from the front passenger side (front near side = FNS) footwell of a vehicle, for example, the location details must indicate this and include the make, model and vehicle registration number, for example, 'FNS footwell of Green Vauxhall Vectra, registration "ABC123Z"'.

The position/location of an exhibit from where originally recovered can serve to corroborate or refute versions of events given by offenders/witnesses/victims and be beneficial in any reconstructions of events. A sketch diagram or photograph can be a useful way to expand on such information.

4.5.5 **Details of person recovering the exhibit**

The person recovering the item must record their full name, rank/role, collar number (if applicable) and sign the exhibit label in the correct place. If it is a member of the public or victim of crime handing over an item, it becomes their exhibit and it is their initials that are used to formulate the exhibit number. Their name and signature are required as the person producing the item.

Any investigator receiving such an item from a member of the public must duly sign the continuity section of the exhibit label.

4.5.6 **Continuity recording**

Any person subsequently taking control of or handling an exhibit must endorse the label with their own details and sign, time and date the exhibit label for continuity purposes. When an investigator hands an exhibit to another person, they must ensure that the individual correctly endorses the exhibit label *at the time* it is handed over. If something is later found amiss with the exhibit, it will be the last person who has signed the label that will be questioned regarding this. A note of the time and date and person receiving the exhibit should also be made in the investigator's contemporaneous notes.

KEY POINT—GOLDEN RULES FOR EXHIBIT LABELS

1. Accurate details must be recorded on labels such as item description, location, time, date, name and signature of person recovering exhibit.
2. Every time a different person 'handles' an exhibit they must sign the continuity section on the label at the time. The exhibit label is a key tool in demonstrating the continuity of an exhibit.
3. Many cases have been lost due to errors made on exhibit labels—exercise due diligence when completing labels.

4.5.7 **Sub-exhibiting**

Where an exhibit consists of several separate items, for example a handbag and contents, it is important when initially seizing such an item to state on the exhibit label, 'Handbag and contents'—the individual contents do not necessarily have to be listed on the label, but should be recorded in contemporaneous notes. There is not usually room to list many items on the label, but if a handbag contains, for example, only a red purse, you can itemise this. Items subsequently removed from the handbag or purse for further examination will require exhibiting separately.

In the case of a mobile phone removed from a handbag which is exhibited as ABC/1, the phone will need to be exhibited sequentially as 'ABC/2—mobile phone recovered from ABC/1'.

It is important to always refer back to the original exhibit to maintain continuity. Many computerised property recording systems, including the Home Office large major enquiry system (HOLMES) cannot easily accommodate sub-exhibit numbering systems that give secondary numbers or letters to denote the item as a sub-exhibit, for example the mobile phone from the handbag being exhibited as ABC1/1 or ABC/1a. This is due to the restricted number of characters available for exhibit numbers on such systems.

If forensic analysis is required, it is likely that different parts of the exhibit will require analysis at different locations which is why items require 'splitting' or sub-exhibiting. Figure 4.6 illustrates the concept of sub-exhibiting and the demonstration of the continuity chain.

The continuity of all property seized must be maintained and sub-exhibiting enables an accurate record of all the items seized to be generated and will demonstrate the continuity and integrity of the exhibit(s) throughout the investigation.

Figure 4.6 The chain of continuity generated from one initial exhibit

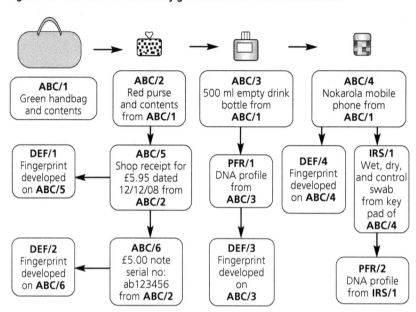

Summary of personnel involved in the continuity chain

PC Arthur Brian Chalk recovers a handbag and contents, exhibited as ABC/1. The bag contains a purse, an empty drink bottle and a mobile phone. The items are sub-exhibited and the following forensic examinations are undertaken.

Daniel Eric Fuller, the fingerprint laboratory technician, recovers fingerprints on some of the items.

The CSI, Imogen Rita Somerton, swabs the mobile phone for possible DNA. The mobile phone is then submitted for fingerprint recovery.

The forensic scientist, Polly Fiona Roberts, generates DNA profiles from the swabs and the water bottle.

Each person must complete the continuity record on the exhibit label and supply a continuity statement detailing their involvement with the exhibit. At each stage of the process there is a record which enables accountability and tracing of an exhibit's movement throughout the investigative process, providing the court with a demonstrable chain of continuity.

4.6 Chapter Summary

The initial recovery of any exhibit in an investigation is perhaps the most important time in its evidential chain. The handling, packaging, labelling and subsequent storage of the exhibit can have a huge impact on the investigation as a whole. If an exhibit is recovered, packaged, labelled and stored incorrectly there is a real risk that any potential forensic evidence will be lost or that a defence team could suggest that contamination and/or cross-transfer of the material has occurred. The key principles that should be foremost in an investigator's mind when handling any exhibits are those of accuracy, detailed, concise recording of item specifics and the principles of continuity and integrity.

The continuity and integrity of exhibits must be proved beyond reasonable doubt in a court of law and the value of these principles is only ever really appreciated when an exhibit is lost, damaged, destroyed or the evidence is devalued through failure to instigate and maintain the correct procedures that prove integrity and continuity of the exhibit at each stage.

It is vital that the continuity and integrity of exhibits can be demonstrated not only for the purposes of the courts, but also for any forensic analysis to be undertaken. Forensic examination may be refused if a scientist is not satisfied that the continuity and integrity of an item is sufficiently robust. Accurate record keeping and appropriate packaging techniques are the first steps to ensuring the continuity and integrity of exhibits.

Investigators must avoid dealing with items from more than one associated scene to prevent cross-transfer of material from a victim to a suspect, for example. Records of vehicles used to transport victims or suspects should be recorded in the investigator's contemporaneous notes.

All exhibits must be handled to the same standards irrespective of whether they are recovered during the investigation of a minor or serious offence.

KNOWLEDGE CHECK—EXHIBIT HANDLING

1. What are the key principles to be maintained when handling items of potential evidence?

   The process of demonstrating the continuity and integrity of the exhibit must be instigated by the investigator who initially recovers the item.

2. State the ways in which the principles in Q1 can be applied.

   The continuity of an exhibit can be instigated by recording concise and accurate details of the item on the exhibit label and in contemporaneous notes. The minimum details required are an identifying reference/exhibit number, a description of the item noting any individualising features, the time and date seized, the location from where the exhibit was taken and the name and signature of the person seizing the item. The continuity label must be completed by all those who subsequently handle the exhibit.

   The integrity of an exhibit begins with the completion of accurate documentation (continuity) and the application of the correct packaging techniques. The correct handling, packaging and storage of an exhibit can demonstrate that no unaccountable interference can have occurred, whether so caused accidentally or deliberately.

3. State the method for packaging items suspected of containing accelerants.

Nylon bags should be used in all cases where analysis for suspected accelerants is required. The exhibit is heated in an oven and the vapour analysed to establish the chemical composition of an accelerant, possibly the quantity of accelerant present in the sample and to potentially link it to other samples from different locations. Nylon bags must be used as they are non-porous and will contain the vapour. The nylon bag must be sealed using the 'twist and tie swan neck' technique, and double bagged. Adhesive tape must not be used to seal nylon bags. Nylon bagged exhibits need to be protected from potential puncture by properly sealing into a box or brown paper evidence sack. A control bag/air sample is required to negate the possibility of atmospheric or other contamination.

4. When should items of potential forensic evidence be moved/recovered by investigators?

When a CSI is unavailable or will not be attending the scene or their attendance is delayed and the item is at risk of being lost, damaged or destroyed if left in its original position. The movement or recovery of such material must be documented and the CSI (if attending) be informed of any actions taken by the investigator.

5. State the method and considerations required to recover a computer that is on.

Prevent users from touching device to prevent them deleting/changing data.

Never search a computer for potential evidence, it may be overwritten, lost or otherwise compromised.

Record what is on screen including the date and time as displayed by the device, and the position of cables, in a sketch diagram or photograph.

If a program or document is running that may contain potential evidence *do not* attempt to turn the device off. Contact the digital forensic unit for advice.

Hard drives can be triggered to be 'wiped' remotely to destroy evidence. If it is believed that the computer has been activated to destroy data, immediately remove power cable from the device (not the wall socket).

If appropriate to do so, remove all cables from the machine itself—never unplug power cable from electric supply point.

Remove battery from laptops before removing any power cable or closing the lid—some laptops automatically turn off or go into standby mode when lid is closed.

Trace cables along their length, they may lead to devices in other rooms/hidden in lofts, for example.

Encryption software can destroy data if the device is powered off.

Allow equipment to cool down before packaging in anti-static bags—paper evidence sacks or cardboard boxes or wrap in paper and sealing into an aerated plastic bag secured with cable ties.

Be mindful of physical forensic evidence and handle items to preserve fingerprints, DNA and other material that may link people/scenes.

Recommended Reading

Crime Investigators' Handbook (2013) Cook, T, Hill, M and Hibbitt, S.

eDiscovery in digital forensic investigations (2014) Home Office CAST Publication 32/14.

Evidence & Procedure (2015) Johnston, D and Hutton, G.

Examination Involving DNA Evidence Recovery (Draft) (2015) Forensic Science Regulator.

Exhibits: A Guide for Forces (2013) Home Office.

General Police Duties (2015) Hutton, G and McKinnon, G.

Good Practice Guide for Digital Evidence (2012) Association of Chief Police Officers (ACPO).

Good Practice Guide for Managers of e-Crime investigation (2012) ACPO.

Managing investigations (2014) College of Policing APP: <http://www.app.college.police.uk/app/content/investigations/managing-investigations/>.

The Control and Avoidance of Contamination in Crime Scene Examination involving DNA Evidence Recovery (Draft) (2015) Forensic Science Regulator.

The Police and Criminal Evidence Act 1984 (2013) Zander, M.

Forensic Evidence Recovery from Persons

5.1 **Introduction**

It is vital that potential evidence is recovered from suspects, victims and witnesses (where a witness may have had physical contact with suspects or victims) in order to corroborate or refute accounts of the incident in question.

There will always be a minimum of two 'scenes' arising from the commission of an offence: the location and the offenders. This number increases where a victim was involved at the time the offence occurred. Material will be transferred between the people, items and the location and vice versa.

The types of evidence transferred will depend on the particular offence. Particulates such as glass, fibres, paint flakes, soils and body fluids are types of potential evidence that may be recovered from victims, scene locations and suspects and where appropriate, witnesses. It is vital that the recovery of such evidence is undertaken as soon as is practicable, in a systematic manner which ensures its integrity, continuity and evidential value.

Although this chapter deals primarily with the recovery of potential evidence regarding suspects, the principles for recovering evidence are valid for a complainant, victim or witness.

The issues of consent regarding victims are such that it is not applicable to recover such samples by force or without consent. For sexual offences, a trained and qualified specialist such as a crime scene investigator (CSI) or specially trained police officer such as a SOLO or a SOTI (see the following definitions) should recover any non-intimate samples; a doctor or nurse must recover intimate samples. For initial responders, the use of an early evidence kit enables the timely recovery of potential evidence.

Definition—SOLO and SOTI

SOLO—Sexual offence liaison officer
SOTI—Sexual offence trained investigator

This chapter covers practical techniques for recovery of non-intimate samples for potential particulate evidence such as fibres, glass and soils for example, swabbing for body fluids, fingernail clippings and swabs, seizure and packaging of clothing and footwear, all of which are activities that may be undertaken by an officer or designated support staff investigator.

5.2 **Forensic Material on Clothing**

One area where the cross-transfer of material can occur is within custody units, particularly in holding areas where material from one detainee is shed to be picked up on the clothing of subsequent detainees. Whilst it can be difficult to avoid such situations, it is not impossible to minimise the potential for cross-transfer of evidence in such situations by taking suspects believed to be involved in the same incident to different custody units, for example.

POINT TO NOTE—MINIMISE TO MAXIMISE

Minimise opportunity for transfer of material.
Maximise the potential evidential value.

Particulate evidence such as glass, fibres, hair or paint flakes and body fluids such as blood or semen, for example, can be retained on the clothing, hair and footwear of a person if they have been involved in an offence or been at the crime scene. The *location* of any potential evidence can be valuable in indicating a person's involvement (or otherwise) in an incident and can serve to corroborate or refute allegations. The location of such evidence is important as it may indicate the scope of their involvement in an incident.

5.2.1 Footwear

Footwear can potentially be matched to footwear marks found at crime scenes. The image of the sole of the footwear, or where applicable the footwear item itself, can be examined and potentially matched to footwear marks recovered from crime scenes. This information can be used to link a series of crimes, such as burglaries and can be beneficial intelligence. Although a 'match' between a suspect's footwear and footwear marks at a crime scene will not, on its own, necessarily put a particular person at the scene, it can provide intelligence which can lead to further lines of enquiry.

Footwear can also provide an investigator with evidence in the form of particulate traces such as glass, soil, fibres, paint flakes, body fluids and other materials from the crime scene or victim, that may be present.

Impressions made by footwear may be recovered from crime scenes and in some cases from the victim (on their clothing or in the form of bruising).

5.2.2 Recovery of footwear evidence

Footwear impressions may be taken in custody units and stored without a person being arrested, charged or reported for an offence where the impression is to be used for elimination purposes. In such circumstances, written consent from the person must be obtained and the person made aware that the recorded marks will be used in the investigation of crime.

POINT TO NOTE—HANDLING FOOTWEAR

Be aware of health and safety considerations. Footwear may be contaminated by body fluids, sharp shards of glass and other material that could cause harm.

Gloves should be worn when handling footwear and the scanner plate must be thoroughly cleaned prior to and following the taking of the impression.

This ensures the decontamination of the scanning area, reducing the potential for suggestions of cross-transfer of evidence and ensures that no grit or other debris creates a distortion of the image.

The two main methods for the recording of footwear impressions in a custody unit are by the use of a dedicated flatbed scanner, which can enable an image to be sent electronically to the analyst for comparison with marks recovered from crime scenes, or by use of a specialist footwear recovery pad.

Avoid taking footwear impressions if it is suspected that there may be body fluids or other pertinent material present on the footwear—seek advice from the CSI. In these circumstances, the CSI will photograph the footwear to include the sole and upper to record the footwear sole pattern and any other potential forensic evidence and recover potential evidence such as glass, fibres or body fluids, for example.

For a comparison with footwear marks at crime scenes, the actual footwear item is far more beneficial for the examiner than a photograph or similar image of the footwear sole.

5.2.3 Trace evidence on footwear

To seize footwear for trace evidence two sheets of clean paper are required. With the person standing on one piece, remove the first shoe ensuring the person then places the foot directly onto the second sheet of paper. Repeat the process with the other foot, as illustrated in Figure 5.1. Clothing can then be removed, where required, while the person remains standing on the sheet of paper.

Figure 5.1 Recovering footwear from persons

This procedure minimises the risk of any material picked up from the custody unit floor on the shoes being transferred to the sheet on which the person stands for the removal of clothing.

The person should then stand entirely on the second sheet of paper. The shoes and the first piece of paper should be exhibited (one shoe per paper bag, paper sheet as a separate exhibit).

The remaining clothes can then be removed with the person standing on the second sheet of paper which is clear of any possible transferred material from the custody unit floor.

POINT TO NOTE—SEIZURE OF SHOES

Where it is only the shoes that are being seized and not the socks or other clothing, the use of one piece of paper is appropriate. It is advisable that the person stands on a piece of paper to remove footwear, as the action of removing the shoes can dislodge microscopic material which may provide potential evidence. Any such material will be dislodged onto the paper which should be exhibited and, if required, forensically examined.

Where shoes are to be searched at the custody desk, stand the person on a sheet of paper as above, and seize the shoes at this point. Provide the person with overshoes to wear to walk them to cells for recovery of clothing if required. Again, remove the overshoes prior to standing the person on a clean sheet of paper. Retain and exhibit the overshoes where local policy dictates.

To seize the shoes of a complainant, the same principle as above can be adopted; however the use of the first piece of paper can be disregarded depending on the circumstances and location when seized. Consider the possibility and implications of any potential transference of possible evidence.

The following principles apply to both a suspect and complainant:

- If glass is apparent on the uppers it is advisable for this to be photographed and removed by a CSI. Where a CSI is not available, carefully tape over the area to retain the glass *in situ*. Make a note of any observations in your contemporaneous notes, and indicate the presence of any possible glass on the exhibit label, for example, '*White "Reebok" trainer, size 9, left foot, with possible glass apparent on upper*'. A sketch diagram or photograph of the shoe indicating where the possible fragments have been observed is also very useful and can assist in the interviewing process.
- If body fluids such as blood are present, the advice of a CSI should be sought. In the first instance, a sketch or photograph showing the location of visible stains should be made.
- If staining is wet, the item must be allowed to dry in a secure drying cabinet or frozen at the earliest opportunity. A CSI should be made aware of the exhibit and can photograph the footwear and undertake a presumptive blood test of the stains to establish if it is blood or not, recovering samples of the stain where appropriate.

Dependent on the offence circumstances and in line with force policies, the stains may either be swabbed to recover potential DNA material or the footwear itself may be submitted to the forensic laboratory for analysis.

5.2.4 **Procedure for seizing clothing**

Outermost layers of clothing should be removed first, as opposed to 'top to bottom' or 'bottom to top' sequences. Where a person is wearing a T-shirt tucked into trousers, for example, the trousers should be removed before the top. This approach ensures that any potential forensic material that is trapped in folds of clothing is not dislodged by the action of pulling a T-shirt out from the waistband, for example. See the illustration in Figure 5.2 which represents an appropriate sequence for clothing removal.

Where it is known that there is a requirement for the clothing to be seized, belts should ideally not be removed when initially booking a detainee into custody. The clothing should, where *safe, applicable and practicable*, be removed as soon as a detainee is put into a cell. There is the potential for a loss of material that could be trapped behind the belt if it is removed from the garment. However, health and safety considerations take precedence. Be mindful that potentially harmful items can also be concealed behind or within belts.

With the person on the second, clean paper sheet following the removal of footwear, as each item of clothing is removed, where practicable, request they drop each item into an evidence bag. Avoid shaking the garment—this will dislodge and lose potential evidence.

Figure 5.2 Example of the appropriate sequence for seizure of clothing

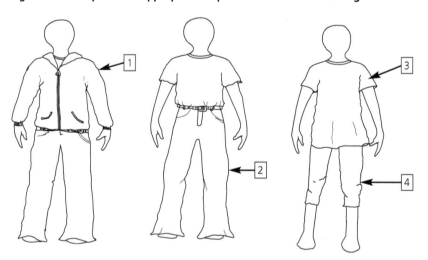

Where an item has an area of interest, such as a possible blood stain, rip or cut, this information should be recorded to show the location of such marks for the interviewing officers. Details of particular marks can go onto the exhibit label, for example:

> 1 x pair light blue Levi jeans, size 38, with apparent blood stain to lower right front hem

A sketch diagram or photograph of the location of areas of interest is helpful for interview purposes and such details should also be documented in contemporaneous notes. The sheet of paper that the person has been stood on throughout the process should be carefully folded to retain any potential trace evidence that may have been dislodged during clothing seizure. This should then be packaged and exhibited.

POINT TO NOTE—INTEGRITY OF SEIZED ITEMS

Ensure all items seized are sealed in front of the donor to ensure continuity and integrity are maintained, where safe to do so. Otherwise seal all exhibits *as soon as is practicable*. Ensure such action is documented in contemporaneous notes detailing the rationale for not doing it at the time of seizure, for example the detainee was violent and posed a risk to safety.

Remember the defence teams have access to CCTV footage in custody units—it is not advisable to leave the cell area with open bags of clothing.

5.3 Recovery of Non-Intimate Samples from Persons in Custody

The following techniques will enable recovery of potential evidence from persons, but *must not* be used where firearm residue/explosives residue evidence may be required. Specialist kits are available for the recovery of such evidence and advice of the CSI or designated officer should be sought in such cases, in line with force policy.

There may be occasions when it would be appropriate to take swabs of possible blood; for example where a suspect is arrested for assault and they have apparent blood on their hands and a CSI is unavailable. This staining may need recovering before the detained person is placed into a cell and has the opportunity to remove it. Record the location of possible blood on a person by way of a sketch or photograph. The Faculty of Forensic and Legal Medicine (FFLM) publishes guidance which is updated twice a year; the most current guidelines for the taking and storage of samples can be downloaded from <http://www.fflm.ac.uk>.

SWABBING TECHNIQUES FOR VISIBLE STAINS

1. Requirements:
   - 2 x swabs;
   - 1 x tamper-evident bag; and
   - 1 x ampoule of sterile water (*Do not* use water from any other source.)

2. Wearing gloves, snap open the water ampoule and drip 3–4 drops of water onto the swab so that it is just moist.

   Drip the water onto the swab—never put swab into water container.

Rub over the stain using small circular movements—ensuring the stain is concentrated on the tip of the swab.

Replace the swab in its tube, complete the label and place in a tamper-evident bag.

3. Use second swab (unmoistened) to rub over same area.

Replace swab in its tube, complete the label and place with first swab in tamper-evident bag.

The swab tubes should be individually labelled, for example:

ABC/1—Wet swab from back of right hand

ABC/1—Dry swab from back of right hand

Both swabs are exhibited as one item, for example:

ABC/1—Wet and dry swabs from . . .

Swabs should be stored in a freezer.

Similarly a complainant or witness may have stains upon them which require recovery as soon as possible to prevent loss or contamination of the potential evidence. The swab modules in the early evidence kits can be used for this purpose, where available.

5.3.1 Intimate and non-intimate samples

The Police and Criminal Evidence Act 1984 (PACE) divides sample types into two distinct categories—intimate and non-intimate samples (summarised in Table 5.1). The taking of intimate samples falls under PACE, s 62. This section

Table 5.1 Summary of intimate and non-intimate samples

Sample type	Description	Conditions for sampling
Intimate samples	Blood, semen, any body tissue, pubic hair or a swab from any body orifice other than the mouth, dental impressions	s 62 and Identification Code D s 6 PACE. Written consent required. Registered medical professional only to recover. In the case of dental impressions only a registered dentist to recover. Donor to be informed that samples may be subject to a speculative search
Non-intimate samples	Saliva, hair (not pubic); samples from a nail or under a nail; body fluid traces on skin (non-intimate areas only); swabs from any part of the body including the mouth but not any other body orifice; footprint or similar impression of part of the body other than the hands	s 63 and Identification Code D s 6 PACE. Can be taken by a police officer or designated police staff. Written consent required or without consent if necessary, with an inspector's authority. Reasonable force may be used. Donor to be informed that samples may be subject to a speculative search

states that, with the exception of urine, intimate samples must be taken by a registered medical practitioner. Dental impressions are classed as intimate samples and must only be taken by a registered dentist (s 62(9)). The taking of intimate samples will therefore not be covered.

Swabbing for visible body fluids and the recovery of hair and fingernail samples are classed as non-intimate samples, as prescribed by PACE, s 63.

Figure 5.3 Fingernail sampling module

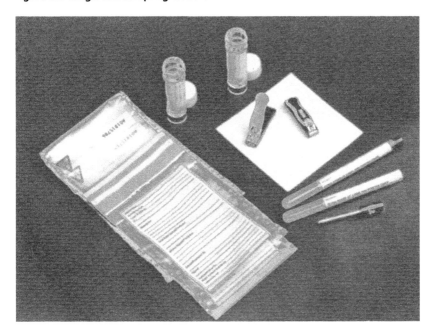

Source: Image with kind permission of Tetra Scene of Crime

5.3.2 **Samples from fingernails**

Evidence such as body fluids, skin, fibres or paint, for example, can be recovered from fingernails. In addition, a physical fit of a fingernail may be undertaken where a broken fingernail is found at the scene.

The following techniques will ensure potential evidence recovery from the fingernails is maximised. Modules for this purpose are available in early evidence kits. Forces differ on where the modules or individual items are kept, however many custody units report holding the items required in the medical examination room. It is advisable to confer with a CSI or forensic submissions officers to establish where the modules are stored within the force. SOLOs/SOTIs will have access to early evidence kits.

As a minimum, the requirements for recovery of potential evidence from fingernails should include two pieces of sterile paper, two pairs of fingernail clippers, swabs, water, and scissors and tamper-evident bags for packaging (see Figure 5.3).

5.3.3 Nail clippings

Open the pack of clean paper supplied with module and lay it out on a clean bench. Place the donor's hand over the paper and using the clippers, clip all the nails of one hand. Some clippers will retain the nails within the body of the clippers.

Return the clippers to the container in which they are supplied and place in a tamper-evident bag.

Carefully fold the paper, ensuring you retain any deposited material. Place this in the same bag as the clippers.

Exhibit as:

ABC/1—fingernail clippings and paper cover from left hand of…

Repeat the process for the other hand, which would be exhibited as, for example:

ABC/2—fingernail clippings from right hand of…

Fingernail clipping exhibits should be stored in a freezer. *Note that if physical fit is required to a broken fingernail recovered at the scene, nails must be cut with scissors.*

Where nails are too short for clipping or it is not deemed appropriate, swabbing is an acceptable method to recover potential evidence.

5.3.4 Swabbing fingernails

You will need one wet and one dry swab.

Place the donor's hand over a piece of clean paper. Using a pointed ended swab moistened with sterile water, run the tip of the swab under each nail rim, the surface of the nails and around the cuticles. Use the edges of the swab as well as the tip of the swab to maximise the available surface area of the swab.

Repeat the process with a dry swab.

Package in tamper-evident bag and label as, for example:

ABC/3—Wet and dry swabs from fingernails of left hand of…

Carefully fold the paper cover, ensuring you retain any debris, and place into a tamper-evident bag with the swabs. Repeat this process with the other hand if applicable.

The nail swabs exhibit should be stored in a freezer.

5.3.5 **Hair collection modules**

Hair can hold valuable evidence such as fibres, glass and body fluids as well as being useful for comparison with hairs recovered at a scene. Hair can also be used for toxicology examinations.

Hair combings should be done prior to removal of any outer clothing in order to minimise any loss of potential evidence and transference onto lower clothing.

Figure 5.4 Hair sampling kit

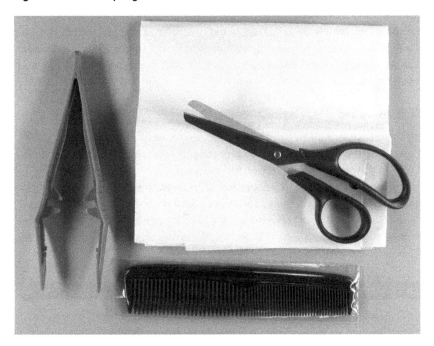

Source: Image with kind permission of Tetra Scene of Crime

Figure 5.4 shows a hair sampling kit. As a minimum, you will require:

- sterile tweezers to remove visible foreign matter (fibres, etc);
- comb;
- sterile paper pack;
- scissors;
- swabs and water (if required); and
- tamper-evident bags, one for each exhibit to be taken.

For all recovery techniques from hair, place the piece of paper on a bench and ensure the donor's head is placed above the paper.

Recover any visible potential evidence such as fibres or glass, for example, using tweezers or gloved fingers and place onto the paper sheet.

Comb through the hair using the comb or fingers of a gloved hand to loosen any particles. Any material should be collected on the paper cover, which should be carefully folded to retain the collected material.

Exhibit the paper and tweezers, scissors and/or comb (whichever has been used) in the same bag as one exhibit.

Depending on the offence/evidential needs, there are different techniques for recovering certain materials from hair.

Body fluids

For the recovery of body fluids (eg, blood or semen) from hair, swabbing techniques can be used to recover any visible stain or the stained area cut out using scissors. Package swabs, paper and scissors if used in tamper-evident bag and store in freezer.

Glass, fibres and other particulate material

For the recovery of glass, paint flakes or fibres, for example, remove any visible material with tweezers or gloved fingers and place on the paper cover. Comb the hair over the paper cover to recover remaining material.

Carefully fold the paper to ensure any debris is retained and place into a tamper-evident bag with the tweezers and/or comb if used. It may also be useful to undertake a taping of the head using a low tack adhesive tape which is then secured to an acetate sheet. For tapings, the items can generally be obtained from your CSI. Exhibits should be stored in a dry store.

KEY POINT—EARLY EVIDENCE KIT MODULES

Details of the module batch number, expiry date and supplier of any kit modules used should be recorded in contemporaneous notes and in subsequent statements.

Hair comparisons

To take a sample for comparison with hair recovered from a scene or for drug analysis, cut a minimum of twenty-five hairs, as close to the scalp as possible, from different places on the head. This ensures a representative sample of lengths and colours is obtained. Do not use tweezers to remove hair for comparison purposes as these may cause crushing to the surface of the hair.

Place the hair onto the paper cover. Carefully fold the paper containing the hair sample and place in a tamper-evident bag. The exhibit should be stored in a dry store.

5.4 **Firearm and Explosive Residue**

Firearm residue can be present on the hands and clothing of suspects. Force policies differ on who may recover such potential evidence, and in many cases such a process *must* be undertaken by a CSI or specifically trained specialist officer.

The techniques outlined are suitable for the recovery of firearm discharge residue from a suspect; however it is recommended that you seek advice from your CSI on the local policy for recovery of such material. Investigators *must not* attempt to recover such residues unless they have received specialist training.

Firearm residue can be present on the hands, face, hair and clothing of a person who has discharged a firearm or has been in close proximity to a discharged firearm.

POINT TO NOTE—USE OF FIREARM DISCHARGE RESIDUE (FDR) KIT

- The sampling kit must be sealed prior to use—never use a kit that has previously been opened.
- Any investigator who has handled or been in the immediate vicinity of firearms, ammunition or explosives within the previous seven days must not recover samples or have contact with recovered items. Also consider whether you have visited the force armory or been in face to face contact with firearms officers in that period, as this may impact on the recovery of samples from a suspect. Do not use the kit if you are a regular user of firearms or explosives.
- Samples need to be recovered as soon as possible after detention of a suspect and prior to fingerprint processing.
- Consider contamination and cross-transfer—use different investigators and locations where there is more than one suspect.
- Roll up sleeves and thoroughly wash hands and forearms and wear a disposable overall prior to opening the kit.
- Read and prepare the included paperwork within the kit before beginning the sampling process.
- Only use the items supplied in the kit. Make a note of the serial or batch number of the kit in contemporaneous notes.
- Follow the instructions in the kit carefully.

Recovery of potential firearm or explosive residue *should* be undertaken by a CSI or suitably trained person.

The kits contain comprehensive instructions which are to be followed accurately to avoid loss or contamination of potential evidence.

5.5 **Smartwater Recovery**

Smartwater is the name of a commercially available solution which contains a unique code specific to a particular location. The solution, called Index solution can be used in a sprinkler type system which can be activated in the event of a burglary, for example. Anyone and anything in the immediate vicinity will be sprayed with the uniquely coded solution. The solution can also be used to invisibly coat valuable items.

Once dry, the solution is only visible by ultraviolet light, where it will fluoresce as blue/white or green/yellow colour (depending on the product). In custody units equipped with ultraviolet light, spray patterns and/or contact staining from where suspects have handled items coated with Index solution may be visible on a suspect's clothing, skin and hair which can link them to a particular scene or item.

5.5.1 **Recovery of Smartwater from scenes and suspects**

Where Smartwater activation has occurred at premises, the CSI will thoroughly examine the area with an ultraviolet light source, to search for any footwear patterns and fingerprints that may be present. The CSI will photograph and/or video the scene and recover samples from key areas. The activated canister must be recovered in order for the scientist to establish the link between the scene and any suspects.

Samples of the solution on larger, less portable items can be taken from any recovered stolen property by the CSI who can either swab or take scrapings from the stained area, although ideally the entire item should be submitted to the scientist for examination where possible.

The recovered samples will be examined and identification made as to the registered owner of the property from which the Smartwater product originated. The comparison of the samples enables a link to be established between suspects and scenes.

The unique serial numbers in the product can then be checked against a database to identify the registered user and establish where the property originated.

Where Smartwater products are located on a suspect, the following points require consideration:

- The fluorescence under ultraviolet light must be recorded by photography or video by the CSI or suitably qualified specialist photographer, prior to the recovery of clothing.
- Other substances can cause fluorescence, such as the whitening products in some washing powders, urine and semen, for example.
- Areas of skin that display Smartwater fluorescence should be swabbed with the appropriate Smartwater swabbing kit. Smartwater products are not water soluble; therefore using water to swab the area will not successfully recover

the required material. Swabbing should be undertaken by a CSI or specifically trained investigator.

- Clothing should be packaged taking into consideration any other potential forensic evidence. Clothing containing Smartwater products must always be packaged in brown paper evidence sacks.

5.6 **Chapter Summary**

People who have been involved in an incident will inevitably have material upon them that can link them to the location(s), to items used and to others involved in the incident. By considering suspects, victims and where appropriate, witnesses as crime scenes, the potential for the recovery of forensic material is maximised, providing links between scenes, people and items that will strengthen a case.

Witnesses who have given first aid to an injured victim or who have held on to a suspect, for example, may have potential forensic material upon them. It is always worth considering this potential where the circumstances of the incident dictate.

As Locard's 'Principle of Exchange' is based on the assumption that 'every contact leaves a trace', it is important that investigators consider the impact of their actions when dealing with persons involved in incidents.

A lot of forensic material is microscopic and can easily be transferred. It is imperative therefore that steps are taken to minimise any cross-transfer by dealing with only one aspect of the incident where evidence of contact is required. Investigators or CSIs who deal with a victim must not then deal with a suspect during that particular shift, for example.

The methods for the recovery of firearm or explosive residues can only be undertaken by a CSI or specifically trained investigator to ensure the integrity of any potential evidence recovered.

KNOWLEDGE CHECK—FORENSIC SAMPLING OF PERSONS

1. A suspect is arrested for criminal damage to a vehicle by spraying paint onto the vehicle and breaking the windows with a piece of rough wooden fencing post. The piece of wood and spray paint can are recovered at the scene.

   What potential evidence could be available to link this suspect with the crime scene?
   Glass on footwear (soles and uppers) and clothing and possibly in hair from the vehicle.
   Paint on the suspect's hands/clothes can be compared with paint at the scene.
   Fingerprints of the suspect on the paint can and/or on the vehicle.
   Comparison of wood fragments on the suspect with the fencing post.

Fibres from the suspect's clothing on the vehicle/paint can/fencing post.
It must be considered that in many cases the potential evidence recovered may not be submitted for forensic analysis.

2. In the scenario given in Q1, what items would you consider for recovery from the suspect, as a minimum?

   Footwear, hair combings, outer layers of clothing for examination for glass, paint and possibly wood fragments, photography of any paint on hands by CSI, fingerprints and DNA.

3. What samples can you recover as non-intimate samples with regard to PACE, s 63?

   Hair (not pubic), urine, swabs from skin from non-intimate areas, swabs from any part of the body, including the mouth but not any other body orifice, saliva.

4. Who can take intimate samples in accordance with PACE, s 62?

   Registered medical professional or, registered dentist for dental impressions.

5. Who can take non-intimate samples in accordance with PACE, s 63?

   Police officers or designated police support staff.

Recommended Reading

Crime Investigators' Handbook (2013) Cook, T, Mill, M and Hibbitt, S.

Managing investigations, College of Policing (2014) <http://www.app.college.police.uk/app/content/investigations/managing-investigations/>.

PACE—A Practical Guide to the Police and Criminal Evidence Act (2013) Ozin, P, Norton, H and Spivey, P.

The Police and Criminal Evidence Act 1984 (2013) Zander, M.

Recommendations for the collection of forensic specimens from complainants and suspects (January 2015) Faculty of Forensic & Legal Medicine (FFLM) <http://fflm.ac.uk/upload/documents/1393618480.pdf>.

Tetra Scene of Crime <http://www.tetrasoc.com>.

6

Fingerprints

6.1 **Introduction**

The use of fingerprints as a means of identification is the oldest forensic technique to be adopted for the purposes of investigating crime. No two persons have been found to have the same fingerprints in over one hundred years of utilising this method systematically. This is because finger/palm prints are created by the friction ridges in the skin that form unique patterns on the fingers, palms and soles of the feet. These ridges are very persistent and do not change over a person's lifetime.

Some people have deliberately tried to 'remove' their prints by burning or applying acid—but superficial damage heals and the ridge detail regrows in its previous position. Cutting into the skin which causes scarring creates another layer of unique identification—therefore any attempt to 'remove' the ridge detail to avoid identification is not generally effective on living persons.

The historic reliability of finger and palm prints to establish/confirm a person's identity makes this forensic technique one of the best forms of identification evidence.

Fingerprints are routinely used to compare marks recovered from surfaces/items at crime scenes with those on the national database to potentially identify an offender, for the identification of an unknown deceased, to eliminate persons from an investigation, and as means of confirming or establishing identity for arrested persons and immigration purposes. Separate crime scenes may be linked by fingerprint evidence.

The skin on the underside of the feet and the palms and fingers of humans and other primates is ridged to ensure a better gripping surface, and the patterns created by these ridges are referred to as 'friction ridge details'. The patterns formed by the ridges contain individual characteristics which has enabled the development of a robust and reliable classification system for the comparison of fingerprints. The patterns and characteristics created by friction ridge skin develop in the womb, remaining unchanged throughout life, and in some circumstances for some time after death.

When an item is touched a transfer of materials secreted from the skin occurs to leave a contact pattern, this can potentially be developed to enhance the visualisation of any fingerprint ridge details, thus making fingerprints an ideal form of forensic evidence to link a suspect to a crime scene.

The underside of the feet contain friction ridge skin which can be used for comparison purposes but as yet there is no national database for the comparison or identification of bare footprints. Direct comparisons, however, can be made between a suspect's bare footprint and a bare footprint found at a crime scene.

This chapter explains the use of fingerprint evidence, the types of potential fingerprint evidence typically found at crime scenes, the techniques used to recover such fingerprints and the legislative framework for taking fingerprints.

6.2 **Types of Fingerprint Evidence at Crime Scenes**

The recovery of finger or palm print evidence at a crime scene can establish the identity of persons who have been there. Palm prints are now routinely used in the same way as fingerprints; for this reason throughout this chapter any reference to fingerprints also includes palm prints.

KEY POINT—FINGERPRINT EVIDENCE CONSIDERATIONS

A fingerprint recovered from a surface is evidence that a particular person has touched the surface *at some time*.The absence of fingerprints does not mean that a person *has not* touched the item.

The absence of evidence is not necessarily evidence of absence.

It is not yet scientifically possible to 'age' a fingerprint and say precisely when it was deposited, so at a burglary scene, for example, asking the victim when the area was last cleaned and obtaining a statement to that effect can narrow down the time scales of when a print may have been deposited.

A person may handle an item and leave no recoverable fingerprints due to many variables that affect the amount of secretions available to transfer to a surface. The amount of residue available tends to be depleted for each successive touch meaning a transferred latent fingerprint will become progressively weaker and more difficult to recover. Some people may not secrete sufficient amounts of specific materials required for the recovery techniques to be successful. The pressure used and the surface handled are also variables affecting the potential recovery of fingerprints.

There are broadly three categories of fingerprint evidence typically recovered from crime scenes.

6.2.1 **Latent**

'Latent' means 'invisible' and such marks cannot be readily seen with the naked eye. Latent fingerprints are made up of the secretions of perspiration from the sweat pores situated along the ridges. Research by Fortunato et al, reported that the perspiration from the sweat glands on the ridged skin of the hands and feet consists of 99.0–99.5% water and 0.5–1.0% organic and inorganic substances such as salts, amino acids, fats, and urea. The deposits left by a fingerprint are typically in the region of a tenth of a milligram, according to research by Menzel et al. When the water constituent in the print evaporates this leaves, at best, nanograms of material for a crime scene investigator (CSI) to detect and recover. Sebaceous oils from the face and hair may also be present in latent prints where a person has touched their face or hair prior to handling an item or surface.

This type of fingerprint requires some form of process to enable it to be visualised. At the scene, a CSI can use powders on clean, dry, smooth non-porous surfaces. Fingerprint powders adhere to secreted fats, oils and water contents, which enables any resulting marks to be lifted with a low tack adhesive tape that is secured to a clear acetate sheet. These are referred to as fingerprint lifts which are then forwarded to the fingerprint unit for comparison with marks available on the national database, Ident1.

Specialist chemical and light source enhancement techniques are available for the visualisation and recovery of fingerprints where powders may not be the appropriate method to employ, for example on porous items such as paper or items that have a textured surface such as a plastic vehicle cowling (steering column cover). It may be that the item in question is very valuable and fingerprint powders will cause damage to the item.

6.2.2 **Visual marks**

Such marks are found where a substance such as paint, ink, cosmetics or blood, for example, is transferred by the fingers onto a suitable surface. These marks can be photographed and the photograph forwarded to the fingerprint unit. The mark may then be subject to further development/enhancement techniques in order to improve the contrast between the mark and the surface it is on and potentially develop further details which are not always visible. Where possible the item containing the mark should be recovered and exhibited.

6.2.3 **Impressed marks**

These are three-dimensional marks which do not rely on the deposition and transfer of a substance. They are formed when a three-dimensional impression of the ridge skin is made in a suitably soft material such as putty, wax, chocolate or part dried paint, for example. Such marks can be photographed and then photographs forwarded to the fingerprint identification team for comparison and identification. Where possible the item containing the mark should be recovered and exhibited.

6.3 **The Role of the CSI in the Recovery of Fingerprint Evidence**

The forensic examination for any potential evidence is a sequential process that begins with the least destructive method being utilised first. The sequential examination process should follow the following steps:

A. Visual examination
    Following a visual search to locate the potential evidence, including a search with the appropriate light sources, the CSI will record an accurate description and sketch diagram of the location of visual marks, including measurements showing the position of the fingerprint in relation to a fixed point, in a contemporaneous scene notebook.

B. Photography

A photograph of the mark *in situ* should be taken prior to any further process being undertaken. This is particularly useful for visible marks that could be destroyed/altered by further processing techniques, for example where the mark is in a substance believed to be blood. Following photography, swabs can be taken from a fingerprint that is not suitable for comparison purposes. A presumptive blood test can be undertaken to establish the likelihood of the substance being blood. It is vital in such circumstances that a photographic record is made prior to and following the swabbing or other technique utilised at each stage in order to demonstrate the integrity and continuity of the mark.

C. Processing

The CSI will employ the most appropriate technique for the recovery of the fingerprint(s). If the surface is clean, dry, inflexible and non-porous such as a window pane or gloss painted door, the CSI will generally use powders to search for and recover marks. The powdered marks when located, may be photographed *in situ* prior to being recovered either on a low tack clear adhesive tape which is then transferred onto a clear acetate sheet or the mark can be lifted onto a gelatine lifter, depending on the surface. Where appropriate, the item containing the mark should be recovered and exhibited.

The CSI has a range of different powders that will be effective in various circumstances and they will utilise the most appropriate technique. Where fingerprints cannot be recovered using powders, such as on porous surfaces like writing paper, cardboard or pliable items such as plastic bags, for example, the CSI will submit these items for the chemical development processes of potential fingerprints.

6.4 Specialist Development Techniques for Fingerprint Recovery

Items recovered from a crime scene can be submitted to the in-force fingerprint development laboratory, or equivalent, which will utilise the application of chemical techniques to recover fingerprints and other marks, such as footwear, from submitted items. Whilst this is a key role of most in-force police laboratories, other techniques may be available depending on the facilities of the laboratory, for example—the examination of documents for indented writing and/or alterations, the initial screening for body fluids or fibres utilising light sources and recovery of erased marks are some of the processes that may be available.

One of the least destructive methods for locating fingerprints is a visual search utilising high intensity forensic light sources. The light sources are an excellent screening tool when searching for body fluids such as semen and can also be used where other techniques are not appropriate to detect traces of fluorescent material that may have been deposited from the hands.

Case study—Locating fingerprints with light sources

Stolen property was recovered from a burglary of a manor house. Many of the items recovered were of extremely high monetary value and rarity, which excluded any use of the traditional fingerprinting techniques such as powders or chemicals.

Some of the items were examined with a range of forensic light sources and areas of ridge detail were located and photographed. These areas were then swabbed to recover any potential DNA material. The light sources enabled a targeted approach to the recovery of potential evidence without causing any damage to the items examined.

Partial fingermarks were found, photographed and swabbed for DNA profiling which obtained a partial profile that could be compared with a known suspect profile.

Five people received a custodial sentence for this offence

6.4.1 Specialist development techniques

Laboratory technicians undergo training from the College of Policing forensic facility, to examine items to establish the most appropriate techniques to use with regard to the nature of the items submitted, the requirements of the case and with full regard for other potential forensic evidence types. The principles of sequential processing are followed—employing the least destructive method first. The techniques applied will be in line with the Home Office Centre for Applied Science & Technology (CAST) 'Fingermark Visualisation Manual' guidelines. CAST are continually researching new processes to recover fingerprints from a range of surfaces/environments that have proved problematic, such as fire damaged exhibits, for example.

The methods utilised will be dependent initially on the type of surface of the item to be examined. Items received into the laboratory typically fall into two distinct categories of surface type—porous and non-porous—which initially determines the process used.

6.4.2 Porous items

Items such as paper (bank notes, envelopes, etc), plasterboard, uncoated cardboard, raw untreated wood etc can be submitted for examination and chemical techniques to establish if they contain latent fingerprints or to enhance weak or partial visible marks. Following a visual examination, photography and recording of any visible marks, the following techniques are available:

• 1,8 Diazafluoren-9-one (DFO) and Ninhydrin

These two reagents react with amino acid secretions in latent fingerprints and can also be useful for developing marks in blood. The use of both these techniques, in sequence, can lead to the development of more fingerprints than may be possible with just one of the methods. DFO must be used before ninhydrin if both methods are to be employed. For the development of blood marks, DFO can be used for porous surfaces only whereas ninhydrin may be used on porous or non-porous surfaces.

- Physical Developer (PD)

This technique can be used after DFO and ninhydrin. The physical developer reacts with non-soluble sebaceous materials, which can generally be recovered after an item has been wet. It is important to inform the laboratory technicians when it is known an item has been wet between the time of the incident and its recovery as an exhibit.

6.4.3 Non-porous items

Items in this category include bottles, vehicle cowlings and plastic bags, for example. The techniques available for these items are as follows:

- Vacuum metal deposition (VMD)

This process is the most effective single process that can be employed for recovering fingerprints on many non-porous items even when the fingerprints are very old and small deposits of secreted or deposited material are present. It can also be successfully employed on items that are known to have been wet. It is a relatively expensive process, and not every in-force laboratory will have the capability to undertake this process. This process is generally utilised for serious cases rather than for routine volume crime work.

- Superglue (cyanacrolate) fuming

The exhibit is placed into a purpose built humidifying cabinet with a foil dish containing a small amount of superglue. The superglue fumes bind to the aqueous (water) components of a fingerprint to form a hard white coloured crust on the available ridge details. This can then be stained with a fluorescent dye and any viable marks photographed. As superglue adheres to the aqueous (water) component in a fingerprint it cannot be used to successfully develop fingerprints on items that have been wet at the time of or following commission of an offence. The use of the superglue should be undertaken as soon as is practicable—prolonged storage of an item may result in the evaporation of the small amount of aqueous component in any fingermark secretion and therefore a reduction in the opportunity to recover viable fingerprints.

- Sudan black

Sudan black is a dye which stains the fat content of latent fingerprints and is particularly useful for the development of greasy marks such as those on food packaging such as takeaway boxes, crisp packets and dried residues of soft drinks on cans or bottles.

- Small particle reagent (SPR)

This adheres to fatty components in a fingerprint secretion and can be used where an item has been previously wet. It is more effective on recent marks rather than older ones.

- Powder suspensions

This technique is a simple and effective technique, particularly useful for recovering fingerprints on the sticky side of adhesive tapes, and can be used on items that have been wet.

- Gentian violet

This process is effective for the development of latent marks on the sticky side of adhesive tapes and on surfaces contaminated with oils and grease. As gentian violet contains a toxic chemical—phenol—the use of large quantities is to be avoided.

6.4.4 **Marks in blood**

When an item is received in the laboratory, and there is no prior forensic confirmation that the stain is blood, a presumptive test for blood may be undertaken. Depending on the circumstances of the case, the laboratory technician may contact the investigator in the case to inform them of the presence of possible blood as consideration needs to be given to preserving the exhibit for potential DNA.

Where an item contains potential body fluids, the outer packaging must be clearly labelled to indicate a biohazard may be present.

POINT TO NOTE—ITEMS THAT HAVE BEEN WET

It is vital to indicate, where known, if an item *has been* previously wet between the time of offence and the recovery of the item, even if dry when recovered. Be aware that substantial moisture (dew) can be absorbed by a porous item if left out overnight even when the weather conditions are dry.

If the item is known to have been wet it is advantageous to inform the technicians to maximise the opportunity for developing marks.

Some items will not fall neatly into one category, for example a cardboard box that has a glossy surface and an interior of matte porous cardboard. The laboratory technicians will ensure the sequence in which items are processed will maximise the forensic potential.

6.4.5 **The impact of chemical development techniques on other forensic evidence**

When an item is received into the laboratory, it should be closely examined for any other potential forensic evidence such as the presence of fibres, body fluids such as blood and any other evidential material that may be appropriate to the investigation. In many cases the laboratory technician will recover such material in the appropriate manner in consultation with the CSI or officer in charge (OIC).

When an item is recovered that bears possible body fluids, it is important that consideration is given to whether any possible DNA material needs to be recovered. Swabbing an item to recover DNA material can destroy any latent fingerprint ridge detail that may be present on the item, so the issue of maximising potential evidence requires consideration prior to submitting for chemical development techniques.

Research reported by Lee and Gaensslen and CAST has shown that DNA material can be recovered from blood and latent fingerprint secretions on items following one single chemical development technique.

Where an item is to undergo any chemical development techniques and DNA analysis is required, it is important to discuss the particular case with the appropriate FSP who will advise on the best sequence to follow. Once an investigator (OIC/senior investigating officer (SIO)) has the available information, they must decide, in the context of the particular case circumstances, the best route for securing the best evidence.

Where chemical development techniques are utilised prior to DNA analysis it is vital that the forensic service provider (FSP) receives the item as soon as possible following a chemical development process in order to maximise the potential for recovery of DNA material.

....

Case study—Chemical fingerprint process and DNA recovery

Several snap-seal plastic bags containing white powder were recovered and exhibited by police officers. The exhibits went first to the FSP to establish the identity of the powder in the bags with a request to 'preserve packaging for fingerprints' made on the submissions form.

The FSP decanted the powder from the snap-seal bags, which were then sub-exhibited and returned to the in-force laboratory for fingerprinting.

The superglue technique was employed on the bags and areas of ridge detail were developed. Unfortunately the quality of the developed ridge detail was insufficient for the fingerprint to be searched on Ident1.

The bags were then returned to the FSP with a request that DNA analysis be undertaken on the developed areas of ridge detail. This enabled the scientist to target the search for potential DNA material with the result that two DNA profiles were recovered from these areas beneath the superglue.

In serious/complex cases forensic strategy meetings will be held with the OIC/SIO, the crime scene co-ordinator, a laboratory technician and an FSP at least, to discuss and agree the best procedures and sequence for the forensic examination.
....

Many of the chemicals used to develop fingerprints can be hazardous to health, and it is important to be aware of the force policy in place regarding the return of items to the lawful owner after such processes have been employed. Some forces have a blanket policy which dictates that no items can be returned to the owner after chemical development techniques have been utilised. It is recommended that a victim of crime is made aware that such processes can lead to the item being permanently damaged. Recovered stolen property may have sentimental value to the owner and it is important that care and consideration is shown with how this is processed. Ensure the laboratory technicians are aware of any such issues in order that consideration can be given to employing least destructive methods where appropriate.

It is possible for many of the chemical development techniques to be utilised at a crime scene by fully trained operatives. However, there are health and safety implications with such procedures including the requirement to decontaminate any premises in which chemical development techniques are used. Such examinations would typically be used for serious incidents and require the authorisation of an SIO.

Once fingerprints have been recovered, the next stage is to submit the marks to the fingerprint expert for the comparison and identification procedure.

6.5 The Role of the Fingerprint Expert

The fingerprint expert will receive the fingerprint lifts from the crime scene and/or photographs of any chemically developed fingerprints from the laboratory. These marks will be checked against any elimination marks provided and then, if not eliminated and of sufficient quality, they will be scanned onto the national fingerprint database known as 'Ident1'.

When a fingerprint identification expert receives a fingerprint mark, the individual classification characteristics present in the mark are highlighted and the mark is then scanned or transferred onto the database. The Ident1 system searches the database to present a list of at least fifteen people with marks that bear close similarity to the crime scene mark(s).

The expertise of the fingerprint expert will determine which, if any, of those listed in the search results has left the crime scene mark. Where identification is made, it will then require a rigorous system of triple checking by a further two fingerprint experts. Only where all three fingerprint experts independently agree, will a notification of identification be given.

6.6 National Fingerprint Database—Ident1

The national fingerprint database is a fundamental part of the criminal justice system and as such, all forces have a duty to populate and maintain the database by providing high quality fingerprint sets and accurate information of those fingerprinted. People that have been arrested and charged, reported or summoned for a recordable offence will have their fingerprints taken to confirm their identity, where the person is already on the database. If they are not shown on the database, where appropriate their fingerprints are taken and added to the database. These can be searched against all the unidentified crime scene marks in what is termed a speculative search. Taking fingerprints from persons is also the method employed to prove previous convictions of those arrested, warned, cautioned, reprimanded or invited into a police station in connection with all recordable offences.

The fingerprints of those in custody are placed onto Ident1 via Livescan or by the scanning of inked 'ten print' forms. Fingerprints recovered from crime scenes are compared with those held on Ident1 and can potentially lead to the identification of an individual. Figure 6.1 summarises the procedure typically utilised in the comparison and identification of fingerprints.

POINT TO NOTE—FINGERPRINTS

The presence of a fingerprint on a surface is conclusive evidence that a person has, at some time, touched the item in question. There is currently no scientifically accepted method to state when such contact was made. The investigator can narrow down potential time frames by asking questions as to when the surface from which the fingerprint was recovered was last cleaned. The absence of fingerprints on an item is not conclusive evidence that a person has not handled an item. There are many factors concerning whether a fingerprint is deposited, including successive handling of items, leading to the depletion of substances to transfer onto a surface and the fact that some people do not leave prints that are developed with the different mediums. It is important to consider the evidential significance, or otherwise of the presence or absence of any fingerprint evidence in the context of the wider investigation.

6.6.1 Searching for fingerprints on Ident1

When taking fingerprints from persons, it is important to ensure that the fingerprints submitted for comparison purposes are of a high standard. Some marks submitted to fingerprint experts cannot be found on Ident1 due to a number of factors including:

- The Ident1 system may attribute characteristics differently from the fingerprint expert. Due to the potential for such variance suspects may not be found. The main reason for the disparity between Ident1 and fingerprint experts attributing different characteristics, is partly due to the poor quality of 'ten print' sets held on the system. It is therefore vital that 'ten print' sets submitted by investigators are of the best possible quality and clarity.
- An offender may not have been fingerprinted in connection with any recordable offence and is therefore not included on the database at the time of an offence. Fingerprint experts regularly undertake 'back searching' where all unidentified scene marks are compared against Ident1 to ensure a more reliable and up to date report of a person's previous criminal activity is available.

- Fingerprints recovered may belong to innocent victims or those with 'legitimate access' to the item or property concerned and not be on the national database. In which case obtaining elimination fingerprints of such persons will be required. Elimination prints enable the fingerprint expert to verify whether any scene marks do not belong to a possible suspect and can be justifiably eliminated as being those of the offender.

Up until 2001, only the fingerprints of those convicted of an offence were retained on the database and there was a numerical standard in place for the identification of a fingerprint to be confirmed. This required that a minimum of sixteen points (characteristics), all in agreement and none in disagreement were present in order for an identification to be confirmed. Since 2001, fingerprint experts no longer have to rely on the comparison of friction ridge detail characteristics alone and other information is now accepted in the identification process, such as the general direction or 'ridge flow' of the ridges, the overall pattern type, positioning of pores (referred to as third level detail) and features such as creases or scars.

Figure 6.1 Summary of crime scene fingerprint identification procedure

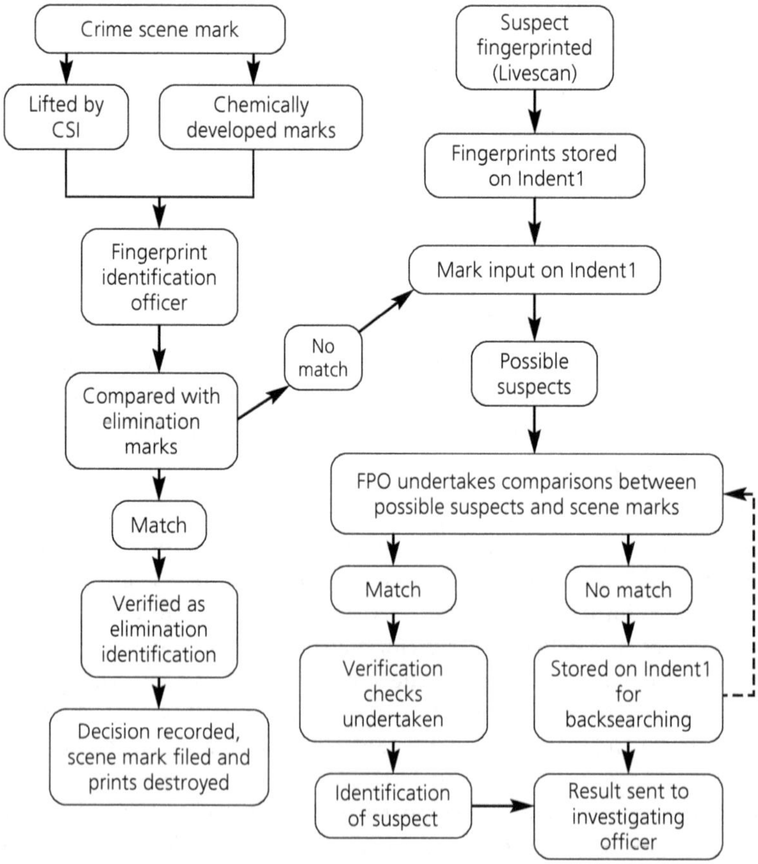

6.6.2 **Police elimination database (PED)**

This database is not linked to the national criminal database (the police national computer (PNC)). All newly recruited police officers and designated police support staff are required to have their fingerprints taken as a condition of their employment so that they can be eliminated from any marks found at a crime scene or on exhibits.

The PED is an important resource. The identification of fingerprints can be a painstaking yet vitally important task. If a mark can be eliminated as belonging to a police officer or support staff member, it will save a lot of time and effort for the investigation team. It also means that such marks are not loaded onto the national database as an outstanding crime scene mark. Fingerprints from a crime scene that remain unidentified can cause problems for the prosecution case as a defence team can imply that the investigation has not been thorough enough and the fingerprint is that of the 'real' offender.

The taking of detainee's fingerprints and DNA buccal swab samples is now a routine aspect of detainee processing within custody. The reasons for the taking of such samples is primarily for identification purposes, and samples are also used to compare with samples from crime scenes and are subject to speculative searching on the appropriate databases. The appropriate methods and considerations to be made for the taking of fingerprints are detailed in the following section.

6.7 **Taking Fingerprints**

The procedure for taking good quality prints is the same whether fingerprints are taken electronically on a Livescan system or whether inked marks are taken. The success of the national database in identifying persons is reliant on consistent good quality fingerprints and the accuracy of the relevant information loaded onto it. The following guidance is applicable whether fingerprints are taken electronically on Livescan or whether inked impressions are taken.

Checklist—Considerations for taking fingerprints

- For inked prints, only a thin layer of ink should be applied to the inking block—too much ink will cause the fingerprint to be overloaded and the resulting impression will be too dark and/or smudged.

- Recover any other potential forensic evidence such as swabs of possible bloodstains and any fingernail samples (where applicable) prior to fingerprinting a person.

- Ensure you have the lawful authority to take the fingerprints.

- Check the hands of the donor for any injuries. If open injuries are present it is important to assess whether prints can be taken. Be mindful of health and safety issues and the contamination of equipment with body fluids.

- Ensure the donor's hands are clean. If it is necessary for the donor to wash their hands, consider whether any other potential evidence may be recovered first, for example swabbing for body fluids, nail scrapings, etc.

- If the skin of the donor's hands is very dry, a small amount of moisturiser can be applied to the hands, allow this to be absorbed before commencing taking prints.

- If the donor's hands are moist, use a tissue to wipe the hands (be mindful of other potential evidence). Repeat this process between taking each impression if the hands are excessively sweaty.

- Take control of the process—do not allow the donor to dictate the pressure and movement during the taking of impressions.

Where a finger cannot be printed due to injury or amputation, this must be recorded on the form.

6.7.1 Types of impressions required

Rolled impressions

This is where the fingertip is rolled from one side of the nail edge to the other. It is vital that the finger does not slip during this process as it will cause smudging to the fingerprint. This process should be repeated with each finger and the thumbs (see Figure 6.2, Figure 6.3).

Plain impressions

This is where all four fingers are printed simultaneously to ensure that the individual rolled impressions are in the correct box, for example to check that the fingers from the right hand have not been placed into the boxes for the left hand, or that the impressions have not been taken out of sequence.

The plain impressions require all four fingers to be placed into the appropriate box. It may be necessary to place the fingers at an angle in the box. A light pressure can be applied to the fingers if required.

Figure 6.2 Taking a rolled fingerprint impression

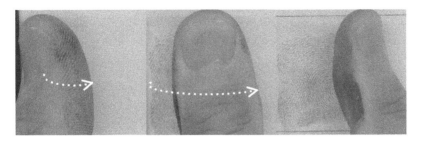

Figure 6.3 Good and poor fingerprint impressions

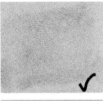

A good mark will be even in tone and appear squared in the centre of the box.

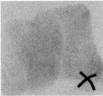

The overlaying of a mark can occur where the finger slips or there is a hesitation during the rolling process. This would render the mark unuseable.

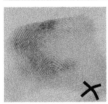

It should be ensured that each finger has a light, even coating of ink before taking the print—the print should not be too dark or too light.

Palm impressions

Clothing should not obscure any part of the palm and the impression is taken by placing the wrist at the bottom of the box and lowering the palm in a smooth movement from wrist to fingertips. Applying a light even pressure to the back of the hand will ensure the natural hollow present in the centre of the palm is captured. A good quality palm print will capture the area of the palm from the base of the fingers to the wrist (see Figure 6.4).

121

Figure 6.4 Good and poor palm prints

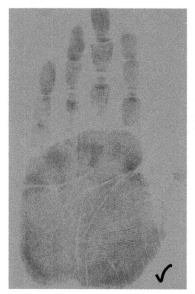 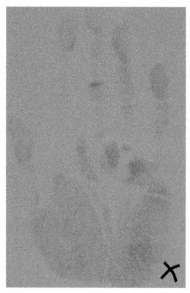

This print has captured the bottom of the palm and the centre area and has a good, even application of ink.

This is a poor quality palm print as there are areas missing due to an uneven pressure when taking the print. The bottom edge by the wrist has not been captured.

The side or edge of the palm must be taken where applicable. Livescan has a space for this, but it may not be possible on forms used for inked prints.

The side edge of the palm is known as the hypothenar, more commonly referred to as 'writer's edge' or 'chop' marks, commonly found where a person has shielded their eyes with the hands to peer through windows, referred to as 'look–in marks' at crime scenes.

It is important to ensure that the palm edge is central within the box when taking such impressions and that the palm is not tilted too far towards the back of the hand. It is the ridge details on the edge of the palm that require capturing and if the hand is tilted too far back there is a risk such details will not be captured.

The importance of taking good quality prints cannot be overstated; the potential consequence of submitting poor prints is a missed identification.

6.8 Chapter Summary

Fingerprints are a key forensic investigative technique and method of identification. The comparison of fingerprints recovered from a crime scene can be made against those held on the national database—Ident1. Fingerprints can also be used to confirm the identity of persons arrested, for immigration purposes and to establish and/or confirm the identity of deceased persons and to link crimes even where the donor of the print is unknown.

Fingerprints are deposited when material from natural secretions or material such as paint, ink or blood, for example, is present on the ridged skin. This is then transferred onto a surface. Marks can also be left by the ridged skin surface to create a three-dimensional impression in a suitably soft medium. The presence of fingerprints on a surface is conclusive evidence showing that, at some time, a particular person has touched that surface. Conversely, the absence of fingerprints on a surface is not evidence that a person has not been in contact with the surface; some people may not deposit sufficient material to be recovered by particular techniques.

Fingerprints are unique to each individual—no two people have been found to have the same fingerprints in over 100 years of the system being utilised. There are many techniques available for the recovery of fingerprints from crime scenes and exhibits, all of which the CSI and laboratory technicians are trained to use. The recovery of DNA material may be possible after the use of one single fingerprint recovery technique. It is important to seek the advice of the CSI or laboratory technician and/or forensic scientist if DNA and fingerprints are required in order to establish the best possible sequence for the recovery of the best potential forensic material.

It is vital that fingerprints taken from persons for comparison purposes are of a high standard, as poor quality fingerprints can lead to an identification not being made even if a person is on the system. It is extremely beneficial for elimination sets of fingerprints to be taken from those who have had lawful access to crime scenes where the CSI has recovered fingerprints. This enables the fingerprint experts to concentrate on establishing the identity of those who have not had lawful access.

KNOWLEDGE CHECK—FINGERPRINTS

1. What are the reasons for taking a person's fingerprints?

   Fingerprints can be taken for identification purposes from those in custody, from those with lawful and legitimate access to a crime scene for elimination purposes, for immigration purposes and to establish or confirm the identification of a deceased person.

2. What would be the chemical development technique used to recover fingerprints from a plastic bag brought to the scene by an offender, which is found inside a premises at a dwelling burglary?

   The superglue technique would be the most appropriate if the bag was dry. If the bag was known to have been wet, then the laboratory technicians need to be made aware of this.

3. Fingerprints are recovered from the plastic bag referred to in question 2 above, and are identified on Ident1. What would be the evidential value of the fingerprints?

The fingerprints will determine that a particular person touched the plastic bag at some time, but not necessarily place them at the crime scene as the bag is an easily transportable item.

4. State the reasons why fingerprints may not be found on Ident1.

There are several reasons why a fingerprint identification officer will not find a person's fingerprints on the national database:

- The main reason for the system and the fingerprint identification officer attributing different characteristics is due, in part, to poor quality sets of ten prints held on the system. It is vital that the ten prints submitted by officers are of the best possible quality and clarity.

- The suspect may not have been fingerprinted in connection with any offence and is therefore not on the database at the time of an offence. Fingerprint experts regularly undertake 'back searching' where all unidentified scene marks are compared against Ident1 to ensure a fuller report of a suspect's previous criminal activity is available.

- Fingerprints recovered may belong to the victim or those with 'legitimate access' and so they may not be on the national database. The submission of elimination fingerprints of those with legitimate access to the scene is required where possible, to enable the fingerprint identification officer to work more efficiently. The elimination fingerprints enable the fingerprint expert to verify that such marks do not belong to a possible suspect, thus such marks can be discounted from any back searching.

Recommended Reading

Advances in Fingerprint Technology, 3rd edn (2012) Lee, HC and Gaensslen, RE.
'Development of Latent Fingerprints from Skin' (1998) Fortunato, SL.
Fingermark Visualisation Manual (2013) CAST.
Fingerprint Detection by Laser (1980) Menzel, ER.
Livescan Good Practice Guide (2010) Association of Chief Police Officers (ACPO)/ National Policing Improvement Agency (NPIA).
Protection of Freedoms Act 2012: How DNA and Fingerprint Evidence is Protected in Law (2013) Home Office.

┌─────────┐
│   │
│   7   │
│   │
└─────────┘

DNA—
Deoxyribonucleic Acid

7.1 **Introduction**

The application of DNA technology has without a doubt had a huge impact on the investigation of crime. In the mid-1980s research undertaken by Dr Alec Jefferies demonstrated that certain areas of the DNA strand contained patterns that would reliably replicate, and the number of these repetitions varied between individuals (except for identical twins/triplets who have the same DNA profiles). Dr Jefferies demonstrated the ability of this technique to reliably identify individuals by comparing samples of their DNA.

The scientific advances since then have enabled a relatively quick and efficient means of identification due to the development of a national DNA database (NDNAD). Investigators of both current and historical cases have access to this key tool for the identification or elimination of persons and to establish links between different scenes.

The technological advances have enabled DNA profiles to be obtained from increasingly small samples. As the sensitivity of the techniques improves, so do the risks of transfer and contamination. It is vital that material that could potentially bear DNA is handled carefully and with due regard to the risks of contamination and cross-transfer. A DNA profile is essentially the sequence in which a combination of particular areas of the DNA occurs.

In simple terms it can be compared to a bar code on retail goods—the overall appearance of bar codes is the same, but individual differences occur which individualise one bar code from another.

One disadvantage of these technological advances is that it can lead to investigators becoming overly reliant on forensic evidence. Whilst the DNA profiling technique and the existence of the NDNAD undoubtedly offers huge benefits and an opportunity to quickly establish or confirm the identity of individuals, investigators must not neglect other aspects of the criminal investigation. There can be numerous defences regarding the presence of forensic material and it is imperative that an investigator is aware of these and ensures a thorough and robust investigation is undertaken in order to put any forensic evidence into the context of the particular circumstances of each case.

At the level of genes and DNA individual differences occur which can enable the identification of an individual from DNA bearing material.

The coding system used enables scientists to calculate a *probability* of two unrelated individuals having the same DNA profiles and the statistical *likelihood* of an individual being the donor of a profile from a crime scene stain.

DNA bearing material recovered from crime scenes is in the form of body fluids or biological matter, such as skin cells for example, and profiles obtained from exhibits/crime scenes can be compared with those on the NDNAD and/with known suspects who may not be on the NDNAD at the time of the investigation. DNA samples taken from persons in custody are loaded onto the NDNAD to be searched against any unidentified crime stains. It is often beneficial to take voluntary samples from those who may have lawful access to an exhibit or location of the crime scene for elimination purposes.

The potential for DNA material to be recovered from body fluids is perhaps the most obvious evidential consideration; there are other investigative benefits in the examination of certain body fluids. The distribution of blood at a crime scene, for example, may benefit from blood pattern analysis (BPA), which can be useful in establishing what has happened, the sequence of events and can corroborate or refute versions of events.

7.2 **Sources of DNA**

Deoxyribonucleic acid (DNA) is present in almost every cell in the body with the notable exception of red blood cells which do not carry DNA material (see Figure 7.1).

Figure 7.1 Diagrammatic representation of the structure a cell

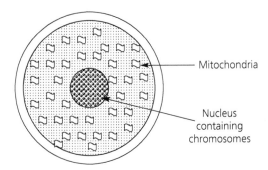

There are many items that can be recovered from crime scenes that will potentially bear DNA—only 'potentially' as there are several factors that mean a sample may not yield a profile. DNA can be degraded by environmental factors and it is also possible that there may not be enough DNA-bearing cells present in the recovered stain.

Millions of skin cells are shed from the body every day, and these will be inevitably contained in other bodily secretions such as saliva, mucus and sweat—it is the skin cells within these fluids that contain the DNA.

The most commonly encountered biological samples recovered for DNA analysis include the following:

7.2.1 **Blood**

Most cells within the body carry DNA with the exception of red blood cells. The role of the red blood cell is to carry oxygen and other nutrients around the body.

It is the white blood cells that are required for DNA analysis. It is often thought that where a large pool of blood is present, a DNA profile will most certainly be obtained.

When a person bleeds, the first defence of the body is to try and stop the loss of blood—white blood cells rush to the wound and are washed out, with damaged skin cells, in the initial flow. Latter bleeding may not contain as high a concentration of white cells or skin cells and therefore a profile may not be obtained. A crime scene investigator (CSI) will therefore generally look for the site of the initial blood loss as this is most likely to contain a higher concentration of the white blood and skin cells and thus potentially lead to a full DNA profile.

All the blood stains present will be sampled, however, as this is a general 'rule' and subject to many variables. It is possible that latter blood stains will yield DNA; however the concentration of the white blood cells present may be one factor in a sample not producing a useable DNA profile.

A CSI will undertake a presumptive blood test to establish if the stain is blood: a negative result indicates the stain is definitely not blood, a positive result indicates the stain may be blood and will warrant the recovery of the stain for analysis. Such tests cannot distinguish between human and animal blood.

On darker coloured backgrounds that may obscure blood, the CSI can utilise a forensic light source to search for potential blood stains. Blood does not fluoresce but absorbs light to appear darker than the background. Chemical screening techniques can be utilised to locate non-visible blood staining.

Blood can be transferred onto parts of clothing after an attack, for example blood on offenders' hands can be transferred to the insides of pockets or on underwear. It should be borne in mind that blood may not always be readily visible; gloves must always be worn if the presence of blood is suspected even if it is not obviously apparent.

7.2.2 Semen

DNA material is present in the heads of the spermatozoa and there are a number of techniques that can be utilised for the analysis of semen for DNA.

Laser micro-dissection (LMD)

Where a sample is likely to contain female cellular material in addition to sperm cells, a technique known as laser micro-dissection (LMD) can separate male cells from any female cellular material. This technique enables the male only cells to be targeted and analysed. Once sufficient sperm cells have been recovered the low template (LT) DNA process can be used to extract the DNA profile.

Fluorescence *in situ* hybridisation (FISH)

This process enables the extraction of non-sperm cells where semen may not contain any sperm, for example as a result of vasectomy. The technique targets the sex chromosomes, identifying the Y (male) chromosomes. LMD is then used to recover male cells to produce a DNA profile.

Both the LMD and FISH techniques can produce profiles that are compatible with the NDNAD.

Identification of semen

Semen stains can be searched for by utilising a forensic light source which will cause the stain to fluoresce as a pale white or yellow stain against the background. Fluorescence properties of semen depend on many variables; a presumptive test for semen can be undertaken by a CSI.

It is possible to identify a stain as semen where no sperm are present. Scientists can analyse the sample for seminal acid phosphatase (SAP) or a protein specific antigen or P30.

7.2.3 **Saliva**

Items such as cigarette butts, drinking vessels, swabs from areas of lick or bite marks, for example, can be sent for analysis. It is the skin cells sloughed off from the inside of the mouth (buccal cells) which is the focus of analysis. Cells are continually lost from the lips; contact such as occurs when smoking a cigarette or drinking from a bottle, will dislodge cells which then adhere to the cigarette filter or bottle opening.

It is important to note that some drinks may degrade any DNA material on the mouth of a bottle—acidic and sugary carbonated drinks are believed to be particularly damaging and may affect the quality of any resulting profile. Smooth surfaces are not generally good for retaining cellular material. The best area for DNA on a drinking bottle is the ridged type tops/caps, as the twisting action required to remove them from the bottle effectively sloughs off skin cells which then adhere to the ridged material.

A presumptive test for saliva is available for use by a CSI.

7.2.4 **Sweat**

Sweat is a liquid secretion which does not carry cellular material in its pure form. As with saliva, sloughed skin cells may be present within the sweat stain. Examples where such skin cells may be present are in the armpits of close fitting clothing and headbands of hats. Any area on an item of clothing that has had close contact with skin may potentially hold sufficient skin cells to yield enough material for DNA analysis.

7.2.5 **Mucus**

Mucus can be a good source of DNA, especially if a used handkerchief is recovered. The force of sneezing, coughing or blowing the nose means a concentration of skin cells from the lining of the nose can be present. For example, mucus material that was swabbed from a pavement (where the suspect was seen to spit) yielded a full profile for a suspect in a series of sexual offences who was wanted in three force areas. This was the only sufficient forensic identification material that had been recovered from the numerous scenes for which this person was believed to be responsible.

7.2.6 **Urine**

Urine will not be routinely submitted for analysis as it is unlikely enough cellular material from the urethra will be present to extract sufficient DNA. However, in serious cases it is worth seeking advice from a forensic scientist as the technology is always improving.

7.2.7 **Hair**

Hair shafts contain dead cells and so are not suitable for analysis for the crime stain database, but may be suitable for mitochondria (MtDNA) analysis. In order to recover sufficient cellular material for nuclear DNA analysis, hair with a root is required.

Hair has three distinct growth phases, with the root gradually reducing in size until the hair falls out naturally. This is generally the type of hair found in hats or on vehicle seats, for example, which have been shed naturally. The presence of a good root on the hair generally indicates the use of some force to remove it.

7.2.8 **Faeces**

Faeces contains a lot of bacteria which can degrade any DNA material present and is not generally suitable for the general DNA profiling unless blood is visible. MtDNA may be able to be extracted from faeces. It is important to discuss any forensic potential of faeces with the forensic provider or CSI.

7.2.9 **Dandruff**

Dandruff and surface layers of skin are not routinely used for standard DNA profiling techniques as it is basically dead skin cells.

The skin cells mentioned in previous sections are 'live' at the time they are removed or sloughed off by some form of friction contact (eg, skin under fingernails where the victim has scratched the offender, the unscrewing of a ridged bottle cap or the rubbing action of a headband on the forehead). Dead skin cells which are shed naturally are not currently suited for the routine analysis. However, in serious offences, further techniques may be available and as techniques are constantly evolving, it is always worth checking potential forensic opportunities with the forensic service provider (FSP). Table 7.1 outlines the potential for DNA recovery from commonly encountered crime stains.

Table 7.1 Summary of sample types and DNA recovery potential

Sample	Source of DNA	Comments
Blood	White blood cells	Good source of DNA.
Semen	Sperm cells/Non-sperm male cells	Good source of DNA.
Hair with roots	Hair follicle cells	Good source of DNA.
Skin/dandruff	Skin cells (dead)	Not a good source for routine analysis.
Shed hair shafts (dead)	Adhering dead skin/follicle cells	Not a good source for routine analysis. MtDNA may be obtained.
Sweat stains	Sloughed skin cells contained in fluid	Can be a good source.
Vaginal fluids	Mainly fluid but may contain sloughed mucosal skin cells	Good source of DNA.
Mucus	Mainly fluid but may contain sloughed mucosal cells	Good source of DNA.
Urine	Mainly liquid but may contain sloughed mucosal cells	Not routinely used as so few cells generally present. Seek advice in serious cases.
Faeces	Sloughed intestinal skin cells	Not usually a good source of nuclear DNA. MtDNA may be used for serious cases.

7.3 What is DNA?

DNA is a self-replicating genetic coding material which determines physical characteristics such as hair and eye colour. DNA remains unchanged throughout life and can remain long after death.

DNA presents its code as four chemical bases arranged to form a twisted ladder-like structure known as the 'double helix' (see Figure 7.2). The four chemical bases are adenine (A) which will always form half of a 'rung' on the 'ladder' with thymine (T), guanine (G) will always form half of a 'rung' with cytosine (C).

131

Figure 7.2 The DNA 'double helix' strand

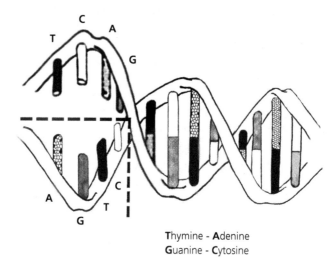

Thymine - Adenine
Guanine - Cytosine

The self-replicating nature of DNA means that each strand (one side of the ladder) of DNA can serve as a template to duplicate the sequence of the bases or 'rungs'. The order (sequence) of these base pairs determines a person's genetic coding. Just as the letters of the alphabet vary to form words, the order of the bases in a DNA sequence form genes. It is the order of these base pairs that are analysed to give the unique DNA profile.

There are three billion bases present in the entire human DNA strand (genome) and approximately 20,000 genes which contain all the genetic information for an individual. However, over 98% of human DNA is non-coding and does not serve as a template for replication. The location (loci) of the markers selected for forensic purposes and suitability for the NDNAD are those that have a high level of variations between individuals. This variation is due to the number of times the short sequence of DNA is repeated along its length; these loci are referred to as short tandem repeat (STR) loci.

The majority of our DNA is sited in the nucleus of cells (nuclear DNA) and a small amount of DNA is found in the mtDNA.

People inherit half their DNA from their mother and half from their father, with siblings inheriting different combinations of the DNA sequence from the same parents. DNA profiles of siblings will have similarities; however individual profiles will differ. Identical twins, triplets, for example, have the same DNA profiles, but different fingerprints—which will uniquely identify one twin from the other.

The main issue with DNA is not so much the scientific techniques and analysis, as courts appear to accept (mostly, but not always) that the statistical methods utilised for DNA identifications are robust. Rather the issues raised increasingly question how the DNA samples are handled from the start of the investigative process, especially regarding issues of transfer and contamination. This is a particular area of concern when low levels of DNA are recovered from crime scenes/exhibits.

7.3.1 Nuclear DNA

The nucleus of a cell contains twenty-two pairs of chromosomes (half from each parent) plus two sex chromosomes (XY chromosomes for males/XX chromosomes for females) which hold our DNA material. It is from the cell nucleus that nuclear DNA can be extracted to provide a 'profile' suitable for searching on the NDNAD.

7.3.2 Mitochondrial DNA (MtDNA)

MtDNA is present in relatively large amounts within a cell, but has fewer features, making it unsuitable for searching on the NDNAD. The fewer points for comparison essentially mean that many people will have the same features within their MtDNA, so it is not highly discriminating.

MtDNA is passed to children via the maternal line, so whilst males have MtDNA, only females can pass it on to their children. MtDNA are essentially the energy source of the cell. During conception the female egg containing MtDNA is fertilised by the sperm, which only contains MtDNA in the tail. As the sperm enters the egg, the tail falls away leaving only the head of the sperm to fertilise the egg, which is why males do not pass on their MtDNA to their children.

Brothers and sisters will have the same MtDNA as their mother and all their relatives linked through the maternal line. As so many related individuals will share the same MtDNA profiles, this system cannot be used for searching on the NDNAD.

The process does have benefits in a forensic capacity, however, and has been used successfully for the identification of degraded and old human remains and bodies involved in mass disasters and familial searches. The technique has been very valuable for cold case reviews where there are only old, degraded samples to work with.

7.3.3 DNA profiles

DNA material, when extracted and processed, will show as a series of 'bars' of differing length and width—similar to the barcodes on retail goods. These are then analysed by a computerised system which accurately measures the 'bars' to produce a series of graphs known as an electropherogram, to show the corresponding lengths, widths and positions of each bar. The data produced is analysed by the scientists to determine the amount of the specific sections of the DNA that are present and enable them to make an interpretation of the results.

Prior to July 2014, the standard DNA profiling technique used a process referred to as SGM*plus* (second generation multiplex) which analysed ten pre-selected sites of the DNA strand plus the sex chromosomes. The examination of the sex chromosomes means a scientist can potentially determine whether the donor was male or female. In mixed profiles, where DNA from two or more individuals contributes to a sample, interpretation of the profiles can be more difficult.

Since July 2014 DNA-17 has become the standard DNA profiling process, replacing SGM*plus*. The new DNA-17 process utilises the same loci as SGM*plus* in addition to six further loci, giving a total of sixteen loci plus the gender marker. This means that profiles generated using SGM*Plus* loaded onto the NDNAD can be compared with DNA-17 profiles and remain admissible for criminal proceedings.

The DNA-17 process enables an improved discrimination between profiles, essentially reducing the probability of a chance match between two unrelated individuals. The improvement in sensitivity means that smaller samples of DNA or degraded samples can now be profiled. A downside to the increase in sensitivity is that there is a greater risk of contamination, transfer and detection of background DNA.

The probability of a chance match between two unrelated individuals is in the order of one in trillions; however for court reporting purposes a random match probability of one in a billion is now accepted as standard, providing very strong evidence that matching profiles have originated from the same person.

However, it must be remembered that a 'match' between profiles is that of probability and is not an absolute certainty, which is why DNA evidence alone may not be admissible as the sole evidence—it must be supported by corroborative evidence that forms part of a thorough investigation which puts the DNA evidence into context. Defence teams are increasingly challenging the 'how' and 'where' a sample was deposited and the actions of the investigator and/or scientist, rather than attacking the reliability of the profiling science. The issue of contamination is frequently raised to cast doubt on DNA evidence.

DNA-17 profiles can be compared with profiles produced in other EU countries that use the same standard DNA profiling techniques, allowing cross-border law enforcement agencies (LEAs) to work together more efficiently.

Access to and uses for DNA profiles are outlined in the Home Office publication from the NDNAD delivery unit (NDU): *The NDNAD Strategy Board Policy for Access and Use of DNA Samples, Profiles and Associated Data*, which states that profiles held on the NDNAD must only be used for the following:

- the provision of intelligence and evidence to support the investigation, detection, prosecution and reduction of crime;
- the identification of a deceased person or of the person from whom a body part came; and
- the protection of an individual who has volunteered a DNA sample as they are potentially at risk of harm.

7.3.4 **Laboratory submission**

Where material potentially bearing DNA is recovered from a crime scene, it has to be sent to an FSP laboratory in order for any DNA to be extracted and subsequently profiled.

It is vitally important that submission to the FSP is conducted as soon as practicable after the collection of samples in order to maximise potential evidence and reduce the opportunity for any degradation of the material to occur.

Submission to an FSP will typically be made via the in-force forensic submissions unit or similar. This ensures the completion of the relevant forms is correct and enables budgetary considerations (cost vs benefit) to be made in order to reach a decision as to whether requests for submission to an FSP are progressed.

Completion of the form MG21 is required for the initial forensic submission and must accompany all samples sent for analysis. It is extremely important the investigator fully outlines the circumstances of the incident, the modus operandi of the offence and the 'points to prove' relating to the samples to be analysed. This enables the forensic submissions unit staff and any scientist to understand the samples in the context of the circumstances of each particular case.

The Prosecution Team *Manual of Guidance for the preparation, processing and submission of prosecution files* advises the following information should be included:

- whether a scientist has attended scene and result of any examination;
- if the case is linked to previous submissions;
- if it forms part of a serious investigation;
- what the main lines of enquiry are;
- result of pre-charge Crown Prosecution Service (CPS) advice;
- crime scene assessment;
- result of forensic strategy group meeting in a major enquiry; and
- when the crime took place.

(See the College of Policing Authorised Professional Practice (APP) internet resources for current guidance on MG completion)

These details and a concise account of the incident under investigation, alongside accounts given by any suspects and other information that would be beneficial for the scientist to be aware of (these are termed 'critical success factors' and a summary of the appropriate success factors should be available alongside the forms in most forces) are required.

It has to be borne in mind that these forms are read by persons who are not personally involved in the incident under investigation and who only rely upon the information provided. It is important that rationale for a submission are stated fully and what outcomes are required to be achieved from the examination are clarified. This information will enable any results to be analysed in the context of the case.

Submission results

Once a sample has been received into the laboratory, any potential DNA material needs to be extracted to obtain a profile of the DNA in the first instance.

Profiles have to be of sufficient quality in order to be loaded onto the NDNAD and not every sample can be loaded for searching and comparison on the database. It may, however, be possible to compare a named suspect sample with a crime stain, or to undertake further analytical processing which may enhance insufficient profiles gained through standard processes. These possibilities can be discussed with the scientist or forensic submissions department; however the authorisation of further work will be subject to the circumstances of the case.

7.3.5 Low template DNA (LTDNA)

Low template (LT)DNA is the term used to refer to what was previously termed 'low copy number' (LCN) or 'touch' DNA. These were commercial terms given to a process whereby degraded or small samples could be replicated by increasing the sensitivity of the profiling technique.

A Review of the Science of Low Template DNA Analysis, known as the 'Caddy Review' defines LTDNA as:

> An ultra-sensitive technique that has the potential to yield a DNA profile from sub-optimal biological samples e.g. Low Copy Number DNA analysis.

LTDNA is more sensitive than standard profiling techniques and can be utilised where very few cells or partly degraded cells are present. The amount of cellular material required to obtain a LTDNA profile is accepted as being between 100–200 picograms (a picogram is a million millionth of a gram). The LTDNA process is potentially capable of producing a profile from a single cell, such as cells left behind in a fingerprint or those present in sweat and from samples previously found to be negative by the routine process. There have been successes in obtaining profiles from items that have been handled by offenders such as tools, weapons and from clothing grabbed by an offender where skin cells have been deposited.

There are two main issues with LTDNA. Firstly, the risk of transfer of minute amounts of cellular material is greatly increased.

KEY POINT—DEFINITION OF TRANSFER

Primary transfer occurs when cells are deposited on an object/surface.

Secondary transfer occurs when a surface containing the primary transfer comes into direct contact with another surface. Typically, there will be less cellular material on the secondary surface.

Factors affecting the amount of cellular material present on a surface include:

- The propensity of a person to transfer their cellular material. (Research has demonstrated that individuals differ in the amount of cellular material they transfer to a surface.);
- The *texture* of the surface. A rough surface like a rusty bar for example, will slough off and retain more cellular material than a smooth surface.

> • The amount of *time* and the *pressure* involved in the contact.
>
> The transferability of cellular material for LTDNA is further increased as it is generally in the form of skin cells or minute stains which are not generally visible to the naked eye.

Secondly, the amplification process of samples can increase any background contamination proportionately, making interpretation of the profile more problematic and less straightforward than where standard profiling techniques are utilised.

LTDNA has undergone some controversy in the past and following the appeal of Sean Hoey in the Omagh Bombing case (discussed later), the use of LTDNA (formerly LCN) profiling techniques were suspended. The Association of Chief Police Officers (ACPO), in consultation with the CPS, recommended a temporary suspension on the use of LCN DNA analysis techniques in criminal investigations following this judgment. The temporary suspension was in order for a review of the process and the procedures to be undertaken.

The CPS reviewed cases involving the use of LCN DNA analysis and found that the problems highlighted in the review had been satisfactorily rectified and concluded that the use of LCN analysis should remain available for the recovery of potential evidence. This view was upheld in the 'Caddy Review' which supported the science behind the LTDNA.

Issues remain regarding the admissibility of evidence gained from profiles that have been obtained from such small samples of biological material. In particular, the interpretation of complex/partial or mixed profiles has been at issue. The critical factor is the quantity of DNA that is available for analysis. Samples for LTDNA analysis are at a lower quantity than those processed with the DNA-17 process, and thus harder to quantify and interpret statistically.

Due to the sensitivity of the LTDNA process, the risk of contamination and cross-transfer is especially high, as is the chance of obtaining mixed profiles and background DNA, which are far more complex to analyse.

Appeal Court Rulings regarding the use and evidential admissibility of LTDNA.

R v Sean Hoey [2007]—The Omagh bombing appeal

LCN DNA (now referred to as LTDNA) played a key role in the conviction of Sean Hoey, accused of the bombing in the centre of Omagh that claimed the lives of twenty-nine people.

Several issues were highlighted within the judgment, most significantly the interpretation of the LCN evidence and the handling, recording and storage of exhibits that potentially contained DNA material.

During the appeal, the interpretation of the DNA evidence was found to be unreliable. Essentially, more weight was attributed to the evidence by the scientists in the initial trial than could be substantiated.

R v Reed and Reed [2009]

The court found LTDNA could provide profiles capable of producing reliable interpretation where the quantity of DNA was above a certain level, referred to as the 'stochastic threshold'. There is currently no scientific agreement as to where precisely this threshold is; however it varies between 100–200 picograms.

The Judge ruled in this case that challenges to the validity of LTDNA evidence at levels at, or above, this threshold would no longer be allowed unless new scientific evidence was available.

R v Broughton [2010]

The court considered the admissibility of DNA evidence where the quantity of the DNA recovered from the crime scene fell below the stochastic threshold. In this case it found that this did not necessarily mean that such evidence would automatically be ruled inadmissible.

R v Kuba Dlugosz, R v Pickering and R v MDS [2013]

The appeals for these cases were heard together although they each had different circumstances. The common issue was that of the admissibility of LTDNA evidence from mixed samples, and in particular whether expert evidence was admissible where the strength of the evidence could not be expressed in statistical terms, relying on evaluative opinion, which can be more subjective than statistical match probabilities. The Appeal Judges disagreed, stating:

> An expert who spends years studying this kind of comparison can properly form a judgement as to the significance of what he has found in any particular case. It is a judgement based on his experience. A jury is entitled to be informed of his assessment.

This is a significant change regarding LTDNA evidence and can have implications for any evaluative expert opinion on a range of forensic evidence, where it is not possible to statistically present their findings. Recommendations from these cases is that such experts should make it clear to the jury that the opinion given has no statistical basis and is an opinion based on experience and is of more limited assistance.

As this means that subjective opinion evidence is admissible regarding LTDNA evidence it makes it essential for investigators to preserve, recover, record and store the evidence in a manner to demonstrate the continuity and integrity and to thoroughly explore the circumstances surrounding DNA profile evidence to minimise any counter-arguments that its presence arose as a result of a transfer of material.

The *Omagh* case highlights the need to ensure any items bearing potential forensic evidence, especially but not exclusively DNA, are handled with care, packaged and stored correctly and accurate continuity records maintained. It is the responsibility of the prosecution to demonstrate, beyond reasonable doubt, that any forensic evidence relied upon in court is reliable and has been handled in a manner in which no contamination could have occurred accidentally or deliberately. Due to recent appeal cases such as this, the systems in place to ensure the continuity and integrity of forensic evidence will be increasingly scrutinised. As forensic techniques become increasingly sensitive the risk of contamination increases.

7.4 The National DNA Database (NDNAD)

DNA profiles generated from crimes committed in England and Wales are loaded onto the NDNAD, which was launched in April 1995 and is managed by the NDU within the Home Office.

The creation of the NDNAD has, without a doubt, proved to be an effective tool for police investigators.

On 31 March 2013 the NDNAD held 6,737,973 profiles from individuals, and 428,634 profiles recovered from crime scenes, numbers that increase daily to provide the UK with one of the largest DNA databases in the world.

DNA profiles obtained from the suspect samples taken in custody are loaded onto the database and compared with unidentified profiles obtained from profiles recovered at crime scenes.

Profiles obtained from crime scenes are also compared with other scene profiles to establish if there are links between scenes even if an individual cannot currently be identified.

7.4.1 Volunteer/elimination samples

There will be occasions where the DNA material recovered has been left by those who have lawful access to the crime scene. As with fingerprints, it is necessary to take a sample from a victim or witness where appropriate, to ensure any profile obtained does not belong to them.

As with fingerprints, if the profile cannot be eliminated it will be loaded onto the database as an unidentified crime scene profile. This can cause costly and time consuming investigations to be undertaken unnecessarily. If a scientist can compare and eliminate the profiles of those with lawful access to that of the crime scene stain, it will prevent the database being loaded with unnecessary profiles and save investigative time. An unidentified profile can cause problems with defence teams who could suggest that the unknown profile is that of the true offender. Investigators must ensure that samples are taken for elimination purposes where material containing potential DNA has been recovered from the scene.

7.4.2 **The police elimination database (PED)**

Within the database framework there is a police elimination database (PED) which holds profiles of police officers and operational staff. This is *entirely separate* from the main suspect or crime stain database.

As with the police fingerprint elimination database, the PED is an essential tool to ensure that any profiles put on the main crime database are those from genuine suspect samples. The increasing sensitivity of the techniques used means that contamination of samples is a real issue.

A search of the PED can only be authorised at the request of an SIO (senior investigating officer), and the search is limited to the comparison of the profiles of personnel who had access to the scene or exhibits in question, with the profile of the unidentified crime scene profile. It must be demonstrated that there are genuine grounds for believing that contamination by an investigator has occurred. The profiles on the PED cannot be speculatively searched against the NDNAD. It must be noted, however, that not all forensic examination personnel/investigators are on the PED.

7.4.3 **NDNAD search results**

When a profile is obtained that can be loaded onto the database, the initial results will report on the suitability of the profile for loading onto the database and indicate where a sample may contain more than one profile as summarised in Table 7.2.

Table 7.2 Summary of the possible initial analysis results

Reported results	Loadable to NDNAD	Note
Full profile—suitable	Yes	All areas analysed are present in the profile
Partial profile—suitable	Yes	Not all areas analysed are present but are above the minimum required
More than one person—distinguishable	Yes	A mixed profile where the individual profiles can be distinguished
Partial profile—unsuitable	No	The sample does not contain the minimum number of areas required. Can be subject to a one-off speculative search at police request or re-analysed with a more sensitive technique
No profile	No	There may not be sufficient material present to obtain a profile
More than one person—indistinguishable	No	A mixed profile where individual profiles cannot be separated
No body fluids present	No	No material is present for the extraction of DNA

Where profiles are of suitable quality to load onto the database, investigators will only be notified where a match between profiles has been made and not where a sample has been loaded but no subsequent match occurs. Where profiles are compared, the strength of the match between them will be reported to the investigating officer as summarised in Table 7.3.

It must be remembered that a 'match' between profiles is that of probability and is not an absolute certainty, which is why DNA evidence alone may not be admissible as the sole evidence in some cases—it must be supported by corroborative evidence and put into the context of a thorough investigation.

Table 7.3 Match report results

Reported results	What it means.
Conclusive association	The crime stain and suspect sample match across all of the comparison markers.
Strong support for association	The crime stain and suspect sample have some areas of comparison. *Discuss the strength of potential evidential value with a scientist.*
Some support for association	The crime stain and suspect sample have very few areas of comparison match.
Inconclusive	Insufficient material or poor quality sample for comparison purposes.
Some support for elimination	The crime stain and suspect sample have some areas of comparison.
Strong support for elimination	The crime stain and suspect sample have very few areas of comparison. *Discuss the strength of potential evidential value with a scientist.*
Conclusive elimination	The profile crime stain and suspect sample are not alike.

7.4.4 Other DNA database functions

In addition to searching of the NDNAD for matches between crime scene and suspect profiles, there are separate databases to assist investigators in the identification of unidentified bodies or body parts in missing persons enquiries, for example, and in investigation into crimes that may involve a victim that is vulnerable or at risk of harm. Figure 7.3 shows summary of a routine NDNAD process.

Figure 7.3 Summary of routine NDNAD process

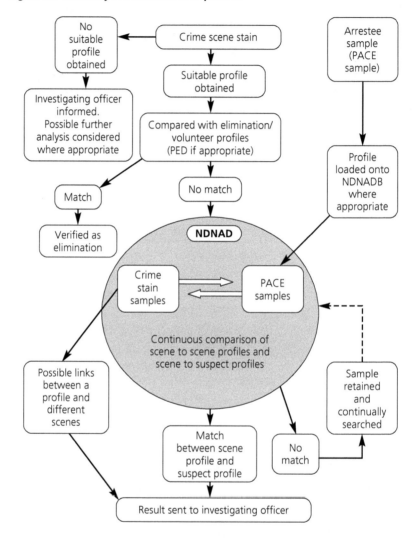

The missing persons DNA database (MPDD)

Held by the UK Missing Person Bureau within the National Crime Agency (NCA) the MPDD holds profiles given with consent by a person's next of kin for the purposes of identification. Samples for profiling can be taken from personal items— such as a hairbrush or toothbrush, of a missing person or DNA sample from a close relative for comparison against profiles from unidentified bodies or body parts.

Vulnerable persons DNA database (VPDD)

Profiles of those considered at risk of harm, for example in cases of 'honour based violence' or 'child sexual exploitation'. Individuals and investigators can request a DNA profile is added to the database—if that person subsequently goes missing their profile can be compared with the main NDNAD to establish whether there is a match with samples such as bloodstains recovered from crime scenes or if an unidentified body/body part is recovered. Vulnerable person profiles are non-searchable until specific reasoning is available to suggest that a vulnerable person has come to harm or is missing.

Familial DNA searches (fDNA)

This search technique can be used where a full DNA profile has been recovered from a crime scene stain that does not produce any matches when loaded onto the NDNAD.

Based on the knowledge that close genetic relatives will share similarities in their DNA profiles, a search of the database can be made for the profiles that most closely match the crime stain. Such a search can produce lists of possible profiles which are then narrowed down by utilising search parameters such as geographic locations and existing intelligence.

This technique is used in serious cases as it is time consuming and expensive, requiring authorisation from the DNA strategy board at the Home Office.

This technique, based on the theory that criminality runs in families, does not provide the name of the offender but may contain the identification of a close relative of them.

....

Case study—Familial searching

Michael Little was fatally injured when a brick was thrown into the cab of his lorry from a footbridge on the M3 in March 2003. The case is the first successful prosecution in England where a killer has been traced through the DNA profile of a relative.

The brick was recovered and using LTDNA analysis techniques (formerly LCN), a partial profile was obtained which was also linked to blood found on a vehicle nearby that the offender had attempted to steal prior to throwing the brick.

The profiles did not produce a match when searched on the NDNAD, nor was a result gained following intelligence led mass screening in the locality. Familial searching (fDNA) was utilised to see if any individuals on the database closely matched the profile obtained from the scene. The search was limited to white males, under 35 years old living within specified geographic parameters.

The search produced a list of twenty-five names with the most closely matching profile having sixteen out of twenty areas of comparison matching the crime stain profile. This included the profile of a family member of the offender, whose details could then be traced and a buccal DNA swab obtained from them was found to be a match with the DNA recovered from the brick and stain on the car.

Craig Harman was sentenced to six years' imprisonment for the manslaughter of Michael Little.

....

Y-STR profiles

The Y-STR analysis technique is helpful where mixed samples are present—such as in sexual offences, for example, that contain both the male and female gender chromosomes.

The Y-STR analysis process targets the Y chromosome, which is inherited through the paternal line, so all related males in a family will have the same Y-STR profile, just as MtDNA is passed via maternal lineage. Whilst not compatible to be searched against the NDNAD it is a useful process where there are specific males to make a comparison with. Due to the fact that many blood related male relatives will have the same Y-STR profiles, the discriminatory power is reduced.

7.5 Recovery and Preservation of DNA Material

The sensitivity of the DNA profiling techniques mean that contamination and cross-transfer are very real risks. The role of the initial responders is to preserve the scene in order to maximise the potential evidence available for a CSI to recover. Where possible, the item bearing the stain should be photographed *in situ* prior being recovered, ideally by CSIs, who have a range of equipment and methods available to them for the recovery of potential DNA material.

Where DNA material is recovered from a crime scene stain and a profile gained which is loaded on to the NDNAD, it can then be searched against the samples from other unidentified crime scene stains and compared to the samples taken from suspects.

7.6 DNA Samples from Persons

There are two routes for taking DNA samples from persons for comparison against profiles recovered from crime scenes. The PACE kits (K505) are for taking samples from arrestees and the volunteer kits (K515) are for those samples taken from victims and witnesses, for elimination purposes and for those involved in intelligence led mass screens.

7.6.1 Intelligence led mass DNA screening

This requires the taking of DNA samples from a number of people, for example, all males between forty to sixty years of age in a particular locality. It will typically be instigated by an SIO in serious cases where the investigation has yielded little information to identify an offender. Intelligence led mass screens aim to recover a sample that can be compared against that recovered from the scene of a crime, to a member of the local population. Much of the information on intelligence led mass screens is restricted. Police and other relevant LEA personnel may access further information from the APP website or via force intranet based document libraries.

7.6.2 Reasons for sample rejection

Samples can be rejected by the laboratory for analysis for several reasons, all of which can be avoided by taking care when undertaking the sampling process. The most common reasons for sample rejection are as follows:

Checklist—Possible reasons for sample rejection

- Where tamper-evident bags are not used or improperly/unsealed bags are submitted.

- Required forms are missing, incomplete or incorrectly completed.

- Barcodes on the form do not match the barcodes on the swab tubes.

- Two swabs are placed in one tube.

- Swabs are missing.

- Part of the swab stick is left on the swab.

- Swab containers are damaged or unsealed.

- Foreign material is found in the container.

- Swab is upside down in the container.

Where samples are rejected due to administrative or documentation errors, it may be possible that these can be rectified. However, this will incur unnecessary delays and have possible cost implications. Samples that have been rejected for reasons other than administrative errors cannot be resubmitted, and it may not be possible in law to retake samples. It is vital that procedures are followed and the relevant documentation completed accurately.

7.6.3 Taking a DNA sample from persons

The DNA sample is taken from the skin cells inside the cheeks, known as buccal cells. Before using any sampling kit, ensure the expiry date, printed on the outer bag has not passed.

Checklist—Taking a buccal swab DNA sample

- Ensure that the person has not consumed any food or drink in the twenty minutes prior to the sample being taken. If they have, investigators must ensure that twenty minutes elapse before taking the sample.

- Make sure the swabs and containers in the kit are fully sealed and undamaged. If they show damage, discard and begin with a new kit.

- Wear the disposable gloves provided and avoid talking or coughing, for example, over the swabs and containers.

- Take one of the two swabs and hold by the stem end. Use the ridged end of the swab to firmly scrape the inside of the cheek of the donor, for at least six passes.

- Open one of the flip top containers, press down on the stem end of the swab to eject the ridged swab piece into the container. Be careful not to bend the swab stem.

- Once the sample has been ejected into the flip top container, seal the top, attach one of the provided barcode labels to the container and place this into the bag provided.

- Repeat this process using the second swab on the other cheek of the donor.

- With both sealed containers in the tamper-evident bag provided, seal the bag in front of the donor.

- Complete the DNA sample form included in the kit in black ink using block capitals. If this is incomplete the sample will be rejected by the laboratory.

- Place the form, the bag containing the two samples and spare barcodes into the larger tamper-evident bag, seal and place in the freezer for storage.

- It is advisable to make a record of the barcode used in the contemporaneous notebook and on the custody record where appropriate, for continuity purposes.

Volunteer sampling

Samples may be required from victims, witnesses or other categories of persons, for elimination purposes or during intelligence led mass screens. The procedure for taking the sample is the same as above, but a volunteer kit (K515) must be used.

Written consent is required for the sample to be taken and if appropriate, any profile obtained to be the subject of a speculative search against the NDNAD. Once consent has been given for the sample to be loaded onto the database it cannot be withdrawn. It is important that those giving the voluntary sample (whether victim, suspect or other) are fully informed of the reasons for taking the sample and the consequences of any consent given. Where consent is not given to load any profile onto the database, samples will be destroyed following the completion of the purpose for which they were taken.

LEGISLATION AND DNA SAMPLES

A DNA buccal swab is classed as a non-intimate sample as defined by the Police and Criminal Evidence Act 1984 (PACE), s 65.

PACE, s 63 is the main overarching legislation regarding the taking of an arrestee's DNA. PACE, s 63(1) states that the DNA of a person may only be taken with consent and, where at a police station, such consent must be in writing in accordance with s 63(2); Identification Code D, s 6.

DNA buccal swabs can be taken without consent with the authority of an inspector or above for a recordable offence and where there are reasonable grounds to believe that the sample will serve to confirm or eliminate the suspect's involvement (s 63(3),(4)). The person must be informed that authority has been given to take a sample without consent and the grounds and nature of the offence in which the suspect is believed to be involved (s 63(6)).

Amendments made by the Criminal Justice Act 2003 extend the powers for taking DNA samples without consent, without the authority of an inspector or above, in the following circumstances:

- from a person in police detention, arrested for a recordable offence;
- who has not had a sample of the same type, from the same part of the body taken during the investigation, or;
- where a sample has been previously taken that has proved insufficient.
- The power is available irrespective of whether or not the sample is required for the investigation of the offence for which the suspect is arrested.

Samples taken under this power can be taken for the purpose of adding the person's profile to the NDNAD. The power confers the same responsibility for informing the person of the reason for taking the sample, but does not require the nature of the offence to be stated.

The Police Reform Act 2002 confers on designated support staff the power to take DNA PACE samples under PACE, s 63.

Under the Criminal Justice and Public Order Act 1994, persons who have their DNA sample taken, with or without consent, must be informed that these may be the subject of a 'speculative search'. This is a search of the appropriate databases to see if their DNA profile can be identified against any crime scene marks.

Reasonable force may be used to take a non-intimate sample by virtue of Code D, para 6.7.

7.7 **Chapter Summary**

The use of DNA profiling is without a doubt a tremendous asset in the investigation of crime. However, as the technology has advanced to enable DNA profiles to be gained from increasingly smaller amounts of material, so the risks of contamination and cross-transfer have risen.

Where DNA material may be required from an exhibit or crime scene, care must be exercised in the preservation, handling, packaging and storage of such. Investigators must *always* wear disposable gloves and dust masks when handling items containing body fluids and should avoid talking, coughing and sneezing over samples. The wearing of a scene suit by all entering the scene of a serious incident is vital to avoid any transfer of DNA bearing material into/out of the crime scene.

DNA material recovered from crime scenes and those taken from persons are processed to obtain a profile. Where the profile is of suitable quality, it can be loaded onto the NDNAD where crime stain profiles are searched against profiles gained from samples of those arrested. A match between profiles can be in the form of a scene to scene match, enabling investigators to link a series of incidents committed by the same person or between a scene profile and a suspect's profile.

A match between a scene profile and a suspect may not, however, provide conclusive evidence (depending on particular circumstances of the case) on its own that the suspect committed that particular crime due to the transferability of DNA material and the microscopic amounts of material that can now yield a profile. Any DNA evidence needs to be supported by a thorough investigation which puts the presence of the profile into the context of the case, and closes down any potential defence assertions that it was as a result of transfer of material from another place that is not related to the crime scene or offence in question.

The evidence that can be gained from a DNA profile is based on a probability match between the suspect sample and the crime scene sample, and the likelihood of anyone else having the same profile. For this reason it is important that other corroborative evidence is available to support the DNA identification, especially where LT profiling techniques are used.

KNOWLEDGE CHECK—DNA

1. What is DNA?

   Deoxyribonucleic acid (DNA) is the genetic coding found in most of the cells of the body, with the exception of red blood cells. We inherit half our DNA from our mother and half from our father which means that an individual's DNA is unique with the exception of identical twins, triplets, for example, who share the same DNA profile.

2. What is a DNA profile?

   A DNA profile is the unique sequence and combinations of certain areas of the DNA at specific points. It can be compared to a barcode found on retail goods, inasmuch as barcodes all have a similar overall appearance but the location, sequence and size of the bars means that they can be identified as being individual. The analysis of a person's DNA profile enables scientists to establish links or eliminations between a profile at a crime scene with a suspect's sample.

3. State the two types of DNA material that can be recovered from cells and their uses and limitations.

   Nuclear DNA comes from the cell nucleus and if a suitable profile is obtained it can be loaded onto the national database and searched against unidentified crime scene profiles and profiles of persons. A DNA match, however, is based on probability and is not an absolute certainty so additional corroborative evidence may be required if it is used evidentially.

   MtDNA can be recovered from bones, teeth and hair shafts. It is inherited down the maternal line only and has low discriminatory value which means it is unsuitable for searching on the NDNAD. It can be used to identify old, degraded human remains and in mass disaster circumstances where nuclear DNA may not be suitable.

4. Under what circumstances can the PED be searched?

   The PED holds the DNA profiles of police officers and operational support staff who will have access to crime scenes and recovered forensic evidence.

   It can be searched at the request of an SIO where a profile from a crime stain remains unidentified, if there is a genuine belief that the profile may belong to a member of the police. The search must be limited to comparing the unidentified crime stain with the profiles of the officers who had access to the scene or exhibits. Profiles on the PED cannot be searched on the NDNAD.

5. Where DNA material does not produce a match on the NDNAD or is unsuitable for searching, what options are available to an investigator?

   Where a profile is insufficient to search on the database, the LTDNA profiling technique can be used in an attempt to recover a usable profile. This highly sensitive technique can provide DNA profiles from extremely small amounts of material. It is generally only used in serious cases.

   If a profile is obtained that is suitable for searching, but no match is produced the techniques of familial searching can be undertaken to potentially identify close genetic relatives. This is generally used for serious crimes.

   Y-STR profiles cannot be searched against the NDNAD but can be compared to samples of specific individuals and can also be used for familial comparisons.

Recommended Reading

A Review of the Science of Low Template DNA Analysis (2008) Caddy, B, Taylor, G, Linacre, A.

'DNA Population Data to Support the Implementation of National DNA Database DNA-17 Profiling': <https://www.gov.uk/government/statistics/

dna-population-data-to-support-the-implementation-of-national-dna-data-base-dna-17-profiling>.

Guidance: Allele Frequency Databases and Reporting Guidance for the DNA (Short Tandem Repeat) Profiling (2014) Forensic Science Regulator.

Practitioner's Guide to Intelligence-Led Mass DNA Screening [RESTRICTED] (2006) ACPO.

The Control and Avoidance of Contamination in Crime Scene Examination involving DNA Evidence Recovery (Draft) (2015) Forensic Science Regulator. London.

The NDNAD Strategy Board Policy for Access and Use of DNA Samples, Profiles and Associated Data (2014) NDNAD delivery unit (NDU).

The Police and Criminal Evidence Act 1984 (2013) Zander, M.

The Prosecution Team Manual of Guidance for the preparation, processing and submission of prosecution files (2011) ACPO/NPIA.

Appeal Court Rulings

British and Irish Legal Information Institute (BAILII) <http://www.bailii.org>.

R v Broughton [2010] EWCA Crim 549.

R v Kuba Dlugosz, R v Pickering and R v MDS [2013] EWCA Crim 2.

R v Sean Hoey [2007] [2007] NICC 49 Ref: WEI7021.

R v Reed, Reed and Garmson [2009] EWCA Crim 2698.

8

Blood Pattern Analysis

8.1 **Introduction**

The analysis of the patterns created by bloodstains during an assault, referred to as blood pattern analysis (BPA), can only reliably be undertaken by a suitably qualified and experienced scientist as outlined in the Forensic Science Regulator (FSR) 'Codes of Practice and Conduct' which details the training, professional development and role of a BPA analyst.

The shapes, size, location and distribution of bloodstains at a crime scene can provide investigators with information that can serve to corroborate or refute the accounts given and provide an interpretation and possibly a reconstruction of the events that occurred.

BPA is based on the physical properties of blood and how it reacts under certain circumstances which can enable the identification of attack sites, establish the locations of items or persons during the attack, aid a reconstruction of the sequence of events, determine the level of force used and, in some circumstances, indicate the type of weapon used.

Investigators should be mindful of the potential that BPA can offer the investigation both at crime scenes and when recovering the clothing of suspects or victims. It is worth bearing in mind that witnesses close to the attack may have bloodstaining on their clothing, and the location of such staining may provide supportive evidence regarding the sequence of events.

Bloodstaining should be accurately recorded by a crime scene investigator (CSI) or appropriate forensic specialist by photography or digital video recording. In the case of serious incidents it is beneficial for an appropriately trained and experienced scientist to attend the crime scene to undertake the BPA rather than having to rely solely on the photographic records of blood stains.

8.2 **Principles of Bloodstain Pattern Analysis**

The direction in which blood has travelled can be useful in establishing the location of the victim and attacker when the blood was shed. When a drop of blood hits a surface at a 90° angle it will generally leave a circular stain. As the angle of impact onto the surface changes, so does the shape of the resulting blood stain, which will become elongated in appearance. The viscosity of blood means that the elongated tail of the drop points in the direction of travel. This property enables a scientist to determine the location from where the blood originated.

Blood dries quickly when exposed to air and within a minute an outer crust will begin to develop around the edge of the stain. Attempts to wipe away the blood will typically leave the encrusted outer ring which remains as a skeletal outline and can be indicative of the time frames of actions.

There are broadly three categories of bloodstain, generally referred to as passive, projected and transfer bloodstains.

8.2.1 Passive bloodstains

Passive bloodstains are formed when a drop of blood falls onto a surface without any force other than gravity acting upon it. For example, blood dripping from the blade of a weapon that is not moving would fall from the end of the blade to leave circular stains as illustrated in Figure 8.1, where the blood hits the surface at a 90° angle.

Figure 8.1 Typical passive bloodstains

The surface onto which the blood drips can alter the appearance of the outer edges of the bloodspot, with hard non-porous surfaces producing a stain with smoother edges.

Textured or porous surfaces can produce a blood spot with scalloped distortion around the edges as illustrated in Figure 8.2. The level of distortion around the edges of a bloodstain is dependent on surface texture.

The diameter of a circular stain created by a free falling drop of blood will increase according to the distance it has fallen, up to a height of around 121–122cm. Above this height the diameter of the fallen bloodspot would remain fairly constant. The diameter of a passive dripping blood spot is typically 4mm or above.

Figure 8.2 Blood spot with scalloped edges

8.2.2 **Projected bloodstains**

Projected blood marks will occur where blood is moving under some force, which can be external or internal in origin. The force of such movement will cause blood to be expelled or projected onto a surface. An indication of the force used to project the blood can be determined by a scientist. Analysis of the size, shape and quantity of the projected stains can enable the amount of force required to create the stain to be established.

When a drop of blood hits a surface at an angle other than 90°, the resultant stain will be elongated. The more acute the angle of impact onto the surface, the longer the stain will become. The resultant 'tail' of the elongated bloodstain will indicate the direction of travel, as shown in Figure 8.3. This information can aid investigators in determining the location of the victim and/or suspect during an attack and serve to corroborate or refute allegations.

Figure 8.3 Direction of travel as indicated by the tail of bloodstain

A BPA scientist can determine the origins of bloodstains by the application of mathematical formulae. The calculations take into account the physical properties of blood which dictate that a drop of blood in flight will take on a spherical shape, resulting in an oval shaped staining on impact with a surface (see Figure 8.4). The width of the stain will be equal to the diameter of the drop before it hit the surface. The length of the resulting stain is dependent on the diameter of the original drop and the angle of impact onto the surface.

Figure 8.4 Angle of impact of projected blood drop and resulting stain

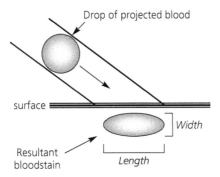

When the direction of travel and the angle of impact of bloodstains have been established, it is possible for the scientist to determine the location from which the stains originated.

This can assist an investigator in establishing where a victim or offender was positioned during an assault, for example, and establish whether the victim was lying down or standing up during the attack.

Projected bloodstain patterns can be separated broadly into three categories: arterial spurt, cast-off stains and impact patterns.

Arterial spurt

When an artery is breached, blood is forced from the body under the force of the pumping of the heart. Arterial spurts will typically display a wave-type, zig-zag pattern caused by the pressure changes of the heartbeat.

Cast-off stains

When an object strikes the skin with enough force to cause bleeding, the initial blow may split the skin; the immediate reaction of the body is for the capillaries to tighten in an attempt to prevent blood loss. There will be a delay between the splitting of the skin and the blood rising to the surface. The effect of clothing can also slow the blood reaching the surface that any weapon will contact, and explains why it is possible for the offender in a stabbing incident, for example, to have no apparent bloodstains on them.

On the second blow, blood will have begun to pool on the surface of the skin, which will then be transferred onto the weapon. This blood is then thrown, or cast from the weapon when it is in motion, as illustrated in Figure 8.5.

KEY POINT—'FIRST BASH—NO SPLASH'

The number of cast-off bloodstains does not always indicate the number of blows, there will generally be *at least* one more.

Cast-off marks will generally form drops of blood that are deposited in a linear manner, (Figure 8.6) illustrating three distinct lines of cast-off staining, which may indicate a minimum of four blows.

Figure 8.5 Blood patterns created from medium velocity impact

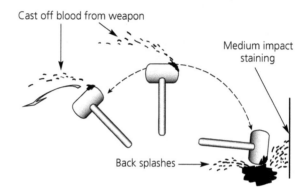

The first blow will not create a cast-off mark as there is no blood on the surface of the weapon. Blood will be picked up on the second and subsequent blows.

Figure 8.6 Typical linear pattern of cast-off stains

Impact patterns

These are caused when force is applied to wet blood causing blood to disperse in small droplets. The size, shape and dispersal patterns of the drops can indicate the level of force used. There are three general categories of impact indicated by blood patterns: low, medium and high velocity impact stains. The size of bloodspots can be indicative of the force of impact. Generally, the greater the impact velocity, the smaller the drops produced will be.

KEY POINT—IMPACT STAINS

- Low velocity stains are created by passive blood drops which are usually about 4mm in diameter.
- Medium impact velocity will result in stains 2–4mm in diameter and would typically be caused by blunt force trauma, cutting or stabbing, for example.
- High velocity impact stains are typically less than 2mm in diameter and are generated as a result of incidents such as gunshot trauma or high speed machinery injury. Such stains appear as a fine spray or mist.

Aspirated bloodstains occur where blood is projected by the action of coughing or gasping, for example, when blood is present in the mouth or airways. In such instances, blood is projected and dispersed in small droplets similar to that which occurs with high velocity impact wounding.

Aspirated blood can generally be distinguished from high velocity impact stains as it will often be diluted with saliva which leads to a weaker colouration. Small air bubbles present in aspirated blood may be visible as small rings within the stain where the bubbles have burst, although these may only be noticeable on smooth non-porous surfaces.

....

Case study—Interpretation of blood patterning

Billie-Jo Jenkins was a teenage girl who was battered to death by being beaten with a tent peg on the rear patio of her home. She was the foster daughter of Sion Jenkins who was sentenced to life for her murder in July 1998.

The blood of Billie-Jo was found on the jacket, trousers and shoes worn by Sion Jenkins on the day of the murder. The blood that was located on the clothing was not readily visible and was present as a fine spray of small drops. Similar blood patterning was located on the front of the leggings worn by Billie-Jo.

The size and distribution of the blood spots located on clothing was reported to be consistent with him being the attacker. Forensic scientists stated that the blood patterns on his clothes were what would be expected if a person was to inflict blows onto wet blood whilst standing over the victim.

....

The defence team submitted the argument that bloodstains resulted from the exhalation from the deceased caused when Mr Jenkins, on discovery of Billie-Jo, went to tend to her. They argued that a passive exhalation occurred when Billie-Jo was moved, depositing blood onto his clothing.

Scientists undertook experiments to replicate the effects of the aspiration of blood and analysed resultant patterns. It was found that exhaled (aspirated) blood can cause a pattern similar to that which would be created with a high velocity impact.

The bloodstain evidence and the research to establish whether the bloodstains could be as a result of impact or aspiration, played a key role in the trial. The jury had the task of deciding which of the complex arguments for either position was correct.

The conviction against Sion Jenkins was quashed in July 2004 and he was released on bail pending a retrial. Mr Jenkins was acquitted of the murder of Billie-Jo in February 2006 following two appeals and three trials.

This case highlights the issue that forensic evidence can, and will, be interpreted in different ways. The BPA evidence was one aspect of this investigation that contributed to the acquittal.

It is vital investigators retain an open mind and consider all the possible scenarios for the presence of forensic evidence. To have any value in a case such evidence must form part of a thorough investigation to put the forensic material into context.

In addition to basic patterns that can be observed, there are other characteristic marks that can assist in the reconstruction and interpretation of events. Trail patterns may be evident at crime scenes where blood has fallen in drips from an injury, object or where a bleeding body has been carried. The trail of blood drops can enable a scientist to establish the direction and speed of travel by assessing the elongation of the individual blood drops and the distance between them. As the velocity of the blood source increases, the elongation and distance between the spots will also increase.

Scenario 1—Observation of absence

The absence of bloodstaining in an area can indicate that something was shielding the area from the bloodstains, and that the object has subsequently been removed.

For example, consider a room, the scene of a fatal assault with medium impact staining on the wall and horizontal surfaces such as tables and chairs. It is observed that there is a small rectangular area on a coffee table that is clean, although the rest of the table surface is covered with medium impact blood patterning.

It is not known what was on the table, but it is clear that it would have blood upon it.

A suspect, a known associate of the deceased, is arrested. The suspect has in his possession a mobile phone of the same shape and size as the clear area (void) on the coffee table. Forensic examination established that the mobile phone, which appeared clean to the naked eye, contained minute traces of the victim's blood on the front outer cover of the phone.

The suspect put forward the argument that he found the victim after the attack, tried to rouse him and then tried to call for help and that is how the victim's blood came to be on the phone.

How does the application of BPA corroborate or refute this version of events?

The phone physically fits the area on the table that is clean of projected blood patterns and traces of the victim's blood were found on the outer cover and not on the keypad. This is supportive of the proposition that the mobile phone was on the coffee table, face down, during the commission of the attack.

8.3 **Transfer Bloodstains**

A transfer bloodstain is created when a surface containing wet blood comes into contact with another surface: for example, a footwear mark created by blood on the sole of the shoe being transferred onto the floor or other surface. It can be possible for a distinct and recognisable image of the item to be observed. Other transfer marks include wipe, drag or swipe marks which can also be used in the interpretation and reconstruction of events.

8.3.1 **Location and recovery techniques for blood at crime scenes**

Minute traces of blood may be present that are not readily observable. This may be due to attempts to clean an area following the commission of an act resulting in bloodshed. There are a number of techniques available to a CSI or forensic scientist for locating such marks.

The initial technique utilised should be the use of high intensity light sources to search for possible bloodstains. An examination with a fluorescent light source may locate possible bloodstaining; although blood will not fluoresce, it will absorb the light to show as darker than the background surface. Where a stain is located that is believed to be blood, a presumptive test should be undertaken. The presumptive test reacts with the haemoglobin constituent of blood, it will not conclusively identify a stain as blood, but it will indicate where a stain is *not* blood. Presumptive blood tests cannot distinguish between animal and human blood.

Any stain that indicates a positive result with a presumptive blood test should be recorded and recovered for examination and analysis by a scientist. Where BPA is required it is advisable for the scientist to visit the scene if appropriate, as it is difficult to undertake such analysis from photographs and/or video. Items bearing possible bloodstains should be submitted to the forensic service provider in their entirety where possible. The CSI can recover the stain by swabbing, scraping or cutting out the area containing the stain if appropriate, but generally speaking it is best to send the entire item for scientific analysis where feasible.

8.3.2 **Chemical enhancement techniques**

Bloodstaining may not be visible to the naked eye and the use of chemical reagents can enable non-visible blood to be located and developed to enable the recovery of further potential evidence.

Blood reagents

Luminol and Blue Star are both commonly used commercially available chemical reagents that react with the haemoglobin in blood to emit a faint light, referred to as chemiluminescence, which is recorded by photography.

These reagents are useful screening tools when searching large areas such as rooms, for traces of blood that are not visible or where it is believed an attempt to clean up any bloodstaining has been made.

The reagents are very sensitive, based on the peroxidase-like activity of haemoglobin in blood, and can detect minute traces of blood even following attempted cleaning of an area.

The main disadvantage with the Luminol technique is that it must be undertaken in darkness in order to observe and record the often faint and short lived chemiluminescence. It is possible to observe chemiluminescence produced by Blue Star in ambient (available) light and the luminescence generally lasts longer, making photography of the reaction easier.

False positives can occur with certain cleaning solutions, such as bleach, painted/varnished surfaces and some foodstuffs; however an experienced operative may be able to distinguish from the intensity and duration of the chemiluminescence whether such interference is occurring, but it is vital that a confirmatory test utilising another type of presumptive test for blood is undertaken where a positive reaction is encountered.

These blood reagent are best utilised on porous surfaces such as carpets and clothing as their aqueous nature means it will run off non-porous surfaces and can wash away any potential stains and any detail that may be present in the form of footwear patterns or fingerprints in blood.

They are useful as a screening tool to detect minute traces of non-visible blood; however to develop fine detail such as fingerprints in blood, or to search and record any such traces on non-porous surfaces different chemical development processes are required.

....

Case study—Blood reagent use outdoors

Whilst typically Luminol and Blue Star reagents are used to screen for and record any blood traces at serious indoor scenes, it has been used at outdoor scenes, for example to establish the direction an offender took away from the scene.

The scientist in this case used Luminol on the pavement and road surfaces at night time. A 'blackout tent' was used at each section of the examination to ensure that the environmental light was reduced and to better visualise any chemiluminescence. Street lighting was also turned off.

Traces of blood, not visible to the naked eye, were discovered on the pavement outside the premises where the offence took place and a trail was observed going across a dual-carriageway, over the central barrier of the carriageway and into a field.

....

The Luminol reaction on the central barrier meant that further examination with different reagents was undertaken which recovered a partial palm print that identified a male. This lead to a fairly swift apprehension of the offender and recovery of further evidence linking him to the offence, for which he was subsequently successfully prosecuted.

Enhancement techniques for marks in blood

The techniques used to develop bloodstain patterns, fingerprints and footwear marks in blood include protein stains such as Acid Black 1, Acid Yellow 7 and Acid Violet 17. Table 8.1 summarises the chemical reagents approved for use by the Home Office Centre for Applied Science and Technology (CAST). These applications can be undertaken within a laboratory and at crime scenes, by trained personnel.

A key consideration where the use of chemical development techniques may be required for the enhancement of marks in blood, is to establish the need for any DNA profiling to be undertaken on the bloodstains.

The most appropriate route should be discussed with the CSI or forensic scientist in context of the circumstances of the case and with a view to maximising all the potential evidence.

Table 8.1 Enhancement techniques for recovery of marks in blood

Chemical reagent	Uses
Acid Yellow 7	Can be used for very light stains on non-porous surfaces. Marks can only be visualised with a fluorescent light source in a darkened area to be effective.
Acid Black 1	Produces a visible impression on porous surfaces.
Acid Violet 17	Produces a visible impression on all types of surface.
DFO	Reacts with amino acids to develop marks in blood on most surfaces. Marks can only be visualised with a fluorescent light source in a darkened area.
Ninhydrin	Reacts with amino acids and will develop marks or fingerprints in blood on most surfaces.

The use of such reagents at crime scenes is undertaken by specifically trained technicians, equipped with the relevant personal protective equipment (PPE). The processes will present hazards to health and non-trained personnel must be kept out of a crime scene when such processes are being undertaken. Investigators should be aware that the application of chemical techniques may be destructive, causing damage to property subjected to any chemical process; therefore the consideration of using such techniques for serious incidents will be decided by the SIO and the forensic team.

8.4 Preserving Items for BPA

As BPA is a non-destructive technique, it should always be undertaken before any other examination. As the scientist will be assessing the size, location and distribution of bloodstains it is vital that the stains are not altered by inappropriate handling, such as the folding of wet bloodstained clothing, for example, which will cause the transfer of bloodstains to other areas of the item not originally stained.

Ideally, if BPA will be a requirement, it is advisable for a CSI to recover any item bearing bloodstains. BPA is not generally utilised for volume crime incidents, therefore it is likely that if it is required it will be a serious case, whereby a CSI will be in attendance to record and recover the items as appropriate.

Footwear marks will be present at *every* crime scene, although they may not be visible. Care must be taken when entering scenes where there has been significant bloodshed not to destroy potential footwear marks. CSI use stepping plates to traverse across the scene in order to preserve potential footwear marks and other evidence that may be present on the floor/ground.

A particular phenomenon referred to as the 'wick effect' occurs in carpeted rooms where investigators stand on an apparently clean area of the carpet/rug, close to a bloodstain. The 'wick effect' occurs where there is a visible bloodstain on a carpet; the blood seeps through to the underside of the carpet and disperses beneath it, unseen. When pressure is applied to an apparently clean area near to the bloodstain this can draw blood up from beneath the carpet to the surface to create an image of the item creating the pressure, such as the footwear marks of investigation personnel.

Such a footwear mark may only become visible following the application of a chemical reagent screening technique. If the blood has seeped onto the surface of the carpet due to the wick effect, there will then be traces of blood on the soles of the investigators' footwear, which can then be transferred to other areas.

The best way to avoid contamination and transfer of material at crime scenes is to stay out unless preservation of life considerations exist.

8.5 **Health and Safety Considerations**

When dealing with scenes containing bloodstaining, whether the scene is the location, weapon, victim or suspect, care must be taken with a view to minimising the risk from potential blood borne infections.

Checklist—Health and safety considerations when dealing with blood

- Always wear gloves when handling items or persons containing blood or other body fluids.

- Always wear disposable over boots at scenes where bloodstains are apparent on the ground/floor.

- Dried blood becomes airborne as fine dust particles when disturbed which can enter the body via mucus membranes. Wearing a disposable mask ensures that the dried blood particles are not inhaled. Avoid unnecessary movement of bloodstained items to prevent dislodging any dried blood.

- Any items exhibited must be clearly labelled on the outer packaging as '*biohazard*'

- Be aware that you may have walked through bloodstains that were not visible, such as occur with a 'wick effect', for example. It is advisable to decontaminate the soles of boots following attendance at scenes where bloodstaining is present in large amounts. This can prevent the transfer and contamination of possible blood to other scenes.

- It may be necessary for the footwear of all who attended the scene to be recorded in the event that comparison and elimination of marks at the scene is required. Some overboots have identifiers on the bottom, words such as 'police' or 'CSI' embossed on the soles to indicate marks of official personnel.

8.6 **Chapter Summary**

BPA can assist investigators to establish a sequence of events and the types of actions involved during an attack involving bloodshed. The information from such an examination can serve to corroborate or refute allegations or differing versions of events.

BPA can only be undertaken by a scientist, usually a biologist, who specialises in the analysis of bloodstains as it is a complex process with many variables. As seen with the Billie-Jo Jenkins case, the interpretation of the staining and how it was formed was a key point during the court procedures. There will inevitably be different interpretations that could apply in a case and investigators must keep an open mind as to the possibilities of differing interpretations being presented.

BPA relies on the knowledge of the physical properties of blood and how it reacts under different circumstances. The scientist will examine the bloodstaining, recording the size, shape, locations and quantity of bloodspots to establish the possible location from which the blood originated, the relative positions of persons involved, possibly the type of weapon and the level of force used where appropriate.

Bloodstaining may not be visible to the naked eye and the use of chemical processes can assist in the locating of minute traces of blood. Care must be taken to ensure that contamination and transfer of blood stains is avoided.

Health and safety precautions must be observed when dealing with blood-stained items or persons due to the risk of blood borne infections. Any items exhibited must be labelled 'biohazard' on the outer packaging.

KNOWLEDGE CHECK—BPA

1. Describe the three basic types of projected bloodstain.

   Impact stains occur when an item such as a weapon impacts into wet blood. Impact stains can establish whether the force used was of low, medium or high velocity.
   Cast-off stains are linear stains which occur as wet blood is flung from an object in motion.
   Arterial spurt stains form wave or zig-zag patterns when an artery is breeched. The pattern created is due to the pressure of blood rising and falling with the heartbeat.

2. What information can potentially be gained from the number of cast-off marks at a scene?

   It can be possible to establish the minimum number of blows that were struck due to the number of linear cast-off stains present. The principle of 'first bash,

---

no splash' may apply where the initial blow does not impact into wet blood, subsequent blows into wet blood will transfer blood onto the object which will then be flung or cast off as the object is moving.

3. How can the direction a blood stain has travelled be established?

A drip of blood falling onto a surface at a 90° angle will generate a circular stain. As the angle of impact decreases, the resulting stain becomes more oval and elongated in shape. The narrower tail end of such an elongated bloodstain will point in the direction of travel. The angle of impact can be determined mathematically using measurements of the width and length of the stain.

4. State the procedures that can be used to locate blood at a crime scene.

BPA should be undertaken (where appropriate to the case) where visible bloodstaining is present. It is a non-destructive technique that should be undertaken prior to any further processing by a qualified and experienced scientist.

The CSI should examine the area with a high intensity light source to search for blood. Blood does not fluoresce but will absorb the light to appear darker than the background. Once located any possible blood should be tested with a presumptive blood test kit. Screening techniques using reagents such as Luminol or Blue Star can be used to search for non-visible blood traces. Fingerprints and other marks in blood can be developed by using different processes.

The need for DNA analysis should be considered prior to the application of any chemical processes.

5. What does a positive result of a presumptive blood test indicate?

A positive presumptive blood test indicates that the stain may be blood, as the test targets the haemoglobin in blood. It cannot distinguish between animal or human blood.

A positive test will warrant the recovery of the stain for further confirmatory testing by a scientist, as no single test is 100% specific for blood. A negative result means the stain is not blood.

Recommended Reading

Bloodstain Pattern Analysis with an Introduction to Crime Scene Reconstruction, 3rd edn (2008) Bevel, T and Gardner, RM.

Codes of Practice and Conduct. *Appendix: Bloodstain Pattern Analysis* (2014).

Criminalistics, 11th edn (2014) Saferstein, R.

Fingermark Visualisation Manual (2014) Home Office Centre for Applied Science and Technology (CAST).

Forensic Science, 3rd edn (2011) Jackson, ARW and Jackson, J.
Principles of Bloodstain Pattern Analysis: Theory and Practice (2005) James, SH and Kish, PE.

Appeal Court Rulings

R v Sion David Charles Jenkins [2004] EWCA Crim 2047.

Death Investigation

9.1 **Introduction**

The investigation into deaths has two main strands—to establish the cause and manner of death, and to investigate the circumstances where the death was unexpected. This chapter aims to provide the investigator with underpinning knowledge regarding the forensic aspects of a death investigation.

When investigators are tasked to attend scenes involving deceased persons, the incident can take a number of forms. It can include fatal road traffic incidents (RTIs), suicides, murders and other unexpected deaths such as drug-related deaths, for example. Crime scene investigators (CSIs) will attend the scenes of all suspicious deaths as well as suicides, and non-suspicious accidental deaths to record the scene and collect evidence on behalf of the coroner. The criteria for CSI attendance at non-suspicious deaths is dependent on force policies and the circumstances surrounding the case.

The key issues at death scenes to be addressed are to identify the deceased and establish the cause and manner of the death. Where it is felt the circumstances surrounding the death are suspicious, access to the scene must be restricted immediately and scene preservation actions put in place.

The investigations of deaths that have occurred in a manner other than by natural causes necessitate two distinct inter-related priorities, as outlined by the Forensic Science Regulator:

> The consideration of suspicious death involves two separate but concurrent investigations. One, by the coroner, seeks to identify the deceased and establish the cause of death and surrounding circumstances. The other, by the police, is to determine whether a criminal offence has occurred and, if it has, to bring to justice those responsible.

Establishing the time of death (referred to variously as the post-mortem interval—PMI, time since death—TSD or time of death—ToD) can be of benefit to investigators to narrow down time frames for investigative trace, identify, eliminate (TIE) parameters.

9.1.1 **Health and safety**

The presence of body fluids presents biological hazards with the risk of infection. The minimum requirement is to wear disposable gloves and mask when required to handle a cadaver under non-suspicious circumstances (eg, suicide).

Where the deceased is known to have an infectious disease such as HIV or hepatitis B it is vital that this fact is relayed immediately to those who will subsequently be handling the body including the CSI, pathologist and undertakers, for example.

In addition to the physical hazards present when dealing with the deceased, there is the impact it may have on the mental health of investigators. Such scenes can be distressing and upsetting. Occupational health units and trauma counsellors are available in-force for those affected by any incident, as well as charitable organisations. It is recommended that investigators are familiar with the impact of such stresses and recognise the behavioural changes that may be indicative of stress and to seek support if adversely affected by any incident.

When dealing with sudden unexpected deaths, whatever the circumstances, investigators must be mindful that the deceased is a member of a family and should be treated with the same consideration and respect that they would expect to be given to their own family members. The discovery of a deceased person can be a distressing event for the person finding the body and such persons should be shown sensitivity, tact and compassion.

9.2 Role of Initial Responders

When dealing with incidents involving sudden unexpected deaths, investigators need to consider whether the death has occurred due to a criminal act, as a result of natural causes or suicide. There may be no apparent outward signs that a criminal act has occurred and investigators must remain open-minded. One example of such a scene involves deaths due to drug overdosing. Such scenes may be regarded initially as a tragic accidental death; however investigators must consider whether the drugs were administered to the deceased by a third party, for example.

....

Case study—Rachel Whitear

Rachel Whitear was a 21-year-old woman, found dead at her home in Exmouth, Devon in May 2000. An open verdict was recorded at the inquest. In May 2003 the Police Complaints Authority (now the Independent Police Complaints Commission (IPCC)) decided to reinvestigate the circumstances and cause of Rachel's death following a complaint from her family regarding the initial response of the police.

The review of the case involved the exhumation of Rachel's body in April 2004 for a post-mortem, as one had not been undertaken during the initial investigation and Rachel's body had been released for burial in May 2000, before results of toxicology analysis had been received. When the results became available, in June 2000, they showed that morphine was present but not in a sufficient quantity to be the cause of death.

The results obtained from the post-mortem, held in March 2004 provided sufficient evidence to indicate a cause of death. Finally, in September 2007 a fresh inquest recorded the verdict that death was as a result of opiate intoxication.

Unfortunately for her parents, however, the question of whether it was a self-injected overdose or the result of a third party involvement could not be answered.

....

The assumption by initial investigators that Rachel's death was as a result of a self-administered overdose meant that scene management techniques were not instigated. This assumption was founded in part, on the observation that there was no forced entry, no undue disturbance and the presence of drug related paraphernalia which lead the initial responders at the scene to feel the death was not suspicious. This lead to many missed opportunities to gather potential evidence. Had Rachel's death been treated as suspicious, until proved otherwise, it may have been possible to gain valuable information which could have enabled a more detailed picture of what happened to Rachel to cause her death.

It is advisable that all incidents that involve sudden, unexpected deaths be approached initially as if they were suspicious deaths, until it becomes absolutely clear that there are no suspicious circumstances surrounding the death. It is preferable to put scene preservation and management procedures in place unnecessarily, than to fail to preserve and manage a scene only to later discover that there may be suspicious circumstances that require investigation.

Where there is any doubt whatsoever that the death may be due to suspicious circumstances this must be communicated to the control room who will inform the appropriate personnel such as the CSI team. Where initial responders are not sure of the circumstances, the attendance of a CID detective or CSI can be requested to get a 'second opinion'.

The initial responders attending a scene must take responsibility for the deceased and ensure that the principles of continuity and integrity are established. The deceased should be tagged with a plastic identity bracelet, similar to those used in hospitals, which should be completed with details of the name of deceased (where known), time, date and location found as a minimum. The investigator who tagged the deceased should ideally be present during transportation to the mortuary. However, this may not be practical as in serious cases a deceased can remain *in situ* for a number of days, to ensure the most thorough of forensic examinations can be undertaken to secure potential evidence. The identity of the deceased needs to be confirmed to the pathologist by an investigator who can testify that it is the body that was at the scene. This is known as a police identification; the forensic methods that can be used to establish/confirm the personal identification of the deceased is covered later in the chapter.

Scene preservation techniques, as outlined in Chapter 2, must be instigated where such scenes give cause for concern regarding the cause and manner of death; however there are additional considerations to be made when dealing with such scenes. Some murder scenes are very difficult to identify initially, for example those committed by the now deceased Dr Harold Shipman, the serial killer jailed for committing multiple murders over a number of years by injecting his victims with lethal doses of diamorphine.

Checklist—Observations for initial responders

- Do not panic or rush—take calm and considered steps in order to assess the scene and gain an insight into what may have happened. If there is any doubt the death is as a result of anything other than natural causes, inform the control room and commence scene preservation actions.

- Make a visual examination, *without touching the deceased*, to check for any wounds on the exposed areas only, such as the head, face, neck and forearms, for example. Document any observations, including:

  - state of dress—clothed/unclothed/partially clothed;

  - obvious injuries and what type they appear to be;

  - presence of potential weapons in the proximity of the deceased;

  - presence of ligatures on the deceased or in the proximity;

  - general condition of the body (eg, is decomposition apparent).

Indoor scenes—make observations of the environment, including:

- entry/exit points;

- if lights were switched on or off;

- if doors/windows were locked/unlocked;

- any signs of a forced entry or disturbance;

- indications that an area has been cleaned/tidied;

- any appliances on/off or mid-cycle;

- alcohol/prescribed or illicit drugs present;

- presence/absence of suicide note;

- presence of mail/newspapers collected beneath letter box.

Outdoor scenes—initial observations of environment/location should include:

- entry/exit points;

- type of location—secluded, industrial, residential, for example, and the identification of any security issues such as being overlooked by offices/homes, for example, which may require the use of additional screening to protect the scene from public/media observation;

- weather conditions;

- if any attempts made to conceal the deceased—buried/covered with vegetation, for example;

171

- any weapons in the proximity;

- any tyre or other such marks nearby that could indicate use of vehicle;

- indications that a struggle may have occurred.

This list is not exhaustive but indicates the types of observations that are beneficial to the investigation.

Actions taken—or not taken—by initial responders at the scenes of suspicious deaths can be crucial in any subsequent investigation. Once the initial responder is satisfied the person is deceased, either by the condition of the deceased (eg, stages of decomposition) or where it has been verified by a doctor/paramedic, it is vital that they then concentrate on securing the scene to ensure the maximum evidence can be gathered.

Checklist—Actions of initial responders

Once it is established that the person(s) are deceased:
- *Do not* touch, move or disturb any clothing of the deceased unless *absolutely necessary.* This can be an area of contention between CSI and investigators. Forensically it is best not to touch the deceased; however investigative priorities may require the deceased's clothing to be searched, for example if an early identification may be obtained (eg, from a wallet that is in a jacket pocket). Consider the risks/benefits of such actions in the context of the particular case—early identification may lead to a swift arrest of an offender against a potential loss/contamination/transfer of evidence resulting in lost forensic opportunities. Where clothing is disturbed investigators must document their actions with their rationale for doing so and inform the CSI exactly what they touched/moved. It is advisable to wait for a CSI who can then ensure all the required steps are taken to record and recover the potential evidence.

- Gloves must always be worn when dealing with deceased persons.

- Dust masks should be worn where body fluids are present (dried blood, for example, can become airborne and inhaled by investigators). Matter that emits odours can form minute particles in the air that is inhaled—be mindful that where decomposition odours are present, inhalation of minute particles that may present biological hazards to health is a risk as many odours from chemicals, gas appliances, for example.

- At indoor scenes, do not open doors/windows (*except* to ventilate premises where carbon monoxide poisoning is suspected—see later in chapter). The temperature of the environment can be an important factor in establishing the time of/since death (PMI).

- Where emergency medical assistance has been provided for the deceased immediately prior to death, any medical consumables (bandages, monitoring pads, blankets) must remain at the scene/on the deceased and the details of any medical crew attending recorded.

- Create a sketch diagram to indicate the layout of the scene, relative position of the deceased and any potential evidence such as a possible weapon or footwear mark in possible blood, for example. Identify potential hazards observed (steep, slippery grassy bank, low hanging thorny branches or the presence of broken glass/used syringes, for example). This can be incredibly useful to brief the CSI before they enter the scene.

- At outdoor scenes, circumstances such as the weather, animal activity or public access/observation areas, for example, can pose real threats to the security of potential evidence and to the investigation (videos being posted online before the deceased can be identified and the next of kin informed, for example).

- Where potential evidence must be moved to protect it from damage or loss, its original location must be recorded either by photographing it before it is moved or recording it on sketch diagram.

- At outdoor scenes, use hard standing where available as much as possible for common approach paths as these are much easier to search.

9.2.1 Sudden death report form

The form required to report sudden deaths must be completed at the earliest opportunity. Where information is not available at the time, this should be recorded on the form. Investigators must not delay the submission of the form until further information becomes available.

9.2.2 Identification of the deceased

A body should ideally only be searched for identification purposes where it is clear there are no suspicious circumstances surrounding the death. Any property with the body must be exhibited by the initial responders and retained for possible forensic analysis or safe-keeping where it is deemed the death is non-suspicious. If during such a search it is realised that there may be cause for suspicion, the search of the body *must cease immediately* and actions taken to preserve the scene.

Where the identity of the deceased is unknown, a detailed description of the body including clothing worn, visible marks, tattoos, scars and any other distinguishing features must be relayed to the control room as soon as possible. These details must also be recorded on the sudden death report form.

There will be situations where a visual identification cannot be made due to the condition of the body or where relatives or those known by the deceased have not been located or may be involved in the death, for example. Where identification cannot be made visually other techniques to establish and confirm identity will be employed.

Checklist—Methods to identifying an unknown deceased

Fingerprints—Taken from the deceased and checked against Ident1 or against fingerprints recovered from personal effects at a deceased's accommodation (where known). Fingerprinting of the deceased will be undertaken by CSIs and typically take the form of inked/powdered lifts or by taking a 3D impression using a casting material similar to that used for recovering fine details of tool marks. Where decomposition 'slippage' or as a result of submersion has left the skin wrinkled, it may be possible to inject the pads of the fingertips with a solution to 'plump out' the area. The 'gloved' method, whereby the skin of the fingers is removed from the deceased, and placed over the gloved fingers of an investigator/CSI enables a rolled impression to be taken. (This can only be done with permission of the coroner and is only ever used as a last resort.)

DNA—The DNA profile of the deceased can be checked against the National DNA Database (NDNAD) and/or the missing persons/vulnerable persons databases or compared with profiles recovered from the deceased's personal items (eg, hairbrush, toothbrush) or with profiles given by close relatives.

Odontology—A Forensic dentist can compare the dentition of the deceased with appropriate dental records where available.

9.3 **Post-Mortem Changes**

The amount of time that has elapsed between a person's death and the discovery of the body can have a great impact on the investigation not least in establishing a time frame for the events that caused the death.

There is no singular scientific method available that can accurately establish the ToD or PMI due to the number of variables that can affect the outcome. In the absence of a witness to the death occurring, it can be difficult to pinpoint an exact time that death occurred.

Changes that take place in a body after death can be used to indicate an approximate time frame and the more observations the forensic pathologist can utilise, the better the determination of the PMI. The combination of observed conditions such as rigor mortis, body cooling, livor mortis and the stages of decomposition can lead to a narrower estimated time frame provided that the necessary records have been made on the initial attendance at the scene, in particular the recording of environmental factors such as the temperature.

The presence or otherwise of any insect activity can also provide valuable information in estimating the PMI.

9.3.1 Body cooling (algor mortis)

A body loses heat following death until it is at an equal temperature to the immediate environment. The rate of cooling can be a useful indicator in establishing the PMI. The environmental temperatures should be recorded where appropriate on at least two occasions by the CSI if the body temperature is to have any meaning. The temperature should be taken from an area close to the body, and the times of each reading recorded.

It is important that the temperature around the body is not altered significantly. At indoor scenes, ensure windows, doors and heating systems, for example, remain as they were on discovery of the body. If doors or windows are left open following discovery of the body this will alter any temperature readings taken, often to the point that they are no longer representative. Where heating systems are on a timer and the body has lain for a few days, it is worth recording the timer settings where possible.

The rate of cooling is subject to many variables including the immediate environmental conditions, body mass, body temperature at ToD and the amount of clothing worn. Generally a clothed body will lose heat at about 1.5°C per hour for the initial six to eight hours and will generally feel cold to the touch after twelve hours. The numerous variables concerning cooling rates make it an unreliable singular method of determining PMI.

9.3.2 Rigor mortis (rigidity)

Rigor mortis is the process whereby the muscle groups stiffen after death. This occurs due to biochemical changes within muscles and has an immobilising effect on the joints. Rigor mortis begins at the same time throughout the body, but is first observed in the head and jaw, it appears to traverse downwards towards lower extremities due to the differing sizes of the various muscle groups. The observation of the stiffening is first apparent in the smaller muscle groups such as in the jaw, neck and fingers. Once a body stiffens it will remain in that position until rigor passes or is 'broken' when a joint is forcibly moved. Rigor mortis is a temporary condition which will subsequently disappear leaving the body limp. Once rigor mortis has fully developed and then subsequently departed it will not recur.

As a general rule, the stages of rigor mortis are that it:

- begins within two to four hours after death;
- is completed within eight to twelve hours;
- begins to reduce between eighteen and thirty-six hours; and
- will have disappeared completely within forty-eight to sixty hours and will not return.

Because of the numerous variables that influence the onset and subsequent departure of this condition, these timings can only be rough guidelines. Factors that can affect the status of rigor mortis are the temperature of the environment and the internal body temperature immediately prior to death (heat can accelerate the onset and the subsequent dissipation of the condition). Persons with reduced muscular development, for example the elderly or young, may have little if any, apparent rigor mortis.

The numerous variables concerning the onset and dissipation rates of rigor mortis make it an unreliable singular method of determining PMI. A condition which can be mistaken for rigor mortis can occur immediately after death. This condition is referred to as a 'cadaveric spasm'.

Extremes of temperature can also affect rigor mortis development. In the case of heat, such as burning or immersion in hot liquid, a phenomenon referred to as the 'pugilistic attitude' develops, which is similar to the stance of a boxer. The proteins in the muscles begin to coagulate at temperatures over 50°c causing them to shorten, the arms and legs then frequently appear to be curled up as in a foetal position. Rigor mortis will not then develop in muscles that have been stiffened by heat, but heat stiffening may occur after rigor mortis has developed.

Extreme cold can also cause muscles to stiffen as the fat and muscles solidify. In temperatures below around 3.5°c, the body will stiffen due to the effect of the cold; true rigor mortis will then develop once a body has been thawed.

9.3.3 Cadaveric spasm

Under certain circumstances the stiffening of the hands or arms can take place immediately after death, this condition can be confused with rigor mortis. The condition is known as a cadaveric spasm and is often associated with violent death or where high emotion is involved. It is not uncommon for people who have held a weapon or such in their hands at the point of death to retain a tight grip on it immediately after death.

Where a suicide has been caused by shooting, for example, the person can retain a very tight grip on the weapon. The observation of such tight gripping of weapons can be a useful indicator to an investigator that the deceased had been holding the weapon immediately prior to death. It would be extremely difficult, if not impossible, to replicate such a tight grip by someone placing the firearm in the hands of the deceased after death in order to give the impression of suicide, for example. Care must be taken, however, not to confuse this with rigor mortis. Cadaveric spasm will remain until onset of putrefaction.

9.3.4 Lividity (livor mortis/hypostasis)

When the heart stops pumping, blood ceases to be circulated causing a gravitational pooling and settling of blood within the blood vessels in the lowermost areas of the body. This leads to a dark purplish discolouration observed at the lowermost unrestricted levels of the body.

For example, a body found lying on its back on the floor would not have any lividity discolouration on the parts of the body that have been in direct contact with the floor, therefore it would be expected that the buttocks, upper back and calves for instance would not be discoloured by lividity as illustrated in Figure 9.1. This is due to the pressure caused by the weight of the body on the small blood vessels which prevents them filling with blood.

Figure 9.1 Lividity development process

Blood settles into vessels in the lowermost point due to the effects of gravity

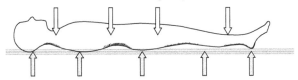

Areas in contact with a surface will restrict the blood vessels meaning that the blood cannot settle in these areas.

When the body is turned, the lividity would typically be present on the back in the shaded areas illustrated below.

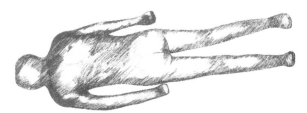

Note how the areas in contact with the surface the body was laid on, such as the shoulders, arms, buttocks, upper thighs, shins and heels are clear of, or display paler lividity.

Similar effects can occur where a person is wearing tight clothing which prevents blood pooling into the vessels in that particular area. Wrinkled bedding or items beneath the body such as coins, for example, may lead to paler areas within the lividity. The observation and recording of such markings can assist the investigator in establishing whether the body has been moved in the time between death and the body being discovered. In cases of extensive blood loss, lividity may be very weak due to the lack of blood in the circulatory system.

The observation and interpretation of the status of the lividity markings should be undertaken and recorded by the pathologist if it is to be used evidentially.

Observation of the positions of discolouration can, in some circumstances, be indicative of whether a body has been moved since death. The settling of the blood to the lowest parts will begin as soon as the heart stops pumping and may be visible within thirty to sixty minutes after death. As blood continues to settle, the intensity of the discolouration increases becoming darker in appearance.

The settled blood will begin to clot and becomes 'fixed' in place. If an area of discolouration is pressed prior to it becoming 'fixed' it will lighten in colour; on removal of the pressure the discolouration will return. This is referred to as 'blanching'. When lividity is fully fixed and the blood has clotted, such blanching will no longer occur on the application of pressure.

The discolouration caused by lividity typically becomes fixed within six to twelve hours of death occurring, although this is subject to variables so can only be a general guide. Once fixed, the lividity will remain until discolouration from decomposition obscures it.

A body may be moved a number of times after death, prior to the discolouration becoming 'fixed' and the blood will resettle to the lowest points in that new position. Once fixed, however, the blood will remain in the original position, and not resettle to another position if the body is subsequently moved. Where lividity is not fully fixed when the body is moved, some blood may resettle to the lowermost areas of the subsequent position and some will remain in the original position, the intensity of the discolouration in this situation will depend on the extent to which the lividity was fixed before the body was repositioned.

Lividity colouration can differ as a result of poisoning, disease or environmental factors. In cases involving carbon monoxide or cyanide poisoning, hypothermia, refrigeration and aerosol inhalation, for example, a bright red or pink colouration can be observed. A browner colouration may be observed where poisoning with oxidants of haemoglobin, such as potassium chlorate and nitrates are involved.

Occasionally, lividity may appear as an unusual pattern or look like bruising from trauma. The forensic pathologist will be able to clarify whether such marks are caused by lividity or bruising by examining the area beneath any discolouration; blood from lividity will seep out from the incised area whereas blood from a bruise will appear as discolouration of tissue. Advanced decomposition can make it increasingly difficult to make this distinction between bruising and lividity.

Case study—Lividity as an indicator for neglect of duty

A 20-year-old male living in a care home was found dead in his bed at 10.00am.

It was reported by staff at the house that the male had been out the previous night and had returned shortly before 11.00pm extremely intoxicated with alcohol. Due to the level of intoxication, it was decided that the male should be checked at regular intervals during the night.

The CSI attended the scene with the investigators. The male was lying flat on his back, and on turning the body, the CSI noted that lividity was well established on the person's back and underside of his arms and legs. The areas of lividity were pressed and did not display any blanching, indicating that it was fixed.

The observation of the lividity indicated that the male had been deceased for some time as lividity was fixed, and that the body had not been moved during that time. This observation was confirmed by the findings of the pathologist during the post-mortem examination.

Due to these observations, it was found that the male had not been regularly roused during the night, as stated by the staff.

The observations made in this case were pertinent in refuting the version of events given by the occupants of the premises.

Care must be exercised, however, as such observations are subject to many variables. It is always worth recording any such observations, but only a qualified pathologist can reliably interpret such markings in conjunction with other factors which come to light during the post-mortem examination.

The numerous variables concerning the development of lividity make it an unreliable singular method of determining PMI.

9.3.5 **Eyes**

The examination of the eyes of the deceased can be a useful indicator in establishing the PMI. The following general observations can assist in establishing the time elapsed since death:

- The cornea becomes slightly milky/cloudy within eight to ten hours after death; however this process is dependent on variables such as whether the eyes are open or closed and the environmental conditions.
- Levels of potassium contained within the vitreous humour (the clear viscous substance behind the lens of the eye) will typically rise after death. A forensic pathologist may take samples in order for the measurement and interpretation of potassium levels to be made.

The numerous variables concerning any changes in the eye make it an unreliable singular method of determining PMI.

9.3.6 **Decomposition**

Decomposition, or putrefaction, begins more or less immediately following death, although the observable appearance of such may not be apparent for a number of hours or possibly days, depending on the particular circumstances.

The activity of bacteria and micro-organisms results in the production of gases and enzymes within the body, leading to the breakdown of tissue.

The decomposition process advances through several observable stages. For bodies on dry land this will typically manifest as a greenish colouration on the skin of the abdomen, due to the breakdown of the haemoglobin contained in the red blood cells. Gases produced as a by-product of decomposition activity can lead to a visible swelling that is particularly noticeable around the face, abdomen and genitals. A green, purple or red 'marbling' patterning of the skin, (subcutaneous marbling) will follow due to the effect of decomposition on the veins close to the surface of the skin. Blisters filled with gases or fluid will begin to appear on the skin, which can later burst leaving large areas of skin detached from the body. The tongue will swell and as the internal organs begin to liquefy, fluid can leak from orifices.

Generally, the timing of the different stages of decomposition for a body on dry land is:

- a greenish discolouration of the abdomen and genitalia occurring between thirty-six to forty-eight hours after death;
- blue, red or purplish subcutaneous marbling of veins may be apparent within seventy-two to ninety-six hours after death;
- once body fluids have dried, a yellow parchment-like membrane forms on the skin;
- the swelling of the body due in part to the build-up of decomposition gases will usually occur within five to six days;
- by three to four weeks following death, facial tissue degenerates making visual identification difficult. Skin slippage and detachment may occur.

Environmental temperature is a major factor in the onset of putrefaction; heat will accelerate the process and cold will retard it. The numerous variables that can affect decomposition rates make it an unreliable singular method for establishing the PMI.

9.3.7 Insect activity and entomology

Entomology is the study of insects and in a forensic context it can be of value as certain insects will colonise dead and decomposing bodies in a fairly predictable manner under certain circumstances.

Entomology can offer the investigator some useful insights regarding the PMI and whether there is the possibility that the body has been moved from the site of death to a deposition site. The observation of insect activity may also provide information on the sites of wounds that may be obscured due to decomposition. The bluebottle (blowfly) is the most commonly encountered insect found colonising on decomposing bodies above ground.

Flies settle on a body within minutes after death to lay eggs in orifices such as the mouth, nostrils, eyes and in sites of open wounds. The blowfly will colonise a decomposing body more readily than other insects and in larger numbers, to be joined later by other insects such as houseflies.

By establishing the age of an insect sample, an entomologist can calculate a time scale that can assist in establishing the TSD. An entomologist will have an in-depth knowledge of the life and development cycles of particular insect groups and the variables that may affect the development stages.

Blowflies have a four-stage life cycle involving the egg, larval (maggot), pupal and adult stages. The larval stage consists of a further three sub-stages, referred to as instars. Between each of the instar stages the larvae will shed its skin, allowing growth in the next stage. During the larval stage the maggot will feed on the dead tissue. The timing of the lifecycle from egg to adult fly can vary greatly with the most significant influence being that of environmental temperature. Generally the development from egg to adult fly can vary between seven to eighteen days, dependent on circumstances including temperature, season and type of insect. Blowfly larvae are the most commonly utilised insect stage examined in the investigation of crime scenes. However, other developmental stages and other insect species should not be overlooked. Adult flies are perhaps the least useful as they can have come from anywhere and not necessarily have originated from the body in question.

In some cases, an entomologist may identify species that are not consistent with the body recovery site indicating the possibility that the body may have been moved from the original site. Larvae and insects can remain at the original site, and if located can contain DNA from the body to establish a link.

Some larvae will migrate away from the body. Migrating larvae may be left over from the first wave of flies which have matured and flown off and these can assist in establishing a more accurate PMI. Investigators attending a scene where maggots are present should be mindful of where they walk and take actions to preserve the scene.

The collection of insect samples should only be undertaken by an entomologist or a CSI.

9.3.8 Saponification

Saponification is a process observed on bodies that have been subject to moist environments or submerged in water. The resultant adipocere appears as a soap/wax like substance also referred to as 'grave wax', which develops due to the anaerobic bacterial hydrolysis of body fat. It can develop over a period of a few weeks to several months, depending on the environmental conditions. Once developed, adipocere can preserve the body and internal organs in a relatively well preserved condition for many months.

The development of adipocere is not a good singular indicator of PMI as variables such as temperature, amount of body fat initially present and moisture levels can impact on the saponification process.

9.3.9 **Mummification (desiccation)**

This is a condition of arrested decomposition caused by the absence of environmental moisture. For mummification to occur a warm atmosphere with a constant circulation of dry air is required and in optimum conditions mummification can occur in a matter of weeks. This process leads to body tissues becoming hard and dry as they dehydrate.

KEY POINT—ESTIMATING TIME OF DEATH

The estimation of the time of/since death can *only* be undertaken by a qualified forensic pathologist due to the complex and numerous variables that can affect decomposition rates.

Investigators and CSI are not qualified to do this.

9.4 **Cause of Death Indicators**

Certain causes of death can lead to the display of particular conditions that can assist in establishing or confirming how a person died. Such circumstances include the following.

9.4.1 **Asphyxiation**

Asphyxiation can occur through a number of mechanisms, with the most common causes of death by asphyxiation being:

- compression of the neck—strangulation and hanging;
- inhalation of poisonous gases; and
- suffocation.

There are particular indicators as to the cause of asphyxiation which may be observed in the situations outlined below.

Strangulation

This is caused by the extended compression of the neck by hands or a ligature. There are different categories of strangulation which can display certain indicators. Manual strangulation as a result of pressure on the neck causes death by the blocking of blood vessels and/or airway. The indicators of manual strangulation are generally as follows.

- The presence of external abrasions/bruising of the neck (4–5 lb of pressure is needed to block the veins on the side of the neck to cause asphyxiation).
- Internal damage to neck structures often involving fractures of larynx and hyoid bone.

- Petechiae are small pin-prick haemorrhages which appear as small spots. They are almost always present in the mucous membranes of the inner eyelids, on the eyeballs and/or on the face, particularly the forehead.
- Haemorrhage or trauma to the tongue is common.

Ligature strangulation/hanging

A body that has been subject to ligature strangulation presents with similar indicators as those observed in manual strangulation, with the following exceptions.

- Petechiael haemorrhages are not usually present in hanging where death has been rapid. Where petechiae are observed they should be above the ligature.
- Soft tissue damage within the neck is variable but generally will be less prominent than in manual strangulation.
- Fractures of the larynx occasionally occur; however fractures of the hyoid bone are unusual.
- Ligature strangulation will generally cause marks of a more horizontal appearance than in hangings, due to lack of extended suspension. The ligature marks in hangings tend to be an inverted 'V' shape.
- Hanging victims often have a swollen, protruding tongue which is red/red-black or black in colouration. The protrusion is due to the ligature pressure on the larynx which forces the tongue outward. The discolouration is due to environmental drying.

When dealing with deaths due to ligature strangulation or hangings, it is important that the ligature remains on the body. The only time a ligature must be removed is where there is the slightest chance the person may still be alive. Where possible, ligatures should be removed in a manner that will preserve any knots.

When initial responders attend the scene of a death by hanging, they should first establish that the body is deceased, initiating any life saving techniques as appropriate unless it is absolutely clear death has occurred. Where it is apparent that the person is deceased, the body must remain *in situ* for the CSI examination and steps taken to secure the scene to preserve potential evidence.

There may, however, be the need to cut down a suspended body prior to the CSI attending. Such circumstances would include to undertake life saving techniques if appropriate, where the body cannot be satisfactorily shielded from public view or where there is a danger of collapse of the area the person is suspended from. The ligature should be cut at a point away from the knot and the CSI must be informed of any cuts made and such information recorded in contemporaneous notes. The ligature/noose must remain on the body. This also applies to any bindings on the hands or feet. However, if murder is suspected the circumstances may necessitate a senior investigating officer (SIO)/crime scene co-ordinator (CSC)/forensic pathologist to decide to remove ligatures, prior to moving the deceased to the mortuary, to prevent fluid leakage from the body disrupting other forensic evidence such as DNA, for example, that may be on the ligatures. Removal of any ligatures in such circumstances must only be undertaken by a CSI or forensic pathologist.

The potential evidence that can be gained from ligatures include intelligence information that can be gained from the type and characteristics of the ligature, the type of knots, DNA from skin cells that may adhere to the ligature during the tying or fixing process, the type of ligature used which could be compared with similar material found at the victim's or suspect's home, for example (depending on the case circumstances), fibres and other particulate material can potentially be present on the ligature.

Inhalation of poisonous gases (chemical asphyxia)

This occurs in an atmosphere where the oxygen has been displaced or depleted by a chemical agent or poisonous gas, usually in enclosed, poorly ventilated spaces. It is not uncommon to find multiple victims and there may be no immediate physical signs to indicate the cause of death.

The most commonly encountered deaths by chemical asphyxiation are those involving carbon monoxide (CO), which inhibits absorption and transport of oxygen by the blood.

The most common causes of death due to carbon monoxide toxicity are:

- smoke inhalation during a structural fire;
- inhalation of vehicle exhaust fumes; and
- malfunctioning of gas heating appliances.

Observations in cases of suspected carbon monoxide poisoning include the following.

- A distinct cherry red/pink colouration to any lividity, which is usually visible when a 30% concentration of carbon monoxide is reached in the haemoglobin of the blood. Such colouration can also be indicative of cyanide poisoning, which may be accompanied by an odour often described as being similar to bitter almonds.
- Where bodies are covered in soot, or have a dark complexion, the colouration may be most visible in fingernail beds or the lining of the mouth.
- There may be areas on the body where the surface skin has separated from the deeper layers after death. The underlying tissue may be red or grey/tan in colour. Such areas of skin (epidermal) slippage can be misinterpreted as ante-mortem thermal burns/blistering. Such slippage is not specific for such poisoning.
- Carbon monoxide absorption ceases on death, therefore allowing for accurate post-mortem testing of the levels present.

Carbon monoxide is an odourless and colourless gas, which can be produced by faulty gas boilers/heating systems, solid fuel fires and vehicle exhaust fumes. Where initial responders suspect carbon monoxide as being present at scenes of sudden death, the area must be *vacated immediately*, leaving doors/windows open to ventilate the area. The control room must be informed of the possible presence of carbon monoxide. The area must not be re-entered until it has been declared safe by the health and safety officer or appropriate specialist.

Inhalation of carbon monoxide will manifest as headaches, nausea, abdominal pain, dizziness, sore throat and dry cough, similar to symptoms of flu but without a rise in temperature. Extended inhalation of carbon monoxide can cause the development of symptoms including a fast and irregular heart rate, hyperventilation, confusion, and drowsiness and breathing difficulties. Seizures and loss of consciousness may also occur. The symptoms can occur days or months after exposure and in delayed cases can manifest as co-ordination problems, confusion and memory loss.

Suffocation

Suffocation is caused by the obstruction of the nose and mouth, resulting in the termination of the air supply. Observations that may indicate suffocation include the recovery of material from the item used to cover the nose and mouth from inside or around the nose or mouth and in the throat. The extent of injuries is variable and there may not be any visible trauma present. Where a violent struggle has occurred during the act of suffocation there may be petechiae present. However, this is not an exact indicator of any force used as the absence of petechiae does not necessarily mean there was no force used.

9.5 **Drowning**

Death by drowning is caused by suffocation due to the immersion in a liquid. It is not necessary for total submersion, providing that the nose and mouth are submerged in any type of liquid, for drowning to occur. The cause of death is not necessarily due to the physical obstruction of the airway by the intake of water (classical wet drowning). In some cases death can be instantaneous, for example, caused by a cardiac arrest after entering water, particularly if the water is very cold.

In general the observations that can be made of bodies that have been submerged in water include:

- a wrinkling of the skin on the hands and feet (where exposed) which will generally occur within 30 minutes;
- after several days the hands will begin to swell;
- the outer layer of skin will begin to separate from the body within five to six days, the skin and nails on hands and feet (where exposed) will be separated from the body within eight to ten days;

- possible vegetation growth on the body can occur within eight to ten days depending on the environment;
- in warm water, an unencumbered body will begin to float to the surface within eight to ten days, in cold water this can take two to three weeks. In very cold water, a body may not surface due to retardation of the development of decomposition gases;
- the greenish decomposition colouration is absent;
- lividity is typically most prominent on the face, chest and upper portions of the extremities, reflecting the position an unencumbered body will typically adopt when submerged (bent at the waist with head and limbs dangling downwards).

A key question in cases of apparent drowning is whether the deceased was alive or dead prior to immersion. There are a number of observations that can be useful in establishing a possible sequence of events, which include the following:

- Petechiae are not usually present in drowning cases; however in cases of 'forced' drowning where a person has been held under water, petechiae may be observed, and is particularly noticeable in the lungs.
- The presence of froth in the nose and mouth is usually observed, this can be extruded by gentle pressure on the chest. The froth is formed from the active mixing of air and water. It can be a strong indication that the person was alive on submersion, but the absence of foam does not necessarily indicate death occurred prior to submersion. (Note too that the presence of froth is not specific for drowning and can occur in other circumstances.)
- The diagnostic value of silt, mud and water in the airways, lungs or stomach is of limited value in assessing whether a person was dead on submersion as such substances can passively enter a body after death.

Diatom analysis can possibly indicate whether a person was alive or dead on submersion and may be able to indicate the location that the body entered the water.

Secondary drowning is a phenomenon whereby inhaled fluid or gas, such as helium, irritates the lining of the lungs. A fluid buildup in the lungs can lead to pulmonary edema developing over the following hours, effectively causing a person to 'drown' in their own body fluids. Poisonous vapours or gases or the inhalation of vomit can have a similar effect. Fatality can occur up to seventy-two hours after a 'near drowning incident' although it is a rare occurrence.

A phenomenon referred to as 'dry drowning' can occur when the body reacts on immersion to water, such as when in a struggle, for example. Two instinctive defence mechanisms can occur which involve the swallowing of water, combined with a simultaneous reflex spasm of the larynx preventing entry of water into lungs. This instinctive reaction can lead to unconsciousness and paralysis of the respiratory organs. The post-mortem examination can typically find that the lungs will be relatively free of water.

Dry or secondary drownings are rare occurrences and each can result in death some hours after the exposure to the fluid/gas.

9.5.1 **Diatoms**

There are over 10,000 species of diatoms, microscopic aquatic organisms with exoskeletons of silica which can remain for a considerable amount of time after their death. They are ubiquitous in the environment and can be found in certain soils. Diatomaceous earth is used in some abrasive metal polishes and in the ballast of older safes. Diatoms can be found in areas of open water such as ponds, rivers, lakes, oceans and ditches and in mud, silt and similar damp conditions.

As a result of drowning, a person will take in some water into their lungs, which can enable any diatoms to enter the bloodstream to be transported into the major organs and bone marrow. Where a post-mortem examination recovers the same species of diatom in a deceased's bone marrow, for example, that are found in the water from where the body was recovered this can possibly provide some supportive evidence that the person was alive when initially submerged. The presence of diatoms in the organs such as the brain, for example, may also provide supportive evidence; however it may be possible for diatoms to passively enter the organs where a body is submerged for a length of time. Diatoms in bone marrow can provide stronger evidence that the person was alive when entering the water.

The analysis to establish the presence or absence of diatoms, on its own cannot provide conclusive evidence of whether a person was alive or dead when they entered the water.

The analysis of diatoms can, in certain circumstances potentially distinguish between two separate bodies of water (eg, a garden pond and lake nearby) but may be less helpful in differentiating between two sites, separated by a mile, for example, along a river or canal.

In cases involving submersion, it is worth considering that diatoms:

- may be present on the clothing, vehicle interior or home of an offender, for example, and can remain until the area/item is washed;
- are not normally present in tap water or fresh rainwater, but may be present in water butts or similar;
- are particularly prevalent during spring and autumn.

Preservation of items for diatom analysis

Because of the potentially ubiquitous nature of diatoms in the environment, care needs to be exercised to avoid contamination between samples. In cases of death by drowning, the CSI should recover any such samples from the scene and the pathologist will recover the appropriate post-mortem samples. There may be occasions, however, where investigators are required to recover items from suspects, such as clothing, for potential diatom analysis and comparison.

Diatom samples from suspects

Where a person has been in contact with water containing diatoms, such as by running through a brook or in the commission of a 'forced' drowning, the clothing and other surfaces touched by the offender, for example the interior of a vehicle, may also contain diatoms. Diatoms recovered from these items can be compared with diatoms contained in the control samples from the scene/victim. Diatoms will remain on clothing and surfaces until they are washed.

The following considerations must be made when recovering items for diatom analysis.

- Recovered clothing or textiles ideally should by air dried in a darkened environment. Exhibits should be protected from light as this encourages algae growth which can denature the sample. It is possible, although not ideal, to recover diatoms from damp or mouldy garments.
- Exhibits need to be stored in a fridge, and should not be frozen.

9.6 **Chapter Summary**

The changes that occur in a body after death can be useful to investigators, as the process will generally follow an expected sequence according to the particular circumstances of the case. There is no one singular forensic method for establishing the time that has elapsed between the death and the discovery of the deceased, referred to as the post-mortem interval (PMI), due to the number of variables that can impact on the decomposition process. Only a forensic pathologist can give a possible time and cause of death. This chapter outlines some of the processes to enable initial responders to gain a basic understanding of the processes that can be utilised.

Consideration should be given to the potential presence of forensic material at any scene of a sudden death. The deceased can contain potential forensic material such as fibres, glass, or DNA material upon them and it is vital that this potential evidence is not lost due to unnecessary handling of the deceased or any associated property. The location at which the body is discovered and any associated property may contain fingerprints, footwear marks, body fluids, fibres and other such material.

The preservation of life will *always* take precedence over forensic considerations. However, when it is clear the person is deceased, investigators must ensure that scene preservation actions are instigated where appropriate. The two main considerations initially will be to preserve life then preserve the scene, in that order. Any actions taken within the scene should be documented and the CSI informed. Where there is the risk of infection when dealing with the deceased and associated property, all personnel involved in such processes must wear disposable gloves and a disposable mask. Where it is known that the deceased is infected with HIV or hepatitis B, this fact must be made known to all those who will be in contact with the deceased or any property containing body fluids.

The sudden death report form should be completed as concisely and accurately as possible and submitted to the coroners' officer as soon as possible. The submission of the report form must not be delayed pending information becoming available, but the reasons for any missing information should be stated on the form. Where the identity of the deceased is unknown the form should contain the same details as the body tag, for example: 'unknown female, exit ramp level 3, supermarket car park/date and time'. It can be useful for continuity purposes to include the log or incident number on the form and body tag.

It is preferable to treat any incident involving sudden death as a suspicious death until there is evidence provided to the contrary.

KNOWLEDGE CHECK—SUDDEN DEATH

1. How can establishing a PMI assist an investigation?

   The PMI is the time that has elapsed between a death occurring and the body being discovered. It can be useful in an investigation in order to determine timelines of event, set TIE parametres and possibly to corroborate or refute accounts.

2. State what information a forensic pathologist can use to determine the PMI.

   There is no singular scientific technique that can establish TSD; however a combination of factors can be used to ascertain an approximate time frame. These include observation of conditions such as rigor mortis, body cooling, lividity, condition of the eyes and the stages of decomposition.

3. What considerations should be made regarding a death by hanging?

   Ideally the body should remain *in situ* for the CSI to photograph. A suspended body should only be removed where there is the possibility the person is still alive, where there is a risk of collapse of the structure they are suspended from, or where the body cannot be adequately screened from public view.
   Ligatures must be cut at a point away from the knot, and the CSI informed of any cuts made. The ligature must remain on the body, as must any bindings on hands and feet in most circumstances.

4. State the methods for establishing/confirming the identity of a deceased person where a personal identification cannot be undertaken.

   A personal identification, made visually by relatives or those who knew the deceased may not be appropriate due to advanced decomposition or mutilation. In such cases identification may be made by way of fingerprints, DNA, marks such as scars or tattoos, facial reconstruction, dental records, medical records, checking against missing persons records and descriptions of the deceased's clothing and possessions where applicable.

5. What are the initial duties of initial responders attending the scene of a sudden death?

Preservation of life and preservation of the scene. Preservation of life takes precedence over forensic considerations, but once this duty is fulfilled, action to preserve and manage the scene is paramount.

Any actions taken must be recorded and the CSI and OIC informed of what was done.

Recommended Reading

'Code of Practice and Performance Standards for Forensic Pathology' (2014) Home Office, Royal College of Pathologists, Forensic Science Regulator and Department of Justice.

Criminalistics, 11th edn (2014) Saferstein, R.

Evidence & Procedure (2014) Johnston, D and Hutton, G.

Forensic Science (2011) Jackson, ARW and Jackson, J.

Legal Issues in Forensic Pathology and Tissue Retention (2014) Forensic Science Regulator.

Pathology for Death Investigators (2001) Dix, J.

Time of Death, Decomposition and identification—An Atlas (1999) Dix, J and Graham, M.

The Use of Time of Death Estimates Based on Heat Loss From the Body (2014) Forensic Science Regulator, Royal College of Pathologists.

10

Firearms and Ballistic Evidence

10.1 **Introduction**

Firearm usage in the commission of criminal offences is on the decrease as reported by the National Ballistic Intelligence Service (NABIS); however initial responders can be confronted with a variety of firearms and associated ballistic material such as cartridge casings and bullets, or the requirement to establish if a person has handled or discharged firearms. The health and safety of all personnel who deal with firearm incidents is of paramount importance. Firearms should be considered as loaded until an authorised firearms officer (AFO) or equivalent has assessed the firearm and declared it as safe. Once a firearm has been made safe, any handling must be minimised to preserve the potential evidential material that may be present. Fingerprints, DNA from skin cells or body fluids, fibres and other trace material may be present on firearms and ballistic materials that can lead to identification of persons and/or links to other offences.

When dealing with firearm related incidents, the firearm and any related material such as cartridge cases, bullets, clothing and wound types can potentially provide an investigator with forensic evidence. Typically the questions to be addressed in any incident involving firearms include:

- identifying the type of weapon used;
- establishing the distance between the victim and the weapon;
- determining the direction of impact;
- identifying the type of ammunition used;
- establishing the sequence of shots, where multiple wounds exist;
- whether the discharge was accidental or intentional; and
- identification of any links between other incidents/scenes.

Air weapons use a burst of high pressure air to force a projectile out of the barrel. The air pressure can be created by a mechanical system of a piston being pushed down a cylinder under the force of a compressed spring, between each shot the spring must be recompressed manually.

Pneumatic air weapons use a small tank of pressurised air which can be refilled by means of a hand pump or from a canister of pressurised air. Gas powered weapons utilise compressed or liquefied gas such as carbon dioxide in a replaceable sealed tank which is used to eject the projectile when the trigger is pulled.

Whilst air weapons do qualify as firearms, their use will rarely lead to fatalities, and for this reason, the firearms discussed in this chapter exclude air weapons.

The discipline of firearms and ballistics examination is a vast subject area and this chapter offers a brief overview of the most common types of weapon used, the basic composition of ammunition, ballistic examinations and how to preserve and recover the potential forensic evidence.

NABIS was developed in order to gather and collate information on the criminal use of firearms and also provides a ballistics examination service.

Police personnel dealing with firearm incidents should be aware of NABIS and ensure that they are familiar with force policies regarding its use. It is common for each force to have a NABIS trained officer who would be conversant with each distinct aspect of the services offered.

10.2 **Firearm Definition**

The Firearms Act 1968 defines various offences relating to firearms, including air weapons, shotguns and related ammunition. Section 1 of the Firearms Act 1968 defines a firearm as being:

A lethal barrelled weapon of any description from which any shot, bullet or other missile can be discharged and includes;

Any prohibited weapon, whether it is such a lethal weapon as aforesaid or not; and

Any component part of such a lethal or prohibited weapon; and

Any accessory to such a weapon designed or adapted to diminish the noise or flash caused by firing the weapon

Prohibited weapons are defined by the Firearms Act 1968, s 5 and include CS spray, Tasers, grenades and air weapons with a gas cartridge system. The forensic recovery of Tasers and related material is briefly covered at the end of the chapter due to their increasing use by police firearm officers as a less lethal option for conflict management during appropriate incidents. The criminal use of such weapons is also being encountered.

Imitation firearms can cause a high level of operational risk to initial responders as it is very difficult to distinguish between an imitation and a real firearm where an incident is in progress.

10.2.1 **Imitation weapons**

Imitation firearms

These are defined by s 57(4) Firearms Act, 1968 as:

anything which has the appearance of being a firearm (other than such a weapon as is mentioned in section 5(1) (b) of this Act), whether or not it is capable of discharging any shot, bullet or other missile.

Evidence of the firearms officer will usually be sufficient expert evidence in such cases. It is not always necessary to get independent forensic scientific evidence on whether or not the item is in fact an imitation weapon.

Realistic imitation firearms

The definition of a realistic imitation firearm is defined by s 38 as:

an imitation firearm which has an appearance that is so realistic as to make it indistinguishable, for all practical purposes, from a real firearm

An imitation firearm will be regarded as a firearm according to s 1 Firearms Act 1968 where:

- it has the appearance of such a weapon; and
- it can be readily convertible into a weapon from which a shot, bullet or other missile can be discharged (s 1(1) and (2) Firearms Act 1968).

Section 36 of the Violent Crime Reduction Act (2006) means it is an offence, since 1 October 2007 to:

- manufacture;
- bring into or cause to be brought into Great Britain; or
- sell realistic imitation firearms.

The modification of an imitation firearm to make it realistic is also incorporated to cause it to be a criminal offence. It is necessary to obtain expert forensic analysis in cases to show a weapon has or could be modified.

Readily convertible imitations

An imitation weapon is defined by s 1 Firearms Act (1968) as a firearm where:

- it has the appearance of such a weapon; and
- it can be readily convertible into a weapon from which a shot, bullet or other missile can be discharged (ss 1(1) and 1(2) Firearms Act 1968).

'Readily convertible' is defined by s 1(6) Firearms Act (1982) where:

> it can be so converted without any special skill on the part of the person converting it and the work involved in converting it does not require equipment or tools other than such as are in common use by persons carrying out works of construction and maintenance in their own homes.

These include BB guns that have been converted to fire 8mm bullets, for example.

Forensic evidence can establish whether an imitation firearm is 'readily convertible' or if a partially reactivated firearm or its component parts can be fired. It is important to seek the advice of a suitably qualified forensic scientist if you are uncertain as to the status of any weapon.

10.2.2 Antique firearms

From July 2014 changes in legislation have been made to encompass the ownership of antique firearms. The age and obsoletion of the ammunition for such weapons means they are allowed to be held in certain circumstances such as for display purposes. However, the potential for those with the right knowledge to manufacture their own ammunition for some antique weapons has required them to be incorporated into legislation.

The new legislation, under s 1 Firearms Act (1968) prohibits anyone who has served or received a criminal sentence from possessing an antique firearm. This applies to those who has served a custodial sentence of more than three years or has served a custodial sentence or received a suspended sentence, of between three months and three years. It is irrelevant whether such a weapon is used solely for ornamental purposes.

There is no definition of what is considered to be an 'antique' in the legislation. Home Office Guidance states that certain pre-1939 weapons will be classified as antiques including muzzle-loading and certain types of breech-loading firearms. The guidance sets out which weapons may be classified as 'antique' and which are exempt. The current information can be obtained in the Home Office *Guidance on Firearms Law (2014)* and on the Crown Prosecution Service website.

10.3 **Types of Firearm and Ammunition**

Firearms will generally fall into two main classifications of rifled and smoothbore weapons.

10.3.1 **Rifled weapons**

There are numerous styles of rifled weapons with a variety of ammunition available. This class of weapons consists of rifles or pistols, both of which are designed to fire bullets.

Definition—pistols

Pistols can be defined as handguns, a firearm which is designed to be used in one hand. Pistols can be single-shot, self-loading or revolver.

Definition—rifles

Rifles have longer barrels and are designed to be held with both hands.

Typically, the handguns encountered in an investigation will be either revolvers or self-loading pistols as they are more compact and easier to carry around and conceal. Revolvers will retain the cartridge after firing until it is manually removed whereas the cartridge cases used in self-loading pistols are ejected from the weapon after firing. Therefore it is more likely to find spent (fired) cartridge cases at the scene of a shooting incident involving a self-loading pistol than a revolver.

The majority of pistols will have what are termed rifled barrels. The rifling in the barrel is a design structure incorporated in order to give some rotation or spin to the bullet, which in turn increases the stability and accuracy of the trajectory of a fired bullet.

Rifling consists of a series of lands and grooves that spiral down the length of the barrel, enabling the bullet to be gripped and rotated prior to leaving the weapon. The number of lands and grooves (see Figure 10.1) differs according to weapon type, as does the number of twists (rotations) along the barrel length.

Figure 10.1 Cross section of rifled barrel

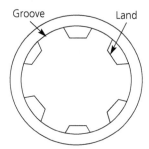

The rifling inside a barrel can leave microscopic scratch marks (striations) on a bullet which can be used to identify the weapon type and establish links between a piece of ammunition and the weapon that fired it. Each class of weapon will possess similar rifling marks to all those of the same make and model. The microscopic scratch marks left on cases and bullets as a result of the rifling and other internal mechanisms, such as firing pins, can be compared to establish if they were fired by the same weapon.

Where a weapon is recovered, marks left on the case and bullet of a test-fired round can be compared to the marks left on cases or bullets recovered from a crime scene.

As the number of lands and grooves and the widths between them, plus the direction and degree of twist of rifling marks on a fired bullet or case differ between makes and models of firearms, this information can enable a firearm examiner to check against a reference database containing technical information on weapons and determine the identity of the weapon to have fired the bullet.

Ammunition

The general design of the ammunition used in rifled weapons consists of four component parts—a cartridge case or shell, bullet (see Figure 10.2), propellant and primer which are generally referred to in their entirety as a 'round'.

Figure 10.2 Typical round construction

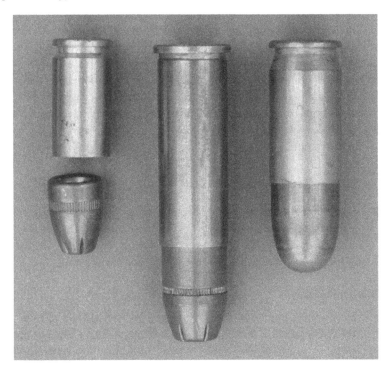

A cartridge case contains a powdered explosive propellant with the bullet clamped into the top of the case. The bottom of the cartridge has a percussion detonator on the base; this is essentially a small metal cup which holds the primer. The detonator (see Figure 10.3) can be situated either centrally (centre fire) or around the edge of the base (rimfire), and contains the primer.

To fire the round, a firing pin strikes the percussion detonator (sometimes referred to as a percussion cap) containing the primer, which in turn ignites the propellant. This creates a relatively large volume of hot gas which causes the bullet and casing to separate, projecting the bullet forward down the barrel. The cartridge case will either remain in the firearm to be removed manually (revolvers and some shotguns) or be ejected from the weapon (self-loading), depending on the weapon type.

Figure 10.3 Cartridge base markings

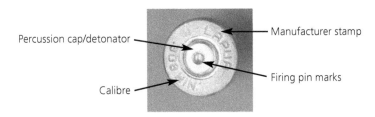

Percussion cap/detonator

Manufacturer stamp

Firing pin marks

Calibre

Bullets

Bullets are manufactured in a range of materials to cater for many different uses, far too numerous to cover in one chapter. The basic types of bullets typically encountered will fall into two categories: those which are jacketed or unjacketed. The most common material utilised to manufacture unjacketed bullets is lead, which may be alloyed with antimony or tin to increase the hardness. Jacketed bullets typically have a lead core which is coated in a harder metal such as copper, zinc or nickel alloy or with copper coated steel. Semi-jacketed bullets are not entirely encased but may have the tip exposed. This tip may be hollowed out.

10.3.2 Smoothbore weapons

Shotguns are typically classed as smoothbore weapons as the inside of the barrel is relatively smooth. Shotguns do not generally contain any rifling in the barrel. Shotguns can be single barrelled or double barrelled with two barrels either 'side by side' or 'over and under' (one barrel above the other).

Shotgun ammunition

Shotgun ammunition is quite variable, and can range from a single ball or cylinder to fit the diameter of the barrel down to numerous small pellets. The pellets are typically constructed of lead hardened with antimony; however due to concerns regarding the impact of lead accumulation in wild animals, substitutes for lead include pellets made of soft steel coated with copper or tungsten or bismuth alloyed with iron.

Figure 10.4 Typical shotgun cartridge components

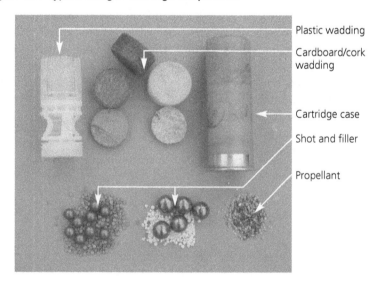

Plastic wadding

Cardboard/cork wadding

Cartridge case

Shot and filler

Propellant

A shotgun cartridge may have a casing of plastic or cardboard type material, attached to a base similar to those of rifled rounds. The base will contain
the detonation cap holding the primer. The propellant is separated from the
shot by wadding. The wadding can be a plastic cup type structure which will
hold the pellet(s) or compressed discs of cardboard, cork or similar material as
shown in Figure 10.4. The wadding keeps the components separated during
storage. Figure 10.5 illustrates how the component parts of a cartridge case are
structured.

When fired, the cartridge will remain in the barrel and the shot and wadding
is discharged down the muzzle. It is typically the shot, any filler and wadding
that will be found at a crime scene involving shotguns. However, cartridge cases
may also be recovered where the firer has reloaded the weapon or if a self-loading weapon has been used.

Figure 10.5 Internal structure of a typical shotgun cartridge

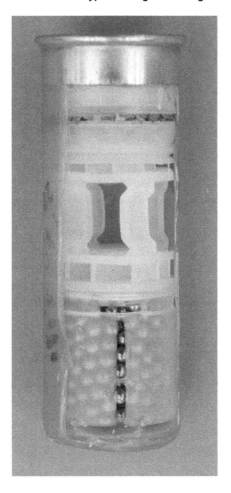

10.4 **Ballistic Examinations**

The forensic examination of firearms can be split into three general areas, referred to as the internal, external and terminal ballistics.

10.4.1 **Internal ballistics**

Internal ballistics deal with the mechanics of what happens inside the weapon from when the firing pin hits the primer to the moment a bullet exits the muzzle. It is at this stage that any imperfections inside the barrel can be transferred onto the bullet or wadding to enable an identification of the weapon used to fire the projectile. In addition to the identification and comparison of such striations (scratch marks), internal ballistic examinations can establish velocity, recoil and barrel pressures.

10.4.2 **External ballistics**

External ballistics is concerned with the behaviour of the projectile in flight, after it has been discharged from the weapon and before it reaches its target. The trajectory, maximum range and momentum of a bullet can be determined by the application of mathematical principles. This is of interest to investigators as it may aid a reconstruction of events and help to establish the relative positions of the firer and any victims and provide information that can corroborate or refute the version of events given.

10.4.3 **Terminal ballistics**

Terminal ballistics refers to the behaviour and effects a projectile has on its target. There are two aspects within terminal ballistics. One involves the penetration potential which is the ability of a projectile to penetrate various materials. The other aspect of terminal ballistics, typically used in the investigation of shooting incidents, is wound ballistics. This is concerned with the effect a projectile has on living tissue. Examination of shooting wounds can be useful in establishing the type of weapon used, the distance between a person and weapon when it was fired and the direction of fire.

....

Case study—Self-defence plea refuted by ballistics evidence

Anthony Edward Martin was the lone resident of an isolated and dilapidated farmhouse in Norfolk. On the night of 20 August 1999, Mr Martin alleges he was disturbed from his sleep by a noise downstairs. He took a loaded 12-bore pump action shotgun with him to investigate the noise. Mr Martin alleges he was blinded by torch light as he was halfway down the stairs, whereupon, fearing for his life he fired the shotgun towards the light.

....

Two males who had entered the house via a downstairs window were hit by the shots. It is believed the intent of the males was to commit burglary.

They both managed to get out of the house, one male sustained injuries to both his legs but made his way to neighbouring premises. The second male sustained injuries to his back and legs, and collapsed and died a short distance from the house.

The prosecution did not accept Mr Martin's assertion that he was in fear for his life and acted in self-defence, proposing instead that Mr Martin had lain in wait for the males having heard their approach to the house and had shot them with the intention of killing or seriously injuring them.

An aspect of the forensic firearm and ballistic evidence in this case was used to establish the relative positions of the parties involved. Mr Martin claimed he was midway on the stairs when he fired the shots.

The position of the cartridge cases and damage caused by the shots to the walls inside a downstairs room, out of the direct line of sight of the stairs showed that at least two of the shots had been fired inside that room and not from the stairway.

The examination of the wounds showed that the distance between the weapon and the males was inconsistent with Mr Martin's assertion that he was on the stairs.

It was possible that the first shot may have been fired from the stairway but the subsequent two shots, based on the forensic evidence, could not have been. They were fired at a closer range than could be achieved from the stairwell.

In April 2000 Mr Martin was sentenced to life imprisonment for murder, with ten years for wounding and one year for possession of an illegal firearm to run concurrently. This was reduced on appeal in October 2001, to manslaughter with three years for wounding, giving a total sentence of five years. Mr Martin was released in July 2003.

The evidence provided by the internal, external, and terminal (wound) ballistics in this case illustrates the way in which such evidence can be used to corroborate or refute different accounts of what has happened and aid a reconstruction of events to be determined.

A combination of the results from the internal, external and terminal ballistics examinations can provide investigators with a clearer picture of what occurred and enable the accounts given to be corroborated or refuted.

10.5 **Scenes of Shooting Incidents**

The preservation of life is paramount. The scene of a shooting incident, once it has been declared safe by AFOs or equivalent, must be preserved for the examination of the crime scene investigator (CSI) or the forensic examiner. Where firearms are present at a scene, investigators must not handle the firearm where it is safe to leave it *in situ*. Only an AFO or equivalently trained personnel should handle the firearm to make it safe. Where a firearm is left at the scene, preserve the scene ensuring that no one remains in the potential line of fire should the weapon discharge.

The evidence to be located and recovered is dependent on the weapon used. Generally the following material may be present:

- bullets/casings (entire or fragmented);
- the weapon itself;
- cartridge cases;
- wadding—card or plastic;
- shotgun pellets; and
- potential ricochet marks that can refute or corroborate claims of accidental discharge or unintentional targeting.

Bullets can travel great distances, the area around the scene can be searched with metal detectors. A ballistics expert can assist in establishing the direction and probable distance of a bullets trajectory in individual circumstances.

10.5.1 National Ballistics Intelligence Service (NABIS)

This is a national database that holds a central registry of recovered weapons and ammunition and has the capability to undertake ballistics comparisons to link incidents, firearms and ammunition and undertake forensic examinations of recovered firearms and related ballistic material. NABIS has an intelligence cell which analyses all the data from recovered material to provide information for strategic and tactical advice to the UK police service, including British Transport Police, Ministry of Defence Police, and agencies such as MI5, National Crime Agency, the UK Border Force and the Police Service of Northern Ireland.

10.6 Forensic Examination of Firearms and Ballistic Material

It is crucial that the examination of a firearm or component part is undertaken in a systematic manner in order to maximise the recovery of potential forensic material. In addition to the firearm and ballistic evidence that may be gained, consideration must also be given to the presence of other potential forensic material such as fingerprints, DNA, fibres and other particulate material.

It is common for firearms to be recovered with their identifying serial numbers erased by drilling or filing them off. Firearms examiners have techniques available to them to possibly recover such erased identifying marks.

10.6.1 Firearm recovery

Any firearm must be left *in situ* to be made safe by an AFO or equivalent, where appropriate. If it must be moved to prevent harm to public or to preserve any potential evidence, then initial responders must seek guidance via the force control room. If in any doubt as to the nature of the weapon regarding whether it is real or imitation, it must be treated as a being real and fully loaded until it can be established otherwise. Once the weapon has been declared safe, a CSI should undertake the recording and recovery of the weapon. The CSI will photograph the firearm *in situ*, making a note as to the position of safety catches and in the case of revolvers, mark the position of the chamber. Any magazine should be removed from the weapon.

The firearm should be secured into a box, preferably one with a transparent window or purpose-specific firearm packaging if available. The box must be securely sealed, labelled and the 'made safe' certificate completed by an AFO (or similar) attached and clearly visible.

If wet, the firearm must not be packaged in plastic as rust will quickly develop and can change the striations created in any test firings. Wet firearms must be packaged into boxes sealed into paper evidence sacks. Firearms must be stored in secure dry locations; typically this will be in a secure purpose-built gun cabinet.

Firearms and ammunition must not be packaged, stored or submitted for forensic analysis together. The firearm and related material should be separated and kept away from other exhibits such as a suspect's or victim's clothing. At no time should anything such as fingers or pens be pushed into a barrel of a firearm. Gloves must be worn when handling a firearm. Investigators should avoid handling firearms where possible, taking action to preserve the scene and weapon for recovery by suitably trained personnel.

10.6.2 **Casings and bullets or shot**

Cartridge cases from rifled weapons or shotguns may be present at a shooting scene. Where the projectiles have not been fired, the recovery of DNA, fingerprints and other transferred material may be possible.

Once a round has been fired, the heat generated in the barrel can be detrimental to the recovery of DNA and fingerprint evidence. However, as techniques are always improving to recover such evidence, the presence of such must not be discounted. The evidence provided by a cartridge case that has been fired can include the identification of the weapon that fired it due to the marks made by the rifling and unique marks made by the firing pin and extractor (in self-loading pistols).

Recovered bullets or pellets can provide potential forensic evidence in addition to the determination of the weapon type that fired them. When a jacketed bullet hits a resistant surface, the bullet coating may peel apart, so all that can be observed is the metal casing. In some cases, the softer metal core of the bullet may be exposed and contain potential forensic material or information that can corroborate or refute versions of events. Trace evidence such as fibres, paint, glass or wood fragments may be embedded in the softer material of a bullet or shotgun pellet (see Figure 10.6).

Forensic recovery of bullets/cartridge cases

Disposable latex gloves must be worn at all times when handling any ballistic material. Cartridge cases should be handled to ensure the minimum amount of contact is made. The case should be placed into a rigid container such as a poly pot or, if it will fit, into a swab tube. The container should be padded out with polythene to stop the case moving about. Movement of the casing in the container must be restricted to prevent any damage occurring to the fragile marks created by the firing pins, rifling and other mechanisms. The microscopic striations can be altered by movement or rough handling. The use of tissue paper or similar is to be avoided as this too may cause microscopic scratches to the casing. The same principles apply to shotgun wadding, whether plastic, card or cork.

Wet ammunition components must be packaged in paper evidence bags and stored in secure dry locations; typically this will be in a secure purpose built gun cabinet.

Figure 10.6 Impact evidence from fired rounds

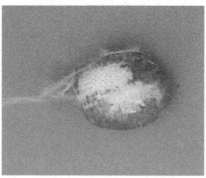

10.6.3 Firearm discharge residue (FDR)

When a firearm is discharged the primer and propellant are expelled in a cloud from the muzzle and any gaps between the working parts of the weapon.

This cloud of particulate material is referred to as firearm discharge residue (FDR) or gunshot residue (GSR) and contains particles of partially burned and unburned propellant and combustion products of the primer in addition to material from the barrel, casing and projectiles.

The FDR will be deposited on the person firing the weapon, typically on the hands, clothes, hair and face, on surfaces in the vicinity including the target (if sufficiently close). The composition of any FDR can provide links between crime scenes, persons involved and weapons.

Recovery of FDR from persons

It is vital that FDR residue is recovered from a suspect as soon as possible as it can be lost fairly quickly.

Delay in recovering samples, washing and movement will reduce the amount of FDR to be recovered. Research has indicated that FDR particle loss is rapid, between one to 48 hours. The best evidence is that which contains the greater number of FDR particles.

FDR particles can remain on clothing and other textile surfaces for considerably longer than they remain on skin. It is vital that FDR recovery from persons is undertaken using a specific FDR sampling kit, the use of conventional swabs is not acceptable.

Hair combings to recover FDR must be done prior to the removal of a suspect's clothing. The presence of FDR can provide supportive information that a weapon has been fired or handled, although on its own it is not possible to say definitively when the weapon was fired.

The issue of contamination and transfer of FDR material is a very real risk. The location, victim and suspect should each be treated as crime scenes in their own right and steps taken to avoid transfer and contamination of material between them. Investigators dealing with one aspect of the incident, such as the location, must not then have contact with the suspect or victim. Any personnel involved with the scene must not have had contact with firearms in the seven days prior to dealing with the incident where the recovery of FDR is likely to be a requirement.

Appeal Court Judgments on FDR Evidence

A key appeal case impacting on the value of FDR evidence was *R v George (Barry)* [2007]. George was convicted in 2001 of the murder of Jill Dando, a TV presenter. Forensic examination revealed that a firearm had been pressed to Ms Dando's head and discharged. The offence occurred outside the victim's home in April 1999.

The Appeal Court considered the evidential weight attributed to the single particle of FDR found in an internal pocket of a coat owned by Mr George. This particle (11.5 microns, or one hundredth of a millimetre in size) was recovered almost a year after the shooting had taken place. The recovered particle was found to be a match with the FDR recovered from the firearm wound and the crime scene.

It was found that such a low level of FDR could have occurred by transfer or as a result of environmental contamination. It therefore carried no real weight as evidence that George had shot Miss Dando. The Police were critisised as it was evident that transfer could have occurred by improper handling of the coat.

The Forensic Science Service published 'The assessment, interpretation and reporting of firearms chemistry cases' guidelines in January 2006. These guidelines state that the weight of evidence for FDR particles should be categorised as:

Low (one to three particles),

Moderate (four to twelve particles),

High (thirteen to fifty particles) and;

Very High (over fifty particles).

A single particle is therefore inconclusive, and in this case the verdict was considered to be unsafe and was therefore quashed.

The issue of the quantity of FDR particles was also raised in *R v Dwaine George* [2014] in an appeal brought about, in part, due to the previous case findings.

Dwaine was a gang member convicted of the murder in 2002 of teenager Daniel Dale in 2001. Four particles of FDR were found on a coat at the home of Dwaine, two of which were found to have components characteristic of firearm residue, the other two particles may have originated from firearm residue but could also have originated from other sources such as fireworks or a nail gun, for example. Again, it is stressed that it is not possible to determine when and how lower levels of FDR are deposited and whether it is as a result of an association with firearms or as a result of other sources. The conviction was declared to be unsafe and therefore was quashed.

10.7 Examination to Establish Cause

There may be a requirement to corroborate or refute allegations or versions of events. It is rare for someone to admit that they have deliberately shot someone; it is quite possible that they will claim that a person was shot due to a deflection or ricochet of the bullet, or that the weapon discharged accidentally. Forensic firearm examiners can establish the likelihood of such actions occurring.

10.7.1 Ricochet

A ricochet occurs when a projectile is deviated from its original course due to impact with a surface. Evidence of ricochet at a scene may be in the form of damage at the impact site or on the bullet or pellet which may have evidence of the surface it has hit embedded upon it. When a projectile ricochets off a surface it loses velocity and as a consequence, its stability. This causes the bullet to wobble or tumble. Bullets ricocheting off smooth surfaces such as glass, steel, concrete or wood will typically have a flat spot where they have made contact with the surface, and this area may have particles of the surface adhering to it.

Wounds caused by a ricocheting bullet will have a distinctive pattern due to the tumbling action of the deflected missile, which will typically result in a ragged entry wound.

10.7.2 Accidental discharge

A forensic firearms examiner can provide valuable information as to whether a particular weapon could accidentally discharge and the circumstances required for this to occur by undertaking a thorough examination of the mechanics of the weapon.

The pressure required to pull the trigger and the condition of any safety catch and firing mechanisms can be established to ascertain the likelihood of any such discharge occurring.

10.8 Conducted Energy Devices (Taser)

A Taser is classed as a s 5 firearm under the Firearms Act (1968) and is used by specially trained police officers, typically firearms officers.

The word Taser stands for 'Thomas A Swift's Electronic Rifle'. The Taser is regarded as a less lethal option to a conventional firearm, to be employed in order to gain compliance without the substantial risk of serious, permanent or fatal injury. The Taser is a hand-held electronic device which can discharge a pair of probes that can attach to a target up to 6.4m (21ft) away. At the end of the probes are sharp barbs which can penetrate clothing or skin. When both barbs are connected via attaching to clothing or skin, an electrical circuit is completed which conducts 50,000 volts down the wires and into the subject. Fatalities occur very rarely with the use of Taser; however the risk is considerably lower than that associated with the use of conventional firearms.

The criminal use of such devices is also encountered by investigators. The following section deals with the procedures and evidence that can be recovered following a police Taser discharge, but the same principles regarding potential evidential material can be applied to criminal discharges. Note that the same considerations as apply to firearm recovery apply to Tasers and similar, that is, they should only be handled and made safe by appropriately trained personnel.

Following a Taser discharge certain materials must be collected for evidential purposes.

Checklist—Materials to collect for evidence following Taser discharge

- Probes embedded in clothing may be carefully removed by an investigator. Probes embedded in skin must ideally be removed by medical personnel; however operational necessity or risk of further injury to the subject may require that the barbs are removed by investigators trained in the correct procedure. In some circumstances, the wire close to the probe can be broken to detach the Taser unit from the subject. Probes that have pierced skin must be treated as biohazards as they will contain body fluids. The barbs must be packaged in rigid containers.

- Forensic information can be gathered from a discharged Taser unit; data regarding the discharge can be downloaded.

- On discharge a Taser will emit numerous confetti type data tags known as AFIDs (anti-felon identification). These contain unique serial numbers which enables the identification and auditing of the unit.

- The wires can be forensically examined to determine distances between a subject and the unit when fired. Under no circumstances should the wires be recovered by wrapping the wires around the cartridge or similar.

Where serious injury or death occurs following the use of Taser, the scene must be secured and preserved as a crime scene.

10.9 Chapter Summary

Firearms and ammunition can contain potential forensic evidence to link projectiles with the weapon that fired it, identify a firearm from a fired projectile, and determine a sequence of events which can corroborate or refute allegations.

In addition to the risks to health and safety, there is a very real risk of the inadvertent transfer of FDR. The only personnel who should enter the scene of a shooting incident where a firearm is present in the first instance, should be AFOs to make the weapon safe and a forensic examiner or a CSI.

The role of the initial responders attending the scene should be to preserve and manage the scene once the duty for the preservation of life has been undertaken. Where a weapon is at the scene, do not allow anyone to stand in the area that is within the line of sight of the weapon. Where any doubt exists regarding whether a weapon is a real or imitation, the assumption must be that it is real and it is fully loaded.

In addition to the potential firearm related evidence that may be available, consideration must also be given to the presence of other potential evidence such as DNA, fingerprints and traces of material such as fibres, glass or paint, for example. Be mindful that the minute striations on a cartridge case or bullet can be easily destroyed by rough handling. Such items must be packaged in a rigid container padded with polythene (piece of clean plastic bag) to prevent movement of the item. Wet items must not be packaged in plastic; with firearms this will encourage rust which can render any forensic analysis invalid.

KNOWLEDGE CHECK—FIREARMS AND BALLISTICS

1. State the definition of a s 1 firearm under the Firearms Act 1968.

   A lethal barrelled weapon of any description from which any shot, bullet or other missile can be discharged and includes:

   (a) any prohibited weapon, whether it is such a lethal weapon as aforesaid or not; and

   (b) any component part of such a lethal or prohibited weapon; and

   (c) any accessory to such a weapon designed or adapted to diminish the noise or flash caused by firing the weapon.

2. What potential forensic evidence can be gained from a fired metal cartridge?

   The make and model and caliber can be indicated on the base.
   Rifling and other mechanically created marks (eg, from firing pin and extractors) can help to determine the make and model of the weapon that fired it. Such marks can be compared with other recovered cases to establish a link between scenes. Where the firearm is also recovered, a test firing will establish if the marks are the same as those on a recovered case.
   FDR can potentially link the case to the firearm, scene, victim, and suspect.

3. What is NABIS?

   NABIS is the National Ballistics Intelligence System, a national database containing information from recovered firearms and ballistic material and intelligence collated from reported incidents (whether a firearm or related material is recovered or not). It has been developed in order to provide a central registry of criminal firearm usage and it can compare material from scenes across the country to establish links between incidents, weapons and ammunition.

4. What is a Taser?

   Taser stands for 'Thomas A Swift's Electronic Rifle'. It is a s 5 firearm as defined by the Firearms Act 1968. It is a hand-held device that is a less lethal option than conventional firearms. It can be deployed by specifically trained, authorised officers for conflict management and its use is directed and controlled by force firearms policies.
   The Tasers can deliver 50,000 volts of electricity when both probes are discharged into a subject's skin or clothing to form a complete electrical circuit. Tasers and similar devices may also be used by criminals.

5. State the forensic evidence that is available following discharge (firing) of a Taser.

When a Taser is discharged, two wires with probes attached at the end are discharged, up to a maximum distance of 6.4m or 21ft. The probes have barbs which can penetrate skin or clothing. Numerous identification tags called AFIDs are also expelled. These have unique serial numbers which can provide an identification of the unit they came from as well as an audit trail and these must be collected from the scene.

Following a discharge, the data held in the device can be downloaded to give technical information regarding the discharge.

The wires must not be wrapped around anything to package them as they can provide evidence of the distance from the unit and subject.

The probes can be carefully removed from clothing by an investigator; however where they have penetrated skin, they must be removed by a medical practitioner and treated as containing biohazard material. Wires can be broken close to the probes in skin in order to detach the Taser from the subject.

Consideration must also be given to fingerprints, DNA, and other potential forensic evidence that may be available.

Recommended Reading

Armed Policing (2014) APP College of Policing—<https://www.app.college.police.uk/app-content/armed-policing/?s=armed+policing>.
Guidance on Firearms Licensing Law (2015) Home Office.
Forensic Science (2011) Jackson, ARW and Jackson, J.
Handbook of Firearms and Ballistics: Examining and Interpreting Forensic Evidence (2008) Heard, BJ.
National Ballistics Intelligence Service— <http://www.nabis.police.uk>.
Understanding Firearm Ballistics, 6th edn (2006) Rinker, RA.

Appeal Court Rulings

R v Anthony Edward Martin [2001] EWCA Crim 2245.
R v Bewley [2012] EWCA Crim 1457.
R v George (Barry) [2007] EWCA Crim 2722.
R v Dwaine George [2014] EWCA Crim 2507.

Footwear, Tyre and Tool Marks

11.1 **Introduction**

Marks and impressions left by footwear, tyres and tools at crime scenes can provide evidence to potentially link scenes and provide intelligence that may lead to the identification of an offender. Marks recovered from crime scenes can then be compared with the actual item recovered to establish if it was the one that made the mark at a scene. These comparisons and potential links can be made by initially looking at the overall shapes of the marks which can indicate a make and model in the case of footwear and tyres. In the case of a tool mark it may be possible to establish the size and generic type of the implement used, for example a 10mm flat-bladed tool.

To link marks from different scenes or marks to items, an examiner will look at the general characteristics such as the type and size of the marks. The unique individualising marks created during manufacture, and then through subsequent wear and tear will then be microscopically examined. Links between a mark and the tyre, footwear or tool can be made by the comparison of such details.

This chapter gives a brief overview into the forensic potential of such marks and guidance on the preservation and recovery of potential evidence.

11.2 **Footwear**

Impressions left by footwear will be present at every crime scene as offenders will have walked in and out of the scene. They may take steps to avoid the law of the land, but they cannot defy the 'law of gravity'. The marks may not always be visible, but they will be there. They can be in the form of impressed three-dimensional marks such as those left in soil or on pieces of paper that have been walked over. The other types of marks frequently encountered at scenes of crime are the two-dimensional marks, those which are left in substances such as dust, paint or blood, for example, that are transferred from the sole of the footwear onto surfaces walked on.

Initial responders need to be aware of where they are stepping when entering a crime scene as it is easy to obliterate footwear marks left by offenders. Avoiding footwear marks at crime scenes can be difficult; assessment of the most likely routes an offender would have used is required and actions should be taken to avoid such routes.

Where life is at risk, the most direct route to the victim should be taken. At scenes of serious incidents, a common approach path (CAP) should be established. The crime scene investigator (CSI) should be informed of the routes taken by initial responders and any other personnel such as paramedics, into and out of a scene.

Although there may be many pairs of the same shoes in circulation, wear patterns differ with each individual. Footwear impressions can provide evidence linking a suspect to a scene, or a series of scenes and can possibly provide an idea of the number of people involved and their movements around the scene. Impressions recovered from a crime scene are typically loaded onto a database such as SICAR (shoeprint image capture and retrieval) or Solemate. The footwear of suspects can also be loaded onto SICAR or equivalent, where available in custody units. A footwear analyst can then classify the characteristics of the sole patterns of the footwear marks from crime scenes and those of recovered suspects' footwear.

The success of the National Footwear Reference Collection led to a privately owned company, Bluestar, to be commissioned by the Home Office to create a National Footwear Database. The database records custody and crime scene marks which can be used by force intelligence units to determine if any links can be established between crime scenes and the footwear of those brought into custody. The database can be used to potentially establish the identity of the make and model of the footwear and an examination and comparison of the unique individual damage and wear characteristics present on footwear from detainees and from footwear recovered during a search of an offenders home, for example, can establish if a link between the shoe and scene marks can be demonstrated.

Appeal Court Ruling—Footwear Evidence

R v T [2010] considered the issue of the identification of footwear marks at the scene of a murder for which T was convicted. An expert, who had recovered the evidence of footwear marks at the scene, undertook the comparison with pieces of footwear recovered in the defendant's house. The examination concluded that a 'moderate degree of scientific evidence' existed to support the view that footwear recovered from the defendant had made the marks recovered at the crime scene. The appeal was launched due to fresh evidence indicating that the expert had used a numerical scale of likelihood ratios (LR) which were not disclosed at initial trial and were more favourable to the defendant, and that the statistical evidence used by the expert at the trial was inherently unreliable.

The court found that there was a discrepancy between the statistics used to make the LR calculations and the figures given at original trial and critisised the lack of transparency, stating that 'an approach based on mathematical calculations is only as good as the data used.' Whilst (LR) calculation as a statistical practice to calculate probability of DNA material originating from a single source (person) is well accepted, the court concluded that LR should not be used where there is no firm statistical basis on which to form such calculations.

11.2.1 Recovery of footwear marks at scenes

Where possible it is preferable for the whole item bearing the footwear mark to be recovered. Where this is not appropriate, several methods are available for the recovery of footwear impressions from non-portable items and the technique utilised by the CSI will be dependent on the type of the impression and the surface it is on.

There are two broad categories of footwear marks found at crime scenes:

- **Two-dimensional transfer marks.** These are marks which are left on a hard, flat surface such as a laminated floor, glass or counter top, for example. Mud, dust and other substances that are present on the sole are transferred onto the surface to leave a two-dimensional impression. These marks may be as a result of a 'dry' deposit—dust or sand, for example, or as 'wet' deposit, such as fluids (eg, blood) where an offender has walked over wet surfaces prior to entering the scene. Once 'wet' deposited marks are dry, it can be difficult to establish if the mark was initially deposited by wet or dry means.
- **Three-dimensional impressed marks.** These occur as marks that leave indentations on soft surfaces such as in mud, snow, sand, paper or on some carpets.

It is important to note that footwear marks may not always be apparent to the naked eye. A CSI will use lighting techniques to search an area of interest, and a variety of options that are available for the recovery of the marks.

Many of the techniques for the recovery of fingerprints can be utilised for the recovery of footwear. In summary, once a mark has been located, the process is as follows.

- The mark should be photographed with a measurement scale. This enables the photograph of the mark to be reproduced to accurately reflect the size of the mark, thus giving the footwear analyst further points of comparison between scenes and suspect marks.
- The use of powders and chemical techniques can be used to enhance the mark. Marks in dust-type materials can be lifted straight from the surface using gel lifters or an electrostatic lifting apparatus (ESLA). The ESLA method involves laying a Mylar foil material over the mark, an electrostatic charge is applied to the foil which attracts the fine dust material onto the foil to give an impression of the sole pattern. ESLA can also be used on vertical surfaces such as walls and doors. Chemical development techniques can also be utilised to recover footwear marks.
- Methods appropriate to a dust deposited mark should be utilised first. If ESLA or gel do not produce a recovered impression it is then possible to use fingerprint powders to recover potential marks. If a dust deposited mark is examined with powders first it can destroy the fragile mark and the evidence will most likely be lost.
- For indented or impressed marks in soil or sand, for example, a casting material is poured into the mark to give a 'life size' three-dimensional copy of the sole. Electrostatic document apparatus (ESDA) is an excellent method for recovering indented footwear marks left on paper which is typically used to

recover indented writing from paper. On some types of close pile carpets that bear an impression, photography and possibly ESLA can be used to recover the mark. ESLA can also be used on walls and other (non-metallic) surfaces, for example where an offender has dropped through a sky light and placed their feet on internal walls to steady themselves.

11.2.2 Footwear marks from suspects

The footwear of detained suspects can be taken by virtue of powers contained within the Police and Criminal Evidence Act (PACE), s 61A(3). Footwear from suspects can also be recovered during a search under warrant.

The footwear of suspects can be electronically scanned onto the SICAR or equivalent database, where available. The scanner plate must be cleaned prior to and following the scanning of footwear, to avoid any potential transfer of material occurring between unrelated items of footwear. Footwear pads can be used to make an impression of the sole of the footwear where electronic scanning is not available. Photocopying of footwear is not appropriate for comparison purposes as the quality can be variable.

Investigators must be mindful of the potential presence of other types of forensic evidence that may be on footwear. Where body fluids or trace evidence are believed to be present, footwear marks must not be taken by scanning or printing. The footwear must be photographed first by a CSI, who can then recover any other potential forensic material such as blood, glass or soil, for example. This will ensure the integrity of any potential evidence by avoiding contamination or transfer of material and ensures the appropriate health and safety precautions are observed with regard to body fluids.

POINT TO NOTE—HANDLING FOOTWEAR

Disposable gloves must be worn when handling items of footwear for reasons of health and safety; there may be biohazards present. Wearing gloves protects the investigator and any potential evidence.

11.2.3 Searching and comparison of scene and suspect footwear marks

The footwear examiner will search a reference database of footwear sole patterns in order to identify the brand and model of the shoe. Many shoes have very similar patterns, so if the examiner only has a small area of a crime scene mark to work with, it can be very difficult to give a definitive answer as to what type of shoe made the mark. The marks recovered from scenes are searched against other crime scene marks in order to identify any linked offences. Footwear impressions taken from suspects are then searched against the scene marks database.

The initial comparison focuses initially on the patterns of the sole. The examiner will then look for any obvious unique wear and damage characteristics, many of which may be microscopic, before making any provisional links between scenes or suspects.

Checklist—Criteria for comparing footwear items to marks recovered from crime scenes

- Pattern types on the sole to determine make and model.

- The particular arrangement of the pattern types, which can be useful where partial footwear marks are present.

- The size of the footwear. This is not a simple task of measuring the length of the mark. The size of footwear is determined by the internal length; therefore different sizes of shoes can have the same external sole length. As shoe sizing can vary between manufacturers it is not a reliable singular comparison point. Marks from scenes are generally compared to test marks made with the same brand and model of footwear in varying sizes. The relative size and positioning of elements in the sole pattern can enable a size to be established. This technique enables the size of footwear to be determined for partial footwear marks.

- The amount and position of wear patterns and areas of damage are compared between the suspect footwear and the crime scene mark. These can be unique and individualising and can in some cases give an indication of the walking style of a frequent wearer of the footwear, for example whether the wear and tear would be consistent with someone walking with a limp, for example.

A conclusive match between a suspect's footwear and marks recovered from crime scenes is possible if sufficient detail is present from the crime scene marks.

The wear and damage patterns on the soles of footwear will change with continued wear, therefore comparisons between scene marks and suspects' shoes may not be valid after a month if the shoes have continued to be worn. However, such potential evidence should not be discounted. The offender may have stored shoes worn to commit an offence and not subsequently worn them. In such circumstances comparison between the recovered shoes and a crime scene mark may provide valuable evidence. The circumstances of each case should be considered individually rather than dismissing potential evidence because of the time that has elapsed since the incident.

11.2.4 Considerations regarding footwear evidence

Two common defences put forward where footwear evidence has been recovered are for the suspect to state that the shoes were worn by someone else on the day in question, or that the suspect acquired the footwear after the offence from the original (usually unknown) previous owner. There are forensic examinations that may corroborate or refute such accounts. A 'feet-in-shoes' or 'Cinderella' examination may be able to establish the regular wearer of footwear items. It is not effective if someone has only worn the shoes for a short period of time. However, if two people have worn the shoes for a period of time it may be possible to detect this through the impressions and wear inside the shoes. This type of examination requires footwear of a similar type and construction as the questioned shoes, along with the barefoot or stocking foot impressions from the persons linked to wearing the shoes. Ideally barefoot impressions should include standing and walking impressions and a three-dimensional impression made in a material such as biofoam.

11.2.5 Preservation of footwear evidence

The techniques required to preserve footwear will depend on the type of mark and the surface it has been deposited upon. The following checklist indicates the most appropriate method for the preservation of the different types of footwear marks often encountered at crime scenes.

Checklist for the recovery of footwear marks

Impressed marks such as those in mud or soil can be covered by a clean rigid cover. Care must be taken to avoid pushing any further soil or debris into the impressed mark.

- Where paper or card has been walked over by offenders, impressed marks may be recovered using ESDA. The item bearing the mark should be placed in a rigid card folder or box to prevent further indentations occurring. Do not lean on the item to write exhibit labels.

- Transfer marks in dust on hard surfaces such as laminate flooring, window sills, and worktops, for example, can be recovered by a CSI utilising ESLA; care must be taken not to disturb these areas.

- Marks on non-porous surfaces can be recovered by CSIs who can employ a variety of techniques to locate and recover footwear marks similar to those used to recover fingerprints. Marks on porous surfaces can be recovered utilizing chemical reagent techniques.

- In areas where public access may be a problem, investigators should establish when the floor or surface was last cleaned. For example, an area in a shop can reasonably be expected to contain a lot of footwear marks; however if the incident occurred prior to the shop opening and the floor was cleaned after closing the previous day, the footwear recovered is likely to be of better quality and forensic value.

11.3 Tyre Marks

The same basic principles regarding footwear marks can be applied to tyre marks located at a crime scene. Tyre marks can be impressed into soil or cardboard or can be transferred marks, made in contaminants such as mud, paint or oil, for example. Tyre marks may also be present on clothing of a hit and run victim for instance. Tyre marks are only of forensic use for comparison purposes where a pattern is discernible, skid marks and scuffs with no apparent detail cannot be linked to a particular tyre by comparison of the patterning.

A CSI will initially photograph the tyre mark to show its relative position in the crime scene, followed by close-up shots to record the detail within the mark. Where a tyre mark has been transferred to a portable surface, such as a piece of board or a victim's clothing, the entire item should be recovered where possible. If a tyre mark has been wet and then subsequently dried onto a surface such as board, hard-coated floorings or plastic, for example, fingerprint powders or chemical enhancement techniques may be utilised to develop any marks.

11.3.1 Suspect tyres

A CSI or forensic vehicle examiner will be responsible for taking any impression from a suspect tyre for comparison purposes. The tyres must not be removed from the vehicle. They will be photographed and then one of two methods will be employed. Either the vehicle will be driven through a similar soft surface to that at the crime scene to replicate impressed marks which will be photographed. A cast will be made of the test mark which can be compared with a cast of the impression from the crime scene.

Alternatively, the tyre could be inked in a manner similar to that of taking a fingerprint. The vehicle is then moved along a roll of paper for at least one full revolution of the tyre, to produce an image of the tread patterns of the tyre.

11.3.2 Tyre marks at scenes

Tyre marks located at a crime scene can potentially lead to an identification of the brand of tyre, provided that enough detail is present in the mark. Marks that do not contain detail, such as skid marks, are of little use for this purpose.

The information on the side wall of tyres, such as brand name and model details, can sometimes be impressed into the side of the mud where a mark is deep enough. A cast of the tyre mark in these circumstances can record such details. Where a number of tyre marks have been left by the same vehicle, it may be possible to establish the width of the wheelbase. The information from the identification of a tyre brand and the width of the wheelbase can be of use to the investigation to establish the types of vehicle that may have been used.

When examining tyre marks to establish links between scenes and suspect tyres, the patterning specific to the brand and the unique wear and damage are compared, similar to the process used for footwear comparison.

Photographs of the tread patterns from a crime scene can be used to allow investigators to make comparisons to eliminate vehicles from the investigation; this is particularly useful where there are large numbers of vehicles to be checked. Care must be exercised, however, as tyres can easily and relatively quickly be changed.

11.4 **Tool Marks**

Tool marks, such as those left by an implement that has been used to force open a window, for example, are regularly found at crime scenes. The CSI should photograph the mark with a scale and take a three-dimensional cast of the mark where appropriate. Such marks can provide evidence that can occasionally lead to the identification of the tool or implement responsible, and by association possibly lead to an offender. Tool marks are also useful for identifying possible linked scenes. Typically, tool marks found at scenes fall into two general categories, lever marks and cutting marks.

11.4.1 **Lever marks**

Lever marks are created in surfaces where a jemmy, crowbar, screwdriver or such has been used to force entry. It may be possible to establish an indication as to the size and shape of an implement used. Lever marks are typically found in the frames of windows and doors. A CSI should photograph such marks with a scale (ruler) so that the image of the mark can be reproduced at actual size, and a three-dimensional cast of the mark should be taken.

Irregularities on the edges of tools, caused by the manufacturing process and the subsequent damage caused by use are uniquely identifiable to a particular tool. This can enable scientists to make a positive match between a tool mark and the instrument that made it. The minute striations and imperfections present in the mark have the most value, and ideally the item bearing the tool mark should be submitted for examination. Where this is not appropriate, a cast of the mark will contain the fine detail required for comparison purposes. Recording a mark by photography alone may not be sufficient for comparison purposes as the microscopic details may not be captured.

Where lever marks exist in a painted surface for instance, the CSI will also take a sample of the paint from the area. When a levering tool is used, it will pick up some of the paint onto the blade and deposit some of its coating/paint onto the area of impact (every contact leaves a trace); if such an instrument is recovered, comparison of the paint located on the tool with the paint recovered from the crime scene can provide further evidence to support a link between a tool and a scene.

11.4.2 **Cutting marks**

Cutting marks will be left when, for example, wire cutters or bolt croppers have been used to cut through padlocks, chains or metal link fencing, for example.

Where cutting tools have been used, the unique, microscopic imperfections from manufacture and damage due to use will be present on the cutting blades. When a cut is made, these imperfections will impart microscopic scratches (striations) on to the cut surface. The cut item such as a padlock, chain or part of a wire fence should be recovered and submitted for examination. The marks can be compared to establish potential links between scenes and where the cutting tool is recovered, comparisons can be made to establish a link between the tool and the cut items recovered from crime scenes.

As with lever marks, where a painted or coated surface has been cut it may be possible to establish links between scenes and the recovered tool through the examination of the paint or other coating material.

As with footwear and tyres, the microscopic details present on a tool will be changed with continued use so may not be capable of providing any comparative value if not recovered soon after the incident under investigation. However, if the tool has not been subsequently used following the incident, the characteristics for comparison may be present indefinitely.

11.5 **Chapter Summary**

Marks made by footwear, tyres and tools can, in the absence of the item that made them, potentially provide valuable intelligence to an investigator regarding the possible make and model of the footwear or tyre, or the generic type and size of a tool, such as establishing that the tool that made the mark is a 25mm flat-bladed or bevel-edged implement, for example. In the absence of an item to compare the marks to, the information provided is of intelligence value. However, when an item such as the suspect vehicle, footwear or tool is recovered, comparison between the marks at crime scenes and the item can provide strong evidence of contact.

There are different techniques available for the recovery of such marks from crime scenes, and by far the best evidence is to seize the item bearing the mark; however this is not always possible. Marks should be photographed to place them in context of the wider scene and then close up, with a scale (ruler) to record the detail in the mark. The next best recovery method for impressed marks, such as footwear in soil or a tool mark on a window frame is for the CSI to take a three-dimensional cast of the mark. There are methods available for the CSI to recover footwear or tyre marks from snow and from soil submerged in water.

Impressed marks in paper can be recovered by the use of ESDA. Surface transfer marks in dust can be recovered from hard surfaces such as laminated or tiled flooring or from kitchen worktops, for example, by the CSI utilising ESLA, which can also be used to recover marks in dust on vertical surfaces such as walls or doors. Conventional fingerprint recovery techniques can also be used to recover such marks.

Footwear marks will be present at every crime scene as offenders will have to have walked into and out of the scene, therefore investigators should be careful where they walk as such marks may not be immediately visible. It is important that CSIs are informed of the routes taken by initial responders, and where the incident is of a serious nature, a CAP should be identified.

Impressed marks in soil, for example, should be protected by covering them with a rigid container such as a box, the cover should not be in contact with the marks and care must be taken to avoid pushing further soil into the marks.

Footwear, tyres and tools can also provide evidence of contact with a crime scene due to transferred material such as body fluids, paint, glass or soil that may be present on them. The comparison of such materials between the scene samples and the item can provide strong evidence of contact. Investigators must be aware of the other potential evidence that may be available on recovered suspect footwear, tyres or tools and must wear gloves when handling such items.

KNOWLEDGE CHECK—FOOTWEAR, TYRE AND TOOL MARKS

1. What potential information can footwear marks at crime scenes initially provide to investigators?

   The make and model of the footwear can be determined by searching a reference database of footwear sole patterns. The size can be established, and if such information is not present in the mark (some footwear will have a size stamped on the sole) the size can be determined by a scientist.

   Footwear marks can indicate the number of people present and their movements around a scene.

   The marks can be searched on a database to establish if similar marks have been recovered from other scenes.

   Searches of footwear marks taken from suspects can be searched to establish the possibility of a link with crime scene marks.

   Where links are made between a suspect's footwear and crime scene marks, a scientist will undertake comparisons of the microscopic detail present on the footwear and in the crime scene marks to determine if the footwear made a particular mark.

2. Tyre marks are located in mud at a scene. What information can this provide to an investigator?

   The brand and model of the tyre can possibly be determined if enough detail is present in the mark. The information on the side wall of the tyre can leave impressions in the side of the mud trench.

   Where several tyre tracks are present from the same vehicle, the wheelbase of the suspect vehicle can potentially be established; this can narrow down the possible identity of the vehicle and eliminate some types of vehicle from an enquiry.

3. How can a recovered crowbar be forensically linked to a crime scene(s)?

The size and shape of the crowbar will initially be compared with the marks recovered at crime scenes to establish if they are similar. Examination of the unique marks left on the crowbar from manufacture and wear and tear will be compared with the scene marks to establish whether they share common characteristics, which could determine if a particular implement could have made a particular mark.

4. Where tyre or footwear marks in mud or soil are located at a crime scene, how should they be protected from adverse weather conditions?

Such marks should be protected with a rigid cover such as a box. The cover must not be in contact with the mark and care must be taken to ensure that soil is not pushed into the impression.

5. What is ESLA?

ESLA is an electrostatic lifting apparatus which can be used on compact surfaces such as laminate or tiled flooring, window sills, counter tops and even walls and doors to recover marks in dust.
A sheet of Mylar film that is black on one side is laid onto the surface and an electrostatic charge is applied to it. This charge attracts the fine dust particles to the sheet, to recover any marks present.

Recommended Reading

Criminalistics, 10th edn (2010) Saferstein, R.
Footwear Impression Evidence, Detection, Recovery and Examination, 2nd edn (2000) Bodziak, WJ.
Forensic Science (2011) Jackson, ARW and Jackson, J.

Appeal Court Ruling

R v T [2010] EWCA Crim 2439.

12

Glass, Paint and Soils

12.1 **Introduction**

Glass, paint and soils are capable of providing intelligence and potential forensic evidence to link persons to crime scenes. Such material may be present in microscopic amounts and as such can be easily lost over time, as it will tend to fall off any surface it initially adheres to.

The issue of inadvertent secondary transfer is a very real risk where microscopic amounts of material are concerned. Different investigators must recover potential evidence from different scenes; for example clothing from a suspect must not be seized by the same person who seizes clothing from a victim. A key area for potential secondary transfer is via police vehicles. Victims, suspects and witnesses should not be transported in the same vehicle where possible; it is advisable for officers to keep a note of the fleet number of the vehicle they use to transport such persons. Alternatively, paper covers should be placed on the seats and backrests to capture any material that may drop from transported persons, this paper can then be retained and exhibited.

This chapter gives a basic overview of the evidential value of glass, paint and soils and the considerations an officer will need to make regarding the forensic viability of glass, including the effects of the time elapsed between the commission of the offence and the recovery of items from a suspect.

12.2 **Glass**

Glass can be a valuable source of forensic evidence as microscopic fragments can potentially adhere to the clothing and hair of any person who breaks any sort of glass whether it originates from vehicles, premises, ornaments, bottles or drinking vessels, for example.

All glass contains traces of other elements due to impurities from the raw materials which contaminate the glass during manufacture. In addition, some elements may be deliberately added to create different colours and finishes in the glass. As glass is often broken in the commission of offences, particularly burglaries, theft of and theft from vehicles and some assaults it is possible to compare the glass at the scene with that recovered from a suspect's clothing.

The value of glass analysis is not restricted to these types of offences, however, and can be employed for incidents such as assault scenes where glass objects such as bottles or drinking vessels have been broken, or to determine if a person was in a vehicle when it crashed, or to provide links between a broken window and the object used.

In addition to the comparison of samples, glass will bear unique breakage features, so a physical fit between two samples may be possible. The way in which glass breaks can also provide information concerning the direction of the force and indicate the number of blows used which can assist investigators in establishing a sequence of events.

12.2.1 **Glass types**

The most frequently encountered types of glass in the environment are:

- soda-lime glass which is used for the manufacture of windows and bottles;
- specialised glass such as Pyrex glass, which contains higher levels of certain constituents (boron oxides);
- 'lead crystal' glass, which contains lead (II) oxides;
- toughened or tempered glass which has been heat treated so when it breaks it creates cuboid fragments, rather than sharp-edged shards. Typically this type of glass is found in the side and rear windows of vehicles;
- laminated glass which is produced by creating a 'sandwich' of plastic film in between two sheets of glass, and is typically used for vehicle windscreens and 'bullet-proof' glass.

The determination of the type of glass is often the first step in the analytical process.

12.2.2 **Glass Analysis and forensic potentials**

Fracture patterns

Figure 12.1 Side view of breaking glass

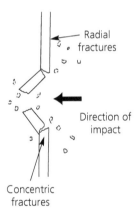

It can often be helpful to know from which side a piece of glass was broken. When a small projectile travelling at speed, such as a stone or bullet, breaks a window, a small crater-type hole will be evident which will be narrower on the side of impact. As the size of a projectile increases and velocity of impact decreases, the shape of the hole will be less likely to be representative of what caused it.

When non-toughened glass is broken by an impact, it will bend slightly under the force. This causes the glass on the side opposite the impact to stretch before breaking. This produces a series of 'radial' fractures which radiate out from the point of impact like spider legs. Figure 12.1 above shows a side view of what happens to glass on impact.

Where the impact is sufficient, the stretching effect causes the glass on the side of the impact to crack again, these cracks occur between the 'radial' fractures, in effect joining the 'spider legs' to form a web type pattern.

Figure 12.2 Fracture pattern to determine sequence of blows

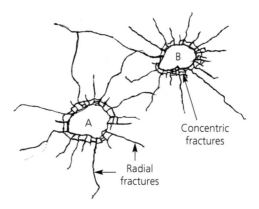

When a pane of glass undergoes successive impacts which do not break it, it is possible to see which impact came first as the radial fractures of secondary impacts will always terminate at the previous fracture. In Figure 12.2, the fracture pattern of (A) terminates when it meets the radial fracture of (B).

The bending and stretching of non-toughened glass during breakage also leaves distinct curved markings on the edges of the break, called chonchoidal lines, or hackle marks (Figure 12.3). At one end of the curve the mark will form an approximate right angle with the surface; the other end will run almost parallel with the opposite surface. The position of the mark can indicate from which side the glass was broken.

Figure 12.3 Chonchoidal lines on broken edge of glass

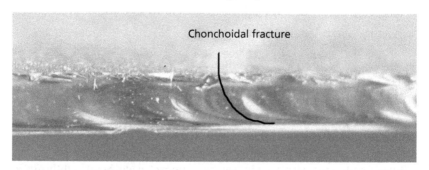

- On the edge of a radial crack the perpendicular side will always be on the *opposite side* of the impact.
- On the edge of a concentric crack it will be on the side of impact.

A simple way of remembering this principle is to consider the 4Cs: 'Concentric Cracks Curve on side of Collision (impact)' or the 3Rs: 'Radial cracks make Right angles on Reverse side of impact'.

There are a number of factors a scientist can consider when analysing glass, and the more points of comparison there are between a questioned sample and a control sample the stronger the evidential value.

- **Physical fit.** No two pieces of glass will break in exactly the same way, therefore it is sometimes possible to fit pieces of glass together to see if they originated from the same source. It is vital where this type of analysis is to be considered that the glass samples are packaged so as not to break further in transit.
- The scientific examination of glass has an established forensic analytical sequence beginning with the visual examination of fragments using microscopy. One key aspect at this stage is to establish if any fragments found are from recently broken glass. The analyst will be looking for clean sharp edges which will indicate that fragments originate from a recently broken source; older fragments will have more rounded edges. The fragments will be measured and then the glass refractive index will be ascertained.
- **Glass refractive index measurement (GRIM).** This analysis enables a scientist to make a comparison between the recovered scene sample and the questioned sample from a suspect, to ascertain if they share a common source. It is imperative that several samples from the crime scene are provided, as the refractive index can display slight variations within the same piece.
- The colour, thickness and density of the glass can be examined.
- The impurities present in the glass can also be analysed to give further support in a comparison of samples.

It is also important to bear in mind the potential presence of other evidence on glass, such as DNA, fingerprints, blood, fibres and footwear marks, for example.

12.2.3 **The persistency of glass**

There may be occasions, however, when despite contact with broken glass, very little if any material will be transferred. The degree of transfer is dependent on the nature of the receptor materials. Close woven smooth materials will not retain many fragments, whereas a fleecy type fabric will retain much more.

Transferred material such as glass fragments will be gradually lost from the surface retaining it; this factor is referred to as the 'persistency' of a material and is a factor that will affect particulate materials such as glass, paint and fibres, for example. The rate of loss for glass fragments is dependent on the size of the fragments, the nature of retaining surface combined with the subsequent use of the item. The amount of glass fragments will reduce where an item has been washed or continually worn following the commission of an offence. However, if an offender removes clothing following the act of breaking glass, and subsequently does not wear the item again, the glass fragments will be retained indefinitely until it is worn or washed.

Factors to consider regarding the retention of glass on clothing include the texture of the fabric as glass will adhere more readily to textured fabrics like wool or fleeces, for example, as opposed to smoother fabrics such as nylon or leather. However, it will settle into creases, seams and pockets where it can remain for longer.

12.2.4 Glass on suspects

When a pane of glass is broken, it will bend slightly under the impact causing fragments to fall both in the direction of the impact and backwards in an outward direction. This is referred to as backward fragmentation.

Glass fragments will fall onto anyone standing in the immediate vicinity with the number of fragments decreasing the further away a person is stood from the breaking glass (Figure 12.4.)

Figure 12.4 Backward fragmentation of breaking glass

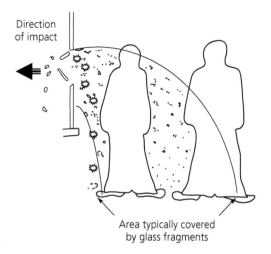

Direction
of impact

Area typically covered
by glass fragments

The distance travelled by glass fragments will vary according to their size and the force of any impact, with smaller fragments travelling further. Therefore, a person standing close to a window when it breaks can be expected to have glass fragments trapped in their hair, upper clothing, lower clothing, uppers and soles of shoes. A person standing further away may only have glass fragments on the lower half of their clothing.

- A person standing within a few feet of a window when it is broken is likely to be showered with hundreds of glass fragments.
- The number of glass fragments decreases as the distance from the impact increases.
- Very few glass fragments will travel as far as 3m from the window, and those that do will generally be very small (less than 0.5mm in size).

The fragments can be microscopic and may also be trapped in areas such as pockets, turn-ups and the seams of clothing and footwear, for example. The location of glass fragments on a person or their clothing may help a scientist to indicate how close a person was standing to the breaking glass. If such information is required, investigators must ensure that clothing is not shaken or handled too much during recovery as this will dislodge glass fragments. Figure 12.5 illustrates the typical potential evidential value that may be ascertained from the location of glass fragments recovered from a person or their clothing.

Investigators should discuss the individual requirements of a case with the forensic service provider or the crime scene investigator (CSI) where the location of recovered glass fragments may be an important factor in the investigation.

Figure 12.5 Decreasing evidential value of glass fragments

- Hair combings and shoe uppers
- Upper clothing
- Lower clothing
- Pockets/turn-ups
- Soles of shoes

Note:
- If a window was broken by being kicked for example, it would be stronger evidence if glass were found in the soles. Always bear in mind the individual requirements of a particular investigation.
- Glass can remain in pockets and turn-ups for some time; it can be possible to distinguish between fresh and old glass fragments as sharp edges of fragments will become blunted over time to become more rounded in appearance.
- Glass can come from any number of sources. Drinking glasses, ornaments, mirrors, and crockery for example can also be sources of glass fragments.

Consider the possibility of glass being on the clothing of witnesses or other third parties if they were in close proximity of where the incident occurred, as this can serve to corroborate or refute the allegations and versions of events being given. The requirement to consider witness clothing will be dependent on the case; it is always better to seize such clothing so all investigative options remain open.

12.2.5 Recovery of glass from scenes

There is a misconception that most window glass is all the same, due to the few sources of manufacture. This is not so. For example, the windows in any given vehicle or premises can differ greatly from each other forensically, due to windows being replaced or some being tinted, for instance. Each piece of glass will have microscopic characteristics that can be examined by a forensic scientist and can have variations across each individual pane; these variations can enable a scientist to link glass from a scene to that recovered from a suspect.

The recovery of glass from crime scenes is required in order to compare with any samples recovered from suspects. Ideally any samples required for forensic analysis should be recovered by a CSI. However, there will be occasions where investigators must recover items from crime scenes. Gloves must always be worn when recovering glass samples and the glass handled carefully by the edges, so as not to disturb any potential evidence.

Pieces of glass recovered from the scene of a burglary may contain 'pick out' marks (finger or glove marks), where offenders have removed pieces of glass from the frame to enable a safe entry into a premises. These marks are usually not visible and can easily be lost by improper handling and packaging.

Glass must never be placed straight into plastic bags as it can puncture the bag, allowing material to be lost, contamination of the sample can potentially occur and it can also cause injury to anyone who handles the exhibit.

POINT TO NOTE—TAKING GLASS SAMPLES FOR COMPARISON

Glass samples taken from broken windows for comparison purposes must always be recovered from the frame for integrity purposes. Samples must never be taken from the ground or from seats of vehicles under any circumstances if the sample is to have any evidential value.

Checklist—Samples required from a broken window of a premises

- Larger pieces of glass found on the floor at scenes can contain footwear marks, fingerprints, fibres and potential DNA material. These should remain *in situ* where possible and be preserved for recovery by a CSI. To protect such pieces from further damage they should be covered to protect them. The cover must not touch the surface of the glass. If the pieces cannot be covered *in situ*, they can be carefully moved to a safe area. Investigators should mark the original position of the glass and inform the CSI of this. If the glass cannot be protected safely and securely then investigators should consider recovering and exhibiting the glass.

- Larger pieces of glass should be secured into a rigid box to ensure further breakage is avoided and that any fingerprints, footwear marks, DNA material and other potential evidence is not rubbed off by friction. Secure the glass in place with string or cable ties. Adhesive tapes should not be used to secure glass into a box, as this can damage other potential evidence types.

- When secured into a rigid container such as a box, the glass should then be sealed into a tamper-evident bag or, if the glass is wet or damp a paper evidence bag. It is important that the glass is packaged in such a way as to prevent movement of the pieces which will cause further breakage and damage.

- At least six pieces of glass are required from different parts of each frame. All pieces from one frame can be one exhibit, labelled as 'Glass samples from frame of kitchen window', for example. For double-glazed panes, at least six pieces from each pane are required.

- One piece of the glass should ideally contain a mark denoting the interior or exterior surface.

- It is useful to take a measurement of the distance between the ground level and the sill of the broken window if possible. A sketch plan of the broken window in relation to other fixed points may be useful.

- Any pieces of glass recovered that contain stains that may be blood must have the exterior of the packaging clearly labelled 'biohazard'.

- This process should be undertaken for each broken window. Samples from several windows must be exhibited separately.

Checklist—Samples of glass required from the broken windows of vehicles

- The windscreen of a vehicle will be made of laminated glass and the side and rear windows are typically toughened glass.

- About fifty 'pebbles' from each window frame, where possible, should be taken.

- Laminated glass from the windscreen should contain both layers, with a piece marked to denote the interior or exterior surface: this piece should ideally be packaged separately in order for the scientist to be able to quickly identify it from the rest.

This can be achieved by wrapping the marked piece in paper or placing it into a small bag which can then be packaged with the remainder of the sample.

- The sample should then be packaged either in a paper envelope that is tightly rolled/wrapped to secure the glass, or into a rigid container such as a poly pot, sealed into a tamper-evident bag.

- Samples from different window frames are separate exhibits and the location of where recovered from should be stated, for example: 'Glass sample from R/O/S (rear off side) window frame'.

- Glass from mirrors and headlamps will contain variations even within vehicles of the same make and model. This can be analysed to provide potential links between a vehicle and a scene.

- Generally, vehicle glass breaks in a manner that is too small for the recovery of fingerprints; however fibres and possible blood may be present.

12.3 **Paint**

Paint is a material that is almost everywhere in our environment in various forms. Although it is mass produced, it displays wide variation as the manufacturing process uses over a thousand differing types of raw materials including pigments, additives, binders, solvents, oils and anti-mildew agents, all in numerous combinations and quantities according to the paint type. The most commonly encountered paint samples submitted for analysis are architectural and vehicle paints. Where an implement such as a crowbar has been used to force open a painted window frame, there is the potential for a two-way transfer. Paint from the window frame can adhere to the tip of the crowbar, and any paint already on the crowbar can also be transferred to the window frame, thus establishing a link between the frame and the crowbar.

An offender who has forced open a painted window or door may have fragments of paint on their clothing. Where force occurs, such as when a tool is used to force a window or a person is hit by a vehicle, paint fragments will be embedded onto the tool or in the victim's clothing. This impacted paint will bear a distinctive appearance and can provide evidence of impact as opposed to a casual light contact.

Where paint has been used in criminal damage or hate crime graffiti cases, for example, samples from the scene can be analysed and may provide intelligence information regarding the make and type of paint. Paint may be present on a suspect's clothing, hair or footwear that can be compared to samples recovered at the scene. Where paint cans are recovered from a scene, these should be submitted to the laboratory as whole items rather than taking a sample from the can, in order to preserve the integrity of the sample and avoid any potential contamination of the sample.

12.3.1 **Vehicle paint**

Where vehicles collide with another surface, paint may be transferred between the vehicle and the surface upon which it impacts. These samples may be present as smears or as flakes or chips which can be forensically analysed to potentially provide links between scenes and persons.

Vehicle paints generally consist of at least four coatings:

- pre-treatment coating—typically a zinc electroplating designed to inhibit the development of rust;
- primer—epoxy resin containing corrosion resistant pigments;
- top coat—which can be a single, multi or metallic colour layer; and
- clear coat—which is an unpigmented coating added for gloss and durability.

It can be possible, in certain circumstances for a scientist to determine the make, model and age range of a vehicle from paint samples left at the scene of an incident. This will be difficult where a vehicle has been resprayed as the reference databases contain information of paint coatings applied at the time of the vehicle manufacture. However, a resprayed vehicle can have a higher evidential value in many situations.

Checklist—Analysis of paint samples

- Physical fit of larger paint flakes recovered from a scene to a suspect's vehicle for example, in a hit and run incident.

- Colour analysis—the multitude and combinations of colours and shades that exist provide paint with its most distinctive forensic viability. The information can provide valuable intelligence to an investigation.

- The number of layers can be microscopically examined—architectural and vehicle paint will most likely display layers of different colours in various combinations. The structure and sequence of these layers can provide good points for comparison to link two or more samples.

- Chemical composition of additives or pigments can be identified.

- Environmental contaminants may be sealed within the paint sample which can possibly be identified and give further points for comparison and intelligence information.

Very often, however, paint samples from scenes are not present in good-sized flakes with distinct layering. It is fairly commonplace to find paint as smears, for which physical fit and layer sequences may not be viable options for analysis. However, the colour, type and chemical composition can be analysed to provide useful information for investigators and determine whether two samples have a common origin.

....

Case study—Paint analysis in series of sexual offences

A series of sexual offences occurred over a period of time at a university student nurse residential halls. No DNA or fingerprint evidence was recovered to identify an offender. Following the last assault, the offender was disturbed by a security guard and escaped in a vehicle. The vehicle scraped against a wooden gatepost at the exit, leaving a small smear of paint on the post. This was noted by the initial responder. Following analysis of the paint, a manufacturer was identified who gave the make and models of the vehicles that had that paint. A check with DVLA gave details of the owners and locations of such vehicles. Investigators could then narrow down the search according to geography and the age of the vehicle.

The offender was apprehended. Damage to his car was consistent with paint left at scene and he also had items belonging to his victims and photographs indicating he had been watching the hall and movement of victims. He was convicted of the offences.

This case highlights how, without DNA and fingerprint evidence, and a good investigation, an offender can still be brought to justice.

....

12.3.2 Recovery of paint samples

Paint samples required for forensic analysis should ideally be recovered by a CSI, as the recovery process requires the use of clean scalpel blades to scrape an area of paint down to the bare surface from the window frame, vehicle or surface in question. Where visible paint flakes are found at a scene or adhering to clothing of a victim or suspect, these can be collected using tweezers and packaged in paper envelopes sealed into tamper-evident bags. If physical fit will be required, it is vital the paint flake does not receive further damage so it must be packaged in a rigid container. Paint samples should not be recovered on adhesive tape as this can interfere with some analytical results.

Clothing required for the examination of paint must not be shaken or unduly handled as material can be lost. The persistency of paint fragments on clothing, hair or implements such as crowbars will depend on the factors as outlined above for glass fragments.

12.4 Soils

Soils are made up of organic matter, minerals and manmade materials such as fragments of brick, glass, concrete or water. Soils can readily adhere to surfaces that are in contact with it and are easily transferred to other sites such as inside vehicles and premises. Soil samples recovered from shoes, clothing, vehicle tyres and wheel arches, for example, may be examined and compared to samples recovered from crime scenes. It can be possible for samples recovered from suspects or their vehicles to be identified as originating from a particular location, which can open up further lines of enquiry for investigators.

Forensically, soils can provide information to an investigation regarding the potential source of a soil sample and may provide evidential links between scenes and suspects. The composition of soil will differ greatly between locations; even neighbouring gardens can have differing soil types due to the variations in what individuals grow or use as fertilizers for instance. At any location soil will also differ in its composition at various depths. The differences observable at varying depths is referred to as the soil profile and will appear as horizontal bands or layers each bearing different characteristics. The checklist below outlines what the forensic analysis of soil samples will typically include.

Checklist—forensic analysis of soil samples

The forensic analysis of soil samples will typically include the following:

- visual observations of the colour and texture;
- microscopic examination of the structure of the soil which may also reveal the presence of man-made, plant or animal material;
- the determination of any minerals and rock fragments;
- determination of the soil particle sizes and distribution.

One difficulty with establishing the evidential significance of soil samples arises due to the natural variation of soil in any given location and between differing areas. The comparison of a sample recovered from a scene with a sample from suspect's footwear for instance, relies on the determination of as many features as possible that are present in both samples. The more points of comparison the samples have in common, the stronger the link. However, unless there is something unique in both samples, that can be shown to only occur in the location of the scene, such a link will not be conclusive evidence.

Soil analysis is not routinely used in the investigation of volume crimes but should be a consideration for more serious cases where appropriate. The samples required from a scene should be recovered by a CSI or forensic scientist. Investigators are more likely to be recovering clothing from suspects or victims for the examination of potential forensic evidence which may include glass, paint and soil.

....

Case study—Soil indicates possible burial site

Soil samples were recovered from the tyres and wheel arches of a vehicle examined during a murder investigation where no body had been recovered.

....

....

The soil was analysed and found to be quite distinctive, the composition of which was analysed and found to originate from a relatively small area of open land. This gave investigators a good indication as to where the body may have been deposited. The area was searched and contained many natural underground tunnels that could be the deposition site for the body.

No body was recovered at this site; however, the soil analysis did give investigators an insight of the movements of the vehicle in the relevant time frames.

....

12.5 **Chapter Summary**

Transferred material such as glass, paint and soil can provide evidence of contact. When recovered from crime scenes and compared with samples recovered from a suspect or victim, links can be established between them.

The analysis of vehicle paint, in the absence of a sample for comparison, can provide potentially valuable intelligence to an investigator regarding the possible make, model and age range of vehicle.

Glass can provide information that can include establishing the number and sequence of blows and the direction of the impact which caused it to break.

The analysis of soil can, in certain circumstances, indicate the possible geographical location of its origin.

The retention of glass, paint and soil on surfaces is dependent on factors such as the nature of the receptor surface, the amount of material transferred, the pressure and duration of the contact and whether the receptor surface is subject to subsequent wear, activity, or washing following the incident.

Trace amounts of glass, paint or soils which are not readily visible can be present on the hair, clothing and shoes of victims and suspects. As such small amounts of material are easily transferable, this makes them extremely susceptible to inadvertent cross-transfer. Where evidence of contact is required, it is vital that there can be no allegation or suggestion that any evidence found on one item is as a result of cross-transfer from another item. Investigators must not recover such potential evidence from more than one person involved with the incident. Victims, suspects and witnesses should not be transported in the same vehicle; it is advisable for investigators to keep a note of the fleet number of the vehicle they use to transport such persons. Alternatively, paper covers should be placed on the seats and seat backs to capture any material that may fall from transported persons, this paper can then be retained and exhibited.

KNOWLEDGE CHECK—GLASS, PAINT AND SOIL

1. A vehicle has had all its windows smashed, what samples would be required for analysis?

Samples are required from each broken window and should consist of about fifty 'pebbles' of glass taken from the frames.

Each sample from different windows will be a separate exhibit.

The exhibit label should denote which window the sample came from.

Laminated glass from the windscreen should contain both layers and one piece marked to indicate internal or external surface.

The samples should be either securely wrapped in a paper envelope or placed into a rigid container such as a poly pot, and then sealed into a tamper-evident bag.

2. State the factors that determine the presence and retention rates of glass fragments on a person.

Glass fragments will adhere more readily to textured surfaces such as wool or fleecy material. Close woven fabrics such as nylon or leathers will not generally retain glass fragments readily; fragments that have been impacted into the fabric by use of force may be retained for relatively longer periods.

The distance of a person from breaking glass will determine how many glass fragments will be present on hair and clothing.

The activity following the breaking of the glass will impact on how much can be recovered from hair or clothing, but in general most fragments will be lost after an hour of normal wear. However, if clothing is removed and not worn or washed following the incident, glass can still be present.

Fragments can settle into pockets, turn-ups and seams and will be retained for longer; it can be possible to distinguish between fresh and old glass fragments as sharp edges of fragments will become blunted over time to become more rounded in appearance.

3. What considerations should be made regarding the evidential value of the positioning of glass fragments on a person?

The position of glass fragments on a person can provide information to corroborate or refute versions of events. Where a person has stood by a window and smashed it, glass fragments would be expected to be recovered from the following:

- hair and shoe uppers;
- upper clothing;
- lower clothing;
- pockets/turn-ups; and/or
- soles of shoes.

The evidential value will be determined according to where the fragments are found. Thus, if they are only found in the soles of the shoes, this would not be strongly supportive of a person standing next to the window, as they could have merely walked through the fragments on the floor.

However, if a window was broken by being kicked, for example, it would be stronger evidence if glass were found in the soles of the shoes. The individual requirements of a particular investigation must be considered when assessing the evidential value of glass.

4. A smear of paint is left on a gatepost as a result of an impact with a vehicle being driven away from the scene of a dwelling burglary. What can forensic analysis of the paint provide to investigators?

Vehicle paint can be analysed to determine colour and the chemical composition of the sample. This can then be checked against a reference database which contains most of the paint compositions used during manufacture of the vehicle. It may be possible to determine a particular make, model and age range of an unknown vehicle from the sample.

This becomes increasingly difficult to determine where a vehicle has been resprayed with paint other than that used for the factory finishes.

Such information can provide investigators with lines of enquiry to follow up.

Recommended Reading

Criminalistics, 10th edn (2010) Saferstein, R.
Forensic Examination of Glass and Paint: Analysis and Interpretation (2001) Caddy, B.
Forensic Science, 3rd edn (2011) Jackson, ARW and Jackson, J.

Appeal Court Ruling

R v T [2010] EWCA Crim 2439.

13

Hair and Fibres

13.1 **Introduction**

The human body contains millions of hairs which can be shed naturally or pulled out during a struggle. In a forensic capacity, head and pubic hair are the most commonly encountered hair at crime scenes and can be a valuable source of evidence.

Hair that has a root with a sheath containing cellular material from the skin can potentially provide DNA that can be profiled and searched on the national DNA database (NDNAD). Where no root is present, there is the possibility that mitochondrial DNA (MtDNA) could be recovered. In addition to possible DNA evidence, the length and colour of hair can be of some use for intelligence purposes and a microscopic examination can, in some cases, provide investigators with the racial origin of the donor.

A scientist can establish whether the recovered hair is human or animal in origin by examination of the physical characteristics. Hair can also provide information on drug usage to establish whether a person has regularly ingested a particular substance over a period of time.

Fibres can provide evidence of contact between people and textile items; for example in cases of assaults involving close contact, fibres from the offender's clothing will be transferred onto the victim's clothing and vice versa. Scientific analysis of fibres can determine the type of fibre, the colour and in some cases may also be able to extract pigments which can be analysed to establish a possible origin; for example, a dye that may have be used by a particular manufacturer to produce certain items. However, due to the mass production and distribution of textiles, this is not always possible. Each case must be assessed on the particular circumstances.

Hairs and fibres are capable of providing intelligence and potential forensic evidence to link persons to crime scenes. The presence of hairs and fibres may not be readily visible and such material can be easily lost over time as it will tend to fall off the surfaces it initially adheres to. As such material may not be readily visible to the naked eye, inadvertent secondary transfer of material is a real risk. Different investigators must recover potential evidence from different scenes; clothing from a suspect must not be seized by the same person seizing clothing from a victim, for example.

A key area for potential secondary transfer is via police vehicles. Victims, suspects and witnesses should not be transported in the same vehicle where possible. It is advisable for investigators to keep a note of the fleet number of the vehicle they use to transport such persons. Alternatively, paper covers should be placed on the seats and backrests to capture any material that may fall from transported persons, this paper can then be retained and exhibited.

This chapter gives a basic overview of the evidential value of hairs and fibres and outlines the considerations an officer will need to make regarding effects of the time elapsed between the commission of the offence and the recovery of items from a suspect.

13.2 **Hairs**

Hair can be recovered from crime scenes and examined to provide information to investigators and establish links between scenes and people

Hair grows from follicles in the skin and has three distinct growth stages.

- The active 'anagen' phase, where hair is growing at the maximum rate. During the anagen phase, the hair has a good root and it requires some force to remove the hair. If a root sheath is present and the hair is in the anagen growth phase, a scientist may be able to conclude that the hair has been subject to forcible removal, which can include vigorous brushing or combing and inadvertent snagging as well as being pulled out during a struggle.
- The 'catogen' phase where growth is slowing and the root begins to reduce in size.
- The 'telogen' phase where the hair has ceased growing and the root has reduced to a size that will no longer anchor the hair in the follicle. It is during the 'telogen' phase that hair falls out naturally. At this stage the hair has no root sheath and is not viable for obtaining material that can be searched on the NDNAD; however, MtDNA may be obtained. A root without a sheath indicates that the hair fell out naturally. If the root is not present, an even break with regular edges indicates that it was cut off, and an irregular break generally means that the hair was broken off.

Hairs recovered from crime scenes will typically be in the first or third stage of growth, where they have been naturally shed or pulled out by force. Consider the potential for hairs to be present on weapons that have been used; for example, where someone has been hit over the head with a baseball bat, their hair may be transferred onto the bat to offer corroborative evidence of the assault.

13.2.1 **Analysis and evidential potentials of hair**

The physical characteristics of hair and the chemical isotopes that can be found in hair can provide valuable information to an investigator, which can serve to open up lines of enquiry, eliminate or implicate suspects, lead to identification of a person and provide links between suspects, victims and scenes which can be used as evidence.

Physical analysis of hair

A scientist will examine the hair microscopically to determine whether the hair is human or animal in origin. The microscopic examination of the physical characteristics of hair will determine the colour(s), the width of the hair, the structure of the central core (medulla), and the structure of the scales on the outer surface of the hair, which make it possible to determine whether the hair is human or animal in origin. In the case of human hair, examination can also potentially determine the following.

241

- The possible location on the body that the hair has come from, for example, pubic hair has different characteristics from the hair from the scalp.
- Hair can display characteristics which can indicate the racial origin of the donor.
- Animal hair will display variations according to species, making it possible to identify which species a sample originates from.
- A scientist can examine the shape of the root, which can indicate whether force was used to remove the hair.

The examination of hairs recovered from crime scenes can provide intelligence to investigators, by indicating the colour(s) and length of the hair of a possible offender, for example; however this can be of limited value as hair can be cut or dyed different colours.

The analysis of hair can provide evidence that varies in its strength: good evidence may be provided from hair that has been dyed and has an area of undyed regrowth available, whereas undyed hair of a mid-brown colour, for example, may provide less evidential strength. Each case must be assessed on the particular requirements.

Chemical analysis of hair

Hair will generally grow about a centimetre a month, and as hair growth is essentially fed by the bloodstream, it stores traces of substances that flow through the blood, including the chemicals that are present in water, food, the air we breathe and drugs ingested. The hair therefore can act as a record of the diet and/or drug use of a person through analysis of the isotopes in the hair.

The physical and chemical analysis of hairs can provide investigators with valuable information. However, if the donor of the sample is unknown and there is no DNA material present, identification of the donor is not possible. It also must be borne in mind that whilst hair can differ from person to person, wide variation can also be observed in the hairs from one individual.

Recovery of hair samples

An offender's hair may be snagged on a window frame at a burglary, caught in jewellery or pulled out during an assault, or found in a hat, face covering or mask that has been dropped at a crime scene, for example. It will be necessary for officers to recover hair from a suspect if a comparison with hair recovered from the scene is required. To recover a sample for comparison purposes with hair recovered from a scene (whether a victim's or suspect's hair) or for drugs analysis, a hair collection module should be used.

Checklist—Considerations when taking hair samples

- Hair combings for glass, paint or other such evidence, if required should be done first.
- Hair samples taken from a person should be from the same area of the body as the hair at the scene. Comparison of head hair cannot be undertaken with pubic hair,

for example. (Head hair samples are classed as non-intimate whereas pubic hair is intimate and can only be taken by a medical practitioner.)

- A representative sample of at least twenty-five hairs is required, cut from as close to the scalp as possible.

- Do not use tweezers to remove the hair as this may cause crushing to the surface of the hair.

- Cut hair from various sites around the head to obtain a representative sample of lengths and colours.

- Place the hair onto the paper cover provided in the hair collection kit. Carefully fold the paper containing the hair sample and place in tamper-evident bag. The exhibit should be stored in a dry store.

Where hair is observed at a crime scene, such as snagged on a broken window, on a weapon or on the broken window of a vehicle involved in a hit and run for instance, it may be necessary for investigators to recover such samples if they are at risk of being lost. This can be done by carefully removing the hair with clean tweezers or with gloved fingers. The hair should then be placed into a piece of folded paper or an envelope and then sealed into a tamper-evident bag and exhibited. Another method for recovering such samples is to use an adhesive tape, pressed onto the hair. The tape should then ideally be placed onto an acetate sheet, but a piece of clean transparent plastic bag, or paper would suffice. This should then be sealed into a tamper-evident bag and exhibited.

13.3 **Fibres**

Fibre evidence is potentially present at virtually any type of crime scene, although it may not be readily seen with the naked eye. A CSI or forensic examiner can utilise high intensity light sources to search for and locate fibres. This technique is non-destructive and can enable otherwise non-visible fibres to be easily located due to the fluorescent properties in many fibres.

Fibres are everywhere in the environment and can provide good evidence of contact. Fibres in clothing, from vehicle seats, carpets and bedding for instance will potentially transfer onto items that come into contact with them. This two-way transfer can provide some very strong links between a person's clothing, the crime scene and other associated areas.

....

Case study—Fibre links to murderer

Sarah Payne was eight years old when she went missing on 1 July 2000. A suspect was identified and his van was seized for forensic examination. Seventeen days after Sarah went missing, her body was recovered.

....

A shoe was recovered near to the body's deposition site and identified as belonging to Sarah. This was the only item of Sarah's clothing to be recovered. The shoe had a Velcro strap which had trapped 350 fibres. Fibres from the shoe matched fibres from a red sweatshirt recovered from the suspect's van. This evidence was further strengthened by the presence of a multi-coloured cotton fibre on the shoe; this was found to have come from fabric that had been produced for Boots the Chemist as curtains for their baby changing rooms. It was established that only 1,500m of this fabric had been produced, meaning that such fabric was fairly unusual and unlikely to be found in general use. This matched fibres from a clown curtain recovered from the back of the van. In addition other fibre links were established between Sarah's clothing, the suspect's clothing and seats in the van, and at the site at which Sarah was found.

The defence put forward the argument that the number of fibres present was not enough to provide conclusive links. However, the scientist explained that although the fibres may not be unusual in their composition, this did not reduce the value of the links and that the combination of fibres could provide extremely strong evidence of contact between Sarah, the van and the suspect. Due in part to the evidence provided by one hair and the fibres, Roy Whiting was found guilty of the kidnap and subsequent murder of Sarah and sentenced to life imprisonment in December 2001.

The mass production and wide distribution of many textiles can limit the evidential value of fibres, and only in exceptional circumstances can fibres produce a conclusive identification of an unknown item. However, as illustrated in the above case study, the combination of fibres, even commonly encountered ones, can provide strong evidence of contact.

13.3.1 **Analysis and evidential potential of fibres**

Fibres will fall into two broad categories: natural fibres such as wool, silk or cotton and manufactured synthetic fibres such as nylon and polyester. Analysis can establish the fibre type in the first instance. With regard to fibres that originate from animals such as wool, the examination will follow the procedures as outlined for hair.

Synthetically produced fibres can also be identified by the microscopic examination of the physical characteristics such as colour, diameter and the shape of the cross-section. In addition, synthetic fibres may contain a delusterant, added during manufacture to reduce shine.

Fibres that have been dyed may be chemically analysed to establish the composition of the pigments. The more points for comparison that can be achieved to link a sample from a crime scene and a suspect sample, the stronger the evidential value.

The significance and evidential value of fibre evidence will depend on the circumstances of the case, and the number, combinations and nature of the fibres recovered.

13.3.2 **Recovery of fibres**

Fibres may be snagged on a window frame at a burglary, caught in items of jewellery during an assault, or on a vehicle that has hit someone, for example. Fibres in some form will be available at almost all crime scenes where contact is made with textile surfaces. Ideally fibres at a crime scene should be recovered by a CSI; however, there may be occasions when it will be necessary for investigators to recover such potential evidence from the suspect, victim, or scene.

Checklist—Considerations when recovering potential fibre evidence from a person

- Hair combings should be done prior to the removal of clothing using a hair collection module.

- Visible clumps of fibres should be recovered with tweezers or gloved fingers if there is a danger they will be lost.

- Place the fibres onto a piece paper (provided in the hair collection kit). Carefully fold the paper containing the fibres and place in tamper-evident bag. The exhibit should be stored in a dry store.

- Fibres can easily be transferred; investigators must not recover the clothing of more than one individual relating to the incident. Different investigators must recover clothing from suspects and victims and different locations must be used to avoid inadvertent transfer of fibres.

- Clothing required for the examination of fibres must not be shaken or unduly handled as material can be lost.

- Where fibres are readily observed at a crime scene, such as when they are snagged on a broken window, a weapon or on the broken window of a vehicle involved in a hit and run, it may be necessary for initial responders to recover such samples to prevent them being lost. Fibres are fragile evidence and can easily be dislodged. Recover fibres by carefully removing them with clean tweezers or with gloved fingers.

13.3.3 **Recovery of fibres from a body**

As hairs and fibres are generally readily transferred during the contact of persons and surfaces, a great deal of potential evidence is likely to be on the clothing on a deceased victim. In serious cases a process known as 1-2-1 taping or fibre mapping can be undertaken by a CSI. As the location of hair/fibres on the body can serve to corroborate or refute versions of events it is vital that they are recovered in a systematic and methodical manner. This method is best undertaken where a body and its clothing has not been subject to post-mortem disturbance since the arrival of initial responders; for example where paramedics or initial responders have moved the body or disturbed clothing.

This task must only ever be undertaken by a CSI or similarly trained investigator.

1-2-1 taping is best undertaken at the scene where at all possible to prevent loss of material during transportation to the mortuary. It is a time consuming process but it does maximise the recovery of potential evidence.

Numbered strips of low tack adhesive tape are applied to the clothing. This allows for the accurate location of every fibre on the body to be determined and enables the scientist to examine the distribution of material and interpret the results in relation to the particular case (see Figure 13.1).

Figure 13.1 Example of tape placement for 1-2-1 taping

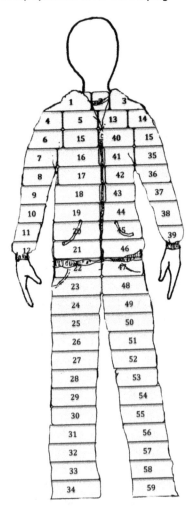

The decision to recover fibres using the 1-2-1 fibre mapping techniques is generally taken in serious cases, although zonal fibre taping, whereby one piece of tape is used to collect hairs/fibres from a particular area, such as the backrest of a vehicle seat, for example, is a routine method of recovering fibre/hair evidence from vehicles, carpets, items of recovered clothing, furniture and possibly even textured wall surfaces. The tape used for fibre recovery must be specific for the purpose and stored in a clean container to prevent extraneous fibres from the environment attaching to the tape during storage.

13.4 **Transfer and Retention of Hairs and Fibres**

Many common fibres are used in manufacture of clothing, household textiles, carpets, rugs, cushions and vehicle seats. In most environmental conditions fibres are resistant to environmental factors such as biological, physical and chemical degradation and can persist intact for long periods of time. However there may be occasions when despite contact, very little—if any—material will be transferred. The degree of transfer depends on various factors, which include:

- the nature of the materials—closely woven materials will not generally retain or shed fibres whereas a fleecy type fabric will retain and shed much more readily; and
- the extent of the contact—a brief brush past two people will generally provide less transferred material than where close prolonged contact has been made. The length of time and strength or pressure of contact will affect the availability of transferred material.

The amount of transferred hairs or fibres will be reduced where an item has been washed or continually worn following the commission of an offence. However, if clothing, for example, is removed soon after the incident, and is subsequently not worn, the hairs and fibres will be retained indefinitely until such items are worn or washed.

13.5 **Chapter Summary**

Transferred material such as hair and fibres can provide evidence of contact. When recovered from crime scenes and compared with hairs and fibres recovered from a suspect or victim, links can be established between them. The analysis of hairs and fibres, in the absence of a sample to compare them with, can provide potentially valuable intelligence to an investigator regarding the possible origin of the material.

Hair acts like a filter and can retain certain substances transported by the bloodstream and in certain circumstances, analysis may determine aspects of lifestyle such as the use of drugs and diet, which can be of value to investigators. Where hair has a root with a sheath attached, it can be possible to obtain a DNA profile suitable for loading onto the NDNAD. Where a root is not present, MtDNA may be extracted from the hair shaft.

The transferability and retention of hairs and fibres is dependent on factors such as the nature of the receptor surface, the amount of material transferred, the pressure and duration of the contact and whether the receptor surface is subject to any subsequent wear, activity, or washing following the incident.

Fibres can be searched for and located by the use of high intensity light sources, which cause many fibres to fluoresce brightly against the background. Screening areas for fibres with such a light source should only be undertaken by an appropriately trained CSI or forensic examiner. It is a non-destructive method for the search and recovery of potential fibre evidence. Fibres can be present on the hair and clothing of victims and suspects which are not readily visible. As fibres are easily transferable this makes them extremely susceptible to inadvertent cross-transfer. Where evidence of contact is required it is vital that there can be no allegation or suggestion that any evidence found on one item is as a result of cross-transfer from another item. Investigators must not recover such potential evidence from more than one person involved with the incident. Victims, suspects and witnesses should not be transported in the same vehicle. It is advisable for investigators to keep a note of the fleet number of the vehicle they use to transport such persons. Alternatively, paper covers should be placed on the seats and backrests to capture any material that may fall from transported persons, this paper can then be retained and exhibited.

KNOWLEDGE CHECK—HAIR AND FIBRES

1. What information can be provided by the analysis of hair?

   The analysis of hair can determine:

   - whether the hair is human or animal in origin (if animal hair, a scientist may be able to determine the species);
   - possibly the racial origin of the donor;
   - information regarding colour, length, and any dyes present, although this is of limited value as hair can be cut and dyed;
   - whether it is head hair or pubic hair;
   - various lifestyle factors such as drugs taken and possible diet;
   - the potential identification of an individual if a root with a sheath is present and DNA can be extracted; and
   - whether hair has been removed by force or has fallen out naturally.

2. Describe the procedure for recovering hair from a person for comparison or drug analysis purposes.

- A hair collection module must be used.

- Hair combings for glass, paint, fibres or other such evidence, if required should be done first.

- Wearing gloves, a representative sample of at least 25 hairs is required, cut from as close to the scalp as possible. Hair should be cut from different areas around the head to obtain a representative sample of length and colours.

- Tweezers should not be used to remove the hair as they can damage the surface of the hair.

- Place the hair onto the paper cover provided in the hair collection kit. Carefully fold the paper containing the hair sample and place in tamper-evident bag. The exhibit should be stored in a dry store.

- It is important that hair samples taken from a person should be from the same area of the body as the hair at the scene. Comparison cannot be undertaken of head hair with pubic hair. Pubic hair is classed as an intimate sample and can only be taken by a medical practitioner.

3. How can investigators demonstrate the integrity of potential hair and fibre evidence?

The transferability of hairs and fibres means that inadvertent transfer can occur which may render any potential evidence inadmissible.

In order to avoid such transfer, investigators must not deal with more than one person involved in the incident. For example, the same officer must not deal with different suspects and victims as the defence may argue that the fibres on a suspect came from the officer who had just dealt with the victim. Investigators must be mindful that a key area for the transfer of such material is in police vehicles, thus suspects and victims must be transported in different vehicles where possible. It is advisable to place a paper cover on the seat which will also cover the backrest for the person to sit on. This paper cover must then be retained and exhibited as it will potentially contain material that has fallen from the person during transportation. Be mindful that this may be upsetting to victims, and ensure that an explanation of why this action is necessary is provided (to preserve the maximum amount of potential evidence in the investigation of the incident).

4. State the factors that influence the transferability and retention of hairs and fibres.

The transferability and retention of fibres is affected by:

- The nature of the receptor surface; for example close woven nylon will not shed or retain fibres readily, whereas a mohair jumper would both shed and retain other transferred fibres for a lot longer.

- The pressure of contact, since more fibres will be transferred during prolonged close contact than when two people swiftly brush past each other.

- The subsequent activity following the contact. Continued wear and washing will reduce the quantity of any transferred hairs and fibres. However, if clothing is removed and stored soon after the incident the transferred material can remain indefinitely.

Recommended Reading

Criminalistics, 10th edn (2010) Saferstein, R.
Forensic Science, 3rd edn (2011) Jackson, ARW and Jackson, J.

Drugs of Abuse

14.1 **Introduction**

There are many types of drugs taken by people for recreational purposes because of the mood enhancing or altering qualities they possess. These can be illegally produced or diverted from lawful sources. The main legislation regarding the control of drugs is the Misuse of Drugs Act 1971, which defines and classifies what are referred to as controlled drugs.

Controlled drugs are categorised in accordance with the harm they can cause to health:

- **Category A** are the most harmful to health and include cocaine, crack, heroin, ecstasy, methamphetamine (crystal meth), LSD (lysergic acid diethylamide), magic mushrooms and amphetamines prepared for injection;
- **Category B** includes amphetamine in powdered form, barbiturates, cannabis, codeine and ketamine;
- **Category C** drugs are regarded as the least harmful of the controlled drugs and include anabolic steroids, some mild amphetamines, khat and cannabis leaf and resin.

There are several key questions that need to be addressed when investigating drug offences. Depending on the case, these will typically include the identification of the substance in question, the quantities of any controlled drug, whether the sample can be linked to other samples to establish a location of origin of the drugs and whether any drugs in body fluid or tissue samples are of a concentration sufficient to have caused intoxication or death.

This chapter will provide a basic overview of the most commonly encountered controlled drugs and the production methods, scene handling and the forensic potentials available.

14.2 **Types of Drugs**

The types of controlled recreational drugs commonly encountered include cannabis, heroin, ecstasy, amphetamines and so-called 'legal highs'. The investigation into the supply and production of controlled drugs can provide evidence which can potentially link scenes, link batches of drugs from different scenes and possibly establish their origin. Forensic examination of the packaging and drug-related paraphernalia and equipment used in the production and supply of controlled drugs can also bear other potential forensic evidence such as fingerprints and DNA which may identify persons.

14.2.1 **Cannabis**

Cannabis is perhaps the most widely used illegal drug worldwide and is increasingly being grown in the UK rather than being imported as a supply option. The main active components in cannabis are present in the leaves and flowering tops of the plant, and are known as THCs (tetrahydrocannabinols). The concentration of THC is dependent on the physical form of the processed cannabis. There are, however, some forty differing active compounds in cannabis, one of which, drobabinol, is prescribed by doctors as an anti-nausea medication for those undergoing chemotherapy. It is believed cannabis interacts with the natural neurotransmitter known as anandamine (in Sanskrit 'ananda' means 'bliss'.)

There are over 100 varieties of the cannabis plant, one of which is 'skunk', commonly regarded as having a higher potency than other forms.

Typically the forms of cannabis are:

- leaves/herbal—the dried, crushed leaves can be mixed with the dried stems, flowers and seeds of the plant. This will typically have the lowest concentration of THCs;
- resin—this is gained from extracting the resin from the plant, usually from the seeds and leaves. It is usually supplied in slab or block form. The THC concentration is typically between that of the herbal and oil forms; and
- cannabis oil—this is typically a dark coloured oil or sticky tar like substance obtained by using solvent extraction techniques on resins or the plant material. It can be potent, with the highest levels of THC of all the forms.

Cannabis cultivation

Cannabis can be cultivated indoors and investigators may encounter the cultivation of a few plants in pots, or larger scale production. When investigating cannabis cultivation incidents, the key questions that need to be addressed include establishing the identity of the plants being cultivated, the actual and possible yield from the plants, the quality of the plants by analysis of the THC levels, whether the scene can be linked to other cultivation scenes or supplied drugs, and to establish the identity of those involved in the cultivation.

The growth cycle of the cannabis plant will develop through five stages, namely:

- Germination—the germination period for cannabis seeds is generally three to ten days.
- Seedling—following germination, the seedling stage will typically last for four to six weeks.
- Vegetative—this is the period of maximum growth with normal rates of one to two inches per day, although reports of four to six inches of growth per day have been reported.
- Pre-flowering—this is a transition phase where growth rates slow down but the flowers have not blossomed.
- Flowering—this is when the plants display flowers for a period of about six weeks. Whilst both the male and female plants produce flowers, only the unfertilised female flowers are retained as these are a good source of THC. It is common for male plants to be removed from the crop.

Like any plant, the growth cycle of the cannabis plant is regulated by the amount of daylight it receives. In natural circumstances the plant will undergo its maximum growth phase during the summer when daylight lasts longer. As the daylight reduces, as in autumn, the plants will flower. Indoor cultivation artificially reproduces the effects of daylight by the use of powerful timed lighting systems. This means that the flowering phase can be regulated; reducing the life cycle of the plant enables successive crops to be grown, so that the number of plants grown in any given period can be increased to maximise the yield.

Plants cultivated in this manner can be grown in pots of compost or by a technique known as hydroponics. Hydroponics is a growing technique that does not use soil. The plants are grown in circulating water which contains added nutrients. The plants may be supported in the water by a material such as vermiculite or rockwool.

Cultivation scenes

There is no one singular method adopted by all growers. In addition to the number of plants being grown, which will indicate the scale of cultivation, the following may typically be present.

- Lighting systems that utilise high powered daylight lamps which are usually operated by a timer system. It is not uncommon for the set up to be replicated in different rooms to produce plants at different growing stages.
- White coated or reflective coverings on walls to maximise the effects of the lighting. Windows and skylights for instance will be covered in order to exclude any natural daylight which can disrupt the timed growing stages.
- Air circulation systems are required to prevent fungal growth on the plants. The air circulation system can include extraction fans to ensure a circulation of fresh air is maintained. Carbon dioxide may be introduced into the circulated air to promote growth.
- Mother plants are specimens of the female plants which are used to supply cuttings for future crops. These are normally kept separately from the main crop.
- Seedling nursery areas where new plants are grown from cuttings or seeds. Typically the number of these young plants will be greater than the number that will be subsequently grown to maturity. A forensic scientist is able to establish whether a plant has been grown from a cutting or a seed.
- There may be documentation detailing growing schedules kept in paper form or on computer.
- Water tanks, trays and pump systems may be present, where a hydroponics system is used. The plants grow by immersing their roots into the nutrient-enriched water in the tank, the pump circulates and aerates the fluid, which may be free flowing or filtered through a medium such as clay pebbles or vermiculite.
- There may be stocks of plant nutrients, insecticides, dehumidifiers, temperature measurement and control devices, scales and packaging materials for instance. All these can provide an investigator with potential forensic evidence and intelligence.

Each cultivation scene will differ according to the sophistication of the operation; however there is a wealth of potential evidence to be gained from such scenes.

Recovery of plants

The process required for the recovery of the plants is dependent on the scale and complexity of the cultivation operation and the evidence required for the charge in question.

For instance, a scene where cannabis is being cultivated on a small scale, and production-only offences are being considered, will require a different approach to a more sophisticated commercial operation where supply and production offences are being considered.

In larger scale operations investigators should establish whether there are plants at different growth stages, and whether there are separate growing rooms with timers set for the different growth stages. In addition, note should be taken as to the appearance of the plants, which can indicate whether they are of the same species. Differences in leaf shape and colour may indicate different types of plant.

Where cannabis cultivation is being investigated, it is important that a crime scene investigator (CSI) is available to photograph and recover potential forensic evidence.

Table 14.1 below outlines general guidance for the recovery of cannabis plants for analysis. It is advisable for investigators to seek advice and guidance from the CSI and forensic service provider (FSP) regarding each case and the particular requirements of an investigation.

Table 14.1 Sampling guidelines for cannabis cultivation scenes

Evidential requirement	Samples required
Identification only (no yield information required)	Up to three plants (whole plant or top only). The roots of soil-grown plants are not required unless a determination of the cultivation method is needed (see below).
Identification and yield	– At least two whole plants (with roots attached if hydroponically grown). Ideally the plants should represent a mid-range height from each room or area.
	– Rooted seedlings or cuttings in propagators—a single plant from each propagator.
	– Mature female plants of similar heights—two whole plants.
	– Mature female plants of differing heights—one plant of each representative size (small, medium and large).
	– Large immature plants which appear to have pieces cut from them— these may be mother plants and must be photographed to show any cut areas. These do not necessarily need to be submitted for forensic analysis unless examination is required to link cuttings with the mother plant.
Cultivation method	Plants with roots need to be submitted to the FSP to establish whether plants have been grown from seed or from cuttings. Most of the growing medium should be carefully removed.

All plants and related vegetable matter should be packaged individually, in paper evidence sacks and submitted to the FSP as soon as possible. Such material must never be packaged in plastic bags. See Chapter 3 for appropriate packaging techniques.

The cultivation equipment does not necessarily need to be submitted to the FSP in the first instance. Investigators should consider the potential forensic evidence that may be present on the equipment such as fingerprints, footwear, and DNA which may be able to be recovered from an in-force laboratory.

The CSI will photograph the scene and take photographs of plants with a scale (ruler) in order to show the actual size of the plant. Photographs taken that do not include a scale (ruler) are of no use evidentially as the size of the plant cannot be determined.

It is advisable for a forensic scientist to visit the scene of large scale complex cultivation sites, as they can indicate the best samples to be recovered and offer advice and guidance regarding potential evidence.

For imported cannabis material, the scientist may be able to offer information regarding the country of origin of the material.

Health and safety at cannabis cultivation scenes

Such scenes must be approached with care as there are particular risks associated with cannabis cultivation sites. It is not uncommon for cultivation scenes to contain booby traps designed to injure any uninvited person entering the premises.

The following are general health and safety considerations to be made at cultivation sites. The list is not exhaustive and investigators must undertake a risk assessment at each stage.

- The risk of booby traps. Investigators should make themselves familiar with intelligence reports on known systems and approach such scenes with caution.
- Electrical risks. Often the electrical systems employed are of a poor standard of construction. Be mindful that the mains electrical supply may have been bypassed; therefore turning off the mains will not make the scene safe. If in any doubt, the electricity service provider can be contacted for advice and guidance. The combination of electricity and water from hydroponic or irrigation systems is potentially hazardous.
- Trip hazards may be plentiful as the wiring and cables supplying the equipment can be draped all over the premises. In addition lighting rigs and temporary partition walls can be hazardous as they may not be securely fixed in place.
- The lamps used to simulate daylight create a lot of heat which may be sufficient to cause burns to unexposed skin.
- Chemicals used in the growing process may be corrosive or they may present a risk by skin contact or inhalation. Cannabis plants and rockwool can cause skin irritation.

- The odour from the plants can become overwhelming and cause breathing difficulties. A disposable mask must always be worn if investigators are required to enter such scenes.
- Legionnaire's disease may be present due to the water and humid conditions.
- Canisters of CO_2 may be present—ensure these are switched off. This gas is heavier than air and can fill cavities below the floor level, avoid entering small spaces where the gas may accumulate.

When dealing with cultivation scenes all personnel must wear a disposable oversuit, disposable gloves and a disposable face mask as a minimum requirement.

14.2.2 Heroin

Heroin is derived from morphine extracted from the opium formed in the unripe pod of certain poppies. Opium is typically brown coloured and contains between 4–21% morphine which is an opiate. Morphine is responsible for most, if not all, of the narcotic effect of heroin and it can be readily extracted from opium. Further processing is required to derive heroin, involving the morphine reacting with acetic anhydride or acetyl chloride to produce a powdered substance that is highly soluble in water, enabling it to be administered by intravenous injection.

When the drug is sold, it will typically contain other substances such as starch, lactose, milk powder, sugars, caffeine and other drugs to increase the apparent amount offered for supply. These are referred to as cutting agents and may be present in other forms of drugs. The presence of cutting agents will impact on the purity of the sample.

Heroin related deaths can be caused by a number of factors and the amount that can cause fatality is dependent to a large degree on individual tolerance to the drug, the strength of the drug and toxic effects of any cutting agents. Death can occur due to a number of reactions including myocardial sensitisation leading to arrhythmia, central/respiratory depression, anaphylactoid reaction causing cardiovascular collapse.

14.2.3 Cocaine

Cocaine is derived from the leaves of the coca leaf and is typically administered by sniffing the powder which is absorbed through the mucous membranes in the nose. Crack cocaine is created by mixing cocaine with baking soda and water. This is then dried and can be broken into lumps known as rocks. Crack is normally smoked.

14.2.4 Amphetamines

These drugs provide the user with a stimulant effect on the central nervous system, and are taken to increase alertness and activity. Amphetamines are typically encountered in powder form and are usually inhaled by sniffing.

Methamphetamine is a chemical derivative of amphetamine capable of being administered by intravenous injection. Forms of methamphetamine can be smoked, snorted, injected or taken orally. Commonly known as crystal, ice, meth, chalk, for example, it is extremely addictive. Methamphetamines increase the levels of the neurotransmitter dopamine, which affects motor function and feelings of pleasure, reward and motivation. It can be produced in clandestine laboratories using relatively inexpensive, freely available ingredients such as pseudoepherine (present in many over the counter common cold medications). Pharmacies and retailers limit the amount of products a person can purchase containing this in one transaction. Other hazardous chemicals are required in the production of methamphetamine and the toxicity of these can remain in the environment for a considerable time after cessation of production.

Indicators of methamphetamine production include odours like ammonia/bleach, cat urine, strong solvents and burnt rubber. Chemicals used in the production process include acids, solvents, iodine, ammonia, cold cure medications, anti-freeze and drain cleaners. Red/brown stained paper coffee filters may be present as well as electric hot plates, funnels and glass jars.

14.2.5 Club drugs

These are synthetically produced and include ecstasy (MDMA), GHB (gamma hydroxybutyrate), rohypnol, ketamine and methamphetamines, for example. These are typically encountered in tablet form.

GHB acts as a depressant on the central nervous system and has anabolic effects (used by some bodybuilders to reduce fat and build muscle). Rohypnol has a sedative-hypnotic effect and is associated with anterograde amnesia and has been reported in connection with drug facilitated crimes such as sexual assaults. Ketamine is a disassociative anaesthetic which distorts audio-visual perception and produces feelings of detachment from the environment and the self. Alcohol can increase the potency of the effect of these substances.

14.2.6 Hallucinogens

LSD (lysergic acid diethylamide) is found in ergot, a fungus found on types of grain fungus, in particular (but not exclusively) rye. A small amount of LSD can cause auditory and visual hallucinations, and is typically ingested on a small piece of blotting paper which has been soaked in a solvent containing the dissolved LSD. The paper is then dried and the solvent evaporates to leave the absorbed LSD. The paper is then cut into small squares for consumption. LSD can also be ingested on small tablets known as microdots or on pieces of dried gelatine. LSD has been found supplied on the back of postage stamps (non-self adhesive types). LSD may also be absorbed via the skin, so it is important investigators wear gloves when handling substrates suspected of being impregnated with LSD. Other hallucinogens include:

- psilocybin which is a naturally occurring substance in a particular variety of mushrooms, commonly referred to as 'magic mushrooms';
- peyote, a small cactus contains mescaline, which can also be synthetically produced. Small disc shaped nodules are cut from the top of the plant and are then dried and either chewed or soaked in water to produce an intoxicating liquid to be taken orally; and
- phencyclidine (PCP) a white crystalline powder that can be easily dissolved in water or alcohol. This liquid can then be impregnated into tablet, capsule or powder forms. It is also possible to smoke PCP by mixing the powder with a dried leafy material—typically mint, marjoram, parsley or cannabis.

The majority of hallucinogens have chemical structures that are similar to natural neurotransmitters and it is believed they react to interfere with serotonin, which is distributed in the brain and spinal cord and regulates behaviour and perception. Mood, body temperature, sensory perception, and muscle control are some of the systems that are controlled by serotonin levels.

14.2.7 New psychoactive substances (NPS)—'legal highs'

'Legal highs' is a generic term that is used to describe psychoactive substances that are intended to mimic the effects of controlled drugs and can pose a real risk to the health of those who take them. They are available to purchase from the internet or from shops (known as 'head shops') which specialise in the sale of drug-related paraphernalia, and can contain synthetically produced or naturally occurring compounds. They are retailed in tablet, powder or capsule form and typically labelled as 'not for human consumption' in an attempt to avoid being controlled under the Misuse of Drugs Act (1971).

Several active ingredients in the NPS, such as mepheradrone (common names include M-Cat, Miaow Miaow, MDPV, for example) and methoxetamine (common names include Moxy, Rhino Ket, Rolfcopter, for example) which were previously sold as 'legal highs' have now been banned under the Misuse of Drugs Act (1971). New legislative powers mean temporary bans on any potentially harmful substance can be instigated whilst investigation by the Advisory Council on the Misuse of Drugs into the risks to health and toxicity of a substance can be undertaken, to establish whether it should be permanently banned.

The forensic examination potentials are the same as for controlled drugs where they may form part of a criminal offence or where the death of a person is related to ingestion of one of the NPS.

14.3 **Illicit Laboratories**

Whilst undertaking unrelated enquiries, investigators may encounter such scenes where an illicit drug production laboratory is suspected. In this instance, investigators must leave the scene immediately. Under no circumstances should a search of such scenes be undertaken unless critical factors such as the preservation of life are necessary.

It is important to be aware that an illicit drug laboratory can also be used for the manufacture of explosives. Much of the information regarding illicit drug laboratories is restricted; however police and other appropriate law enforcement agency (LEA) personnel should be able to access information concerning the indications of such premises.

Illicit drug laboratories are potentially very dangerous, often the premises will be 'booby trapped' to cause harm to investigators, mains electrical supply may be bypassed (to avoid detection by the heavy consumption of power, and avoid paying for such). The electrical supply to equipment will generally be of a poor standard and the risk of electrocution from bare cables is high, especially if water is present such as in a hydroponic set up. The power supplier must be informed and will attend the scene where necessary to ensure the power is disconnected safely.

Where illicit labs or cannabis growing is undertaken in a loft space, the floor can be weakened by the weight of equipment and/or plants and could collapse.

Booby traps are often encountered at such premises and can include the wiring of doors and windows to electricity supply, sharp items being place around frames of doors/windows, hazardous liquids suspended over doors/windows, false floors (eg, a hole cut into the floor and covered with a rug or similar) causing injury and impeding entry. In one extreme case grenades were set amongst containers of chemicals.

In the event of inadvertent discovery of an illicit laboratory, the following actions should be undertaken.

Checklist—actions to take on discovery of illicit laboratories

- Due to the high level of risk involved to health and safety in such circumstances, Investigators and others in the vicinity, must retreat to a safe distance from the scene due to the risk of fire, explosion and chemical contamination.

- Mobile phones and radios must not be used in the immediate vicinity. The control room should be informed of observations made at the premises, including any distinctive odours, and whether it is believed production is in progress at that time.

- Do not switch lights or electrical appliances, or power supplies to any equipment on or off.

- Under no circumstances touch or open any bottles or containers.

- The premises should be kept under observation from a safe distance.

- Management of the scene should be instigated by the use of cordons and a scene log instigated. A sketch plan of the layout observed will be of great benefit to the scene personnel who will be required to enter the scene.

- Only those who are appropriately trained and equipped to deal with such incidents can re-enter the scene.

Initial responders must ensure the preservation and management of the scene is established as a priority. Investigators who have inadvertently entered an illicit laboratory will be considered to be contaminated by drugs residue or chemical traces, and should ensure that this factor is highlighted to the control room, the senior investigating officer and CSI. There should be an avoidance of close contact with other personnel arriving at the scene. Monitor health for any feelings that may occur due to contact with potentially harmful or toxic fumes or residues.

Once the illicit laboratory has been made safe, CSI will examine the scene and recover items for forensic examination. It is beneficial for this to be undertaken in conjunction with a forensic scientist who specialises in illicit drug analysis. Other agencies such as the fire service, environmental department and local authorities may be involved in the scene. Investigators should be mindful that similar set-ups can be used to produce explosives.

14.4 Forensic Potentials from Drugs Packaging

The wrappings of drugs can provide valuable evidence, such as a physical fit between pieces of foil/plastic wrap and the roll it came from, for example. Plastic wrapping and bags can potentially be linked to a single source ('batch match') by examining and comparing microscopic manufacturing marks. Adhesive tapes can be linked to a source roll and may contain fingerprints, fibres or skin cells that may produce DNA profiles. Depending on the type of packaging, there may be the opportunity to recover fingerprints. Investigators should consider the following with regard to drug packaging:

Checklist—Considerations for forensic potentials of drug packaging

- The initial analysis must be one of identification of the substance. The substance must not be decanted into other packaging. The drugs, in the original packaging, should be submitted to the FSP to undertake analysis to establish the identification, quantification and purity of the substance. If the packaging is required for fingerprint examination, the forensic scientist should be informed and they will preserve the packaging for fingerprints.

- Where a physical fit or batch match examination is required to match a piece of packaging to its source, this must be undertaken before any fingerprint development techniques are employed.

- Fingerprints may be developed on plastic bags and cling film using the superglue technique. Where fingerprint ridge detail is developed, it may be possible to also recover DNA material from beneath the superglue deposit. This can be of use where there is not sufficient detail in any fingerprints to make identification possible.

- If DNA analysis is required then the item must be submitted to the FSP as soon as possible.

- Where wrappings such as cling film or tin foil are badly crumpled, it can be very difficult to recover fingerprints and the surface area of the wrapping may be too small to hold sufficient ridge detail to make fingerprint identification possible.

  If in doubt, submit the item and the fingerprint unit can assess the suitability for the potential to recover fingerprint detail.

- Some packages containing drugs may have been secreted in bodily orifices. These will most likely contain bodily fluids and must be handled as biohazards with a high risk of transmitting infectious diseases. It may be possible to obtain DNA profiles from such packaging. Where it is known or suspected packages have been secreted into bodily orifices (referred to as 'plugging'), the exhibit should be labelled as 'biohazard'.

- Gloves must always be worn when searching for and recovering drug packages.

14.5 **Bulk and Trace Analysis of Drugs**

Bulk material is defined as that which can be measured. Trace samples are those that are not readily visible and are present in minute amounts.

Bulk samples are typically analysed to establish the identity of the sample and to determine the composition and ratios of different constituents. Comparison between samples from different scenes can be undertaken to establish if the samples have a common origin.

Trace analysis can be undertaken on a variety of items such as potential packaging materials, banknotes and mobile phones for instance.

14.5.1 **Bulk analysis**

Analysis of bulk samples will typically begin with initial observations regarding the weight and appearance of the sample, followed by presumptive testing. There are several different presumptive tests that can be indicative of a sample's identity. Although such tests cannot provide a conclusive identification, they do serve to reduce the range of possibilities and enable the scientist to undertake appropriate analysis. The techniques utilised can provide information on the combinations and ratios of substances present in a sample. This may enable links to be made with other samples recovered from different scenes.

14.5.2 **Trace samples**

Trace samples are typically required to establish the presence or absence of drugs, for example:

- Biological samples. These are analysed to determine if a person had drugs in their system. The samples that may be examined are blood, saliva, breath samples, urine, stomach contents, hair, nails, sweat and other tissues and body fluids available during a post-mortem examination. The biological samples required for analysis will depend on the individual circumstances of the case.
- Suspected drug-related items such as scales, blades, wrappings and other surfaces that may contain small amounts of a drug that may be linked to a bulk sample or other scenes. Food and drink and relevant containers that may have been adulterated with drugs can also be analysed.
- Mobile telephones, banknotes, vehicle steering wheels and other such items may contain trace amounts of material if they are handled by those who have had contact with drugs. The evidential value of trace samples recovered from such items must be considered in the context of each case, due to the transferability of such trace material.

Due to the microscopic amounts and transferability of trace amounts of material, the inadvertent transfer and contamination of samples are very real risks. Different items recovered from distinct separate locations (eg, from different rooms) that may require trace analysis must be handled by different investigators. Gloves must be worn during any search for such items.

Exhibits that potentially contain trace amounts of a substance need to be analysed as soon as possible as heroin and cannabis for instance, can degrade over time, especially in warm temperatures.

Exhibits containing drugs or potential drug residues must be stored in cool temperatures away from other potential sources of drug contamination.

It is important to keep exhibits for bulk and trace analysis separated. It can be argued in court that a bulk sample has interfered with the trace sample, but it is unlikely that a trace sample can sufficiently contaminate a bulk sample.

14.5.3 **Evidential drug identification testing (EDIT)**

The evidential drug identification testing (EDIT) kits are used by specifically trained investigators in a police station for establishing the presence of morphine, heroin, cocaine and amphetamines. The identification of cannabis, with the exception of the oil form, is generally undertaken by any experienced investigator based on the visual appearance, smell and texture of herbal or resin cannabis. The level of identification confirmation required does, however, depend on the nature of the particular offence.

The EDIT kit can be used for cases of straightforward possession offences. Where a positive result for a controlled drug is obtained and the detainee does not dispute this, then the EDIT test may be sufficient. However, if the detainee disagrees with the result or where there is an offence of conspiracy or intent to supply then independent forensic testing to establish the identity, quantity and purity of the substance is essential.

The EDIT kit requires a small amount of substance to be exposed to Marquis reagent which will generate a colour change. The particular colours indicate the presence of the following:

- orange is a positive result for amphetamines;
- purple is a positive result for opiates; and
- blue/black, green or red indicate a negative result for the presence of controlled drug.

Cocaine is tested with a different specific test kit; these are similar to pregnancy test kits which indicate a positive result for cocaine when a red line appears in the control position of the kit.

There is a very small chance of the kits giving a false positive result.

The results from the test kits can be presented as evidence in court where a guilty plea has been confirmed and there is no dispute regarding the identification. The use of these kits has proved an efficient and effective way of dealing with such cases which has enabled a more expedient approach to dealing with many drug-related offences.

14.6 **Chapter Summary**

The analysis of drugs can provide investigators with an identification of a substance, the quantity and purity of the sample, and determination of any links between substances recovered from different scenes. The cultivation of cannabis and the production of synthetic drugs are increasingly being encountered. The forensic examination of such scenes can provide potential evidence to identify persons involved where fingerprints, DNA, footwear marks and other forensic evidence are recovered from equipment and drug-related paraphernalia which may also link scenes and possibly identify supply networks.

The recovery of potential forensic evidence from such scenes should only be undertaken by a CSI or forensic scientist. The scenes of illicit drug production can be extremely dangerous, booby traps are often set to cause injury to uninvited visitors, the set up of equipment and electrical wiring is most likely to be below safe standards and hazards exist in the form of chemicals that may be present. Where such scenes are inadvertently discovered by investigators, the immediate response should be to secure the scene for CSIs or other specialist personnel. No attempt to undertake a search of the scene should be undertaken, unless preservation of life is an issue, such as where someone in the premises has been injured or overcome by fumes, for example.

The presence of other evidence must be considered, whether dealing with a production scene or recovering smaller amounts from an individual. Care must be taken to ensure that cross-transfer of drug material does not occur. Gloves must always be worn when handling any items potentially bearing drugs.

KNOWLEDGE CHECK—DRUGS

1. How should cannabis plants be submitted to a forensic service provider?

   Cannabis plants should be packaged in paper evidence sacks and stored in a cool, dry store.

   The roots of the plant are not required unless they are grown hydroponically or if there is a need to establish if the plants were grown from seed or cutting (as much soil as possible must be removed from the roots in such cases).

2. What is meant by the term hydroponics?

   Hydroponics is the term used for a method of plant cultivation which does not use soil or compost. The plants have the roots immersed tanks of nutrient enriched water, which is circulated and aerated, either free flowing or through clay pebbles or vermiculite, by a pump.

3. What information can a scientist provide to an investigator regarding a sample of white powder?

   A scientist can identify the substance, determine the quantity and ratios of different constituents, establish the purity (or otherwise) of the sample and potentially provide links with the sample to other samples submitted. This can potentially lead to links between crime scenes and possibly determine a supply chain.

4. What are the possible health and safety risks at a cannabis cultivation scene?

   There is the risk of:

   - booby traps;
   - unsafe electrical wiring;
   - hazards associated with electricity and water from irrigation systems;
   - trip hazards due to wiring and cables which can be draped all over the premises;
   - lighting rigs and temporary partition walls can be hazardous as they may not be securely fixed in place;
   - the lamps can cause burns to unexposed skin;

- chemicals used in the growing process may be harmful;

- cannabis plants and rockwool can cause skin irritation;

- the odour from the plants can cause breathing difficulties;

- Legionnaire's disease may be present due to the water and humid conditions;

- CO_2 may be present in canisters.

When dealing with cultivation scenes all personnel must wear a disposable over-suit, disposable gloves and a disposable face mask as a minimum requirement.

Recommended Reading

Advisory Council on the Misuse of Drugs <http://www.gov.uk/government/organisations/advisory-council-on-the-misuse-of-drugs>.

Commercial Cultivation of Cannabis—Findings from the UK National Problem Profile. (2012) Association of Chief Police Officers (ACPO).

Criminalistics, 10th edn (2010) Saferstein, R.

Evidential Drug Identification Testing in Police Stations (2009) Crown Prosecution Service.

Forensic Science, 3rd edn (2011) Jackson, ARW and Jackson, J.

Guidance on Policing New Psychoactive Substances including Temporary Class Drugs (2011) ACPO.

15

Document Examination

15.1 **Introduction**

A document is any piece of paper bearing written, printed or pictorial forms of communication. However, blank sheets of paper can also be examined to provide potential evidential material. The types of document encountered in the investigation of a crime, referred to as 'questioned documents' typically include forged or altered cheques, vehicle documents, ransom notes, malicious mail, immigration papers and suicide notes, for example; however, with increasing access to photo imaging software and high specification printers, almost any documentation can be forged.

Questioned document examination can provide evidence in the form of fingerprints, footwear marks, indented writing, handwriting analysis and the physical fit of a piece of paper to a pad from which it has been torn, for example. There are a number of facets involved in questioned document examination and the processes utilised will depend on the circumstances of the case. The following examinations are those typically employed in document analysis:

- handwriting analysis;
- forged/altered document examination;
- recovery of indented writing;
- recovery of fingerprints;
- physical fit; and
- comparison of a printed document to printer.

Most paper materials recovered during the investigation of volume crime incidents are generally submitted for fingerprint analysis, for example when an offender has rifled through paperwork during a burglary. Chemical development techniques can be utilised, generally within force chemical enhancement laboratories or equivalent, for the recovery of fingerprints.

Where someone has walked over paper items it can be possible to recover indented impressions of footwear using an electrostatic document analysis apparatus (ESDA). This technique is more commonly used for the recovery of indented writing impressions from apparently blank writing paper (see section 15.4 below). This process is typically carried out in-force by the fingerprint development laboratory (or equivalent).

This chapter will outline the analytical techniques available for the examination of documents and the considerations that an investigator should make regarding the evidential potentials of documents typically encountered and the recovery techniques required to maximise any potential evidence.

15.2 **Handwriting Analysis**

Handwriting analysis enables the comparison of handwriting between items of malicious mail, for example, and the suspect's handwriting. The analysis should be undertaken by a forensic scientist who can potentially:

- establish the author of questioned (crime scene) samples by comparison of the samples provided by suspects;
- determine whether a signature is genuine or forged; and
- determine common authorship between different handwritten documents to establish links.

The basis of this analysis relies on the fact that generally, the writing style of adults tends to be stylised and unique to the author, displaying an individualistic style.

15.2.1 **Handwriting types**

There are four general categories of handwriting that can enable the analyst to classify the style of writing to potentially identify points for comparison:

- **Capitals**—All the letters are written in upper case. This can potentially individualise an author, as the shape of letters and the way they are formed will vary from person to person. An analyst will examine the number of pen strokes and the directions of pen movements.
- **Cursive**—This is 'joined up' writing with no breaks between the letters in words and is the most common form of adult handwriting. There is vast variation in individual styles.
- **Disconnected**—This is a variation on the cursive style where breaks between some of the letters in some of the words exist. The breaks vary from person to person and can be dependent on the word being written. Some people will write certain words with the breaks always in particular places. This style is another common form of handwriting.
- **Signatures**—These are highly stylised and most often illegible. This type of handwriting is frequently examined by scientists due to attempt forgeries. Signatures display enormous variation due to their highly stylised nature. They are often very different from the normal writing style of a person which means it can generally be difficult to link signatures to normal handwriting.

A person's handwriting will display natural variation and will never be identical on two separate occasions. Such variations can be due to simple random variation, the physical state of author, different writing tools being used or different writing surfaces. The natural variations can, however, be characteristic of a particular person. The extent of these variations can potentially be determined by analysis; therefore the more samples provided by a suspect for comparison will increase the reliability of the results.

The examination of handwriting is a systematic and painstaking task which will typically include the following, outlined in the checklist below:

Checklist—Examining handwriting

- The observation of the overall characteristics of the writing, including spelling and grammatical structure.

- Detailed examination of individual words and letters.

- Direction of pen movements determined by observation of changes in ink density and striation marks in the ink lines. Striations are caused by the imperfections in ball point pens due to manufacture, damage or wear through use. Such defects are common. When the damaged tip rotates ink will be unevenly distributed.

- The direction of the striations present in the writing can be indicative of the handedness of the author, as left or right handed people tend to form letters differently.

- The density of ink will tend to be thinner when a pen makes contact with, and leaves, the surface of the paper.

15.3 Forged Handwriting

People may attempt to disguise their handwriting in order to later deny authorship, such as when attempting to forge someone else's handwriting or signature. A person producing handwriting that is disguised will typically attempt to alter the overall appearance of their own natural writing style. Changing the slope, spacing between letters and words, using cursive rather than disconnected writing styles and vice versa are the most common methods used to disguise handwriting.

It is very difficult to disguise handwriting consistently as letter formation tends to be performed subconsciously. There will typically be many changes in style, most commonly between the slope and size of letters, throughout a piece of writing, and as a result altered handwriting is very often untidy, especially where it has to be produced in large amounts and rapidly.

The most frequent form of disguised handwriting encountered by forensic examiners are signatures. These are perhaps the most difficult type of handwriting to analyse due to the small amount of writing available for examination and comparison. The forgery of a signature requires a person to produce a basically correctly-reproduced and smoothly-written signature. The reproduction of signatures will fall into two general categories, depending on the circumstances in which they are made.

- **Rapidly-made disguised signatures.** Such signatures may be made when being watched, such as credit card or cheque transactions in a shop, for example. These signatures will generally be fluently written, and may be of a sufficiently good reproduction to satisfy a shop assistant that it is genuine. When forensically examined, however, such rapidly-made forgeries will typically display incorrect proportions.
- **Slowly-produced disguised signatures.** The accuracy of slowly-made disguised signatures, produced where a person has more time to copy the genuine signature will typically be a good reproduction on general observation. A lack of fluency will become apparent, however, when examined by a scientist. Writing that has been produced slowly and deliberately tends to be angular and shaky in appearance, rather than flowing smoothly. The density of ink will typically be more even when writing slowly.

Another form of slowly-produced forged signatures that may be encountered are those produced using tracing paper to copy over the original, or by writing heavily over an original signature onto a document beneath and then inking in the impression made. Signatures copied in this way can bear good overall similarity to the original signatures, but will display the characteristics of a slowly-written signature.

The forensic examination and comparison of signatures requires as many samples of the genuine and the suspect samples as possible. Signatures are never written exactly the same; a large number of samples enable a more accurate assessment of the natural variations that can occur.

15.3.1 Signature samples

The types of signature required for comparison with samples recovered from the crime scene fall into two categories. Unrequested signatures are the most reliable source for comparisons as these are produced under normal circumstances and will give indication of the natural variations that occur. These can be from a range of documents that have been previously signed by the suspect.

Requested signatures should be obtained where unrequested signatures are unavailable or are limited in number. These are produced by the suspect after the event and may be affected by the circumstances of the case. These are not ideal for comparison purposes but their use may be unavoidable.

When requesting samples from a suspect, an investigator should consider the following:

- The sample should be representative of the person's usual handwriting.

- The sample should contain enough writing to make an effective comparison with the scene samples. Be mindful that letter formation is a subconscious act and it is very difficult to consistently disguise natural writing style.
- If the sample from the scene is written in capital letters, then investigators should request the suspect provide a sample in capital letters. The document examiner can only compare like with like.
- Avoid directing suspects to produce a certain style of writing, for example cursive (joined-up) or disconnected writing, as this will lead to unnatural variations in the sample.
- Where possible the same sort of pen used to produce the scene sample should be used to produce the suspect sample. Avoid using new pens for sample collection.
- Ensure the suspect has a suitable writing surface to produce the samples.

Ideally, take as many samples as possible; the minimum requirements will depend on the case. Typically the following are required:

- for signature comparison, at least twelve samples;
- for cheque fraud, at least twelve signature samples and a further six handwriting samples.

For handwritten document comparison such as in malicious mail cases, it is advisable to discuss the requirements with a document examiner who will offer guidance on the sampling process required for the particular case. The sample required will be dependent on the size of the handwriting sample that has been recovered from the crime scene. Once the size of a suspect sample has been established, investigators should consider the following.

- Where possible, take samples from the suspect at different times.
- The suspect must never be shown the questioned (scene) sample.
- Investigators should dictate what they require the suspect to write at a reasonable pace in order to ensure the suspect produces their natural handwriting style.
- The suspect should sign and date each sample as it is completed.
- As each sample is completed, it must be removed from the sight of the suspect (to avoid any copying of characters or style).
- Each sample must be numbered sequentially as they are produced. The time of each sample must be recorded.

The potential evidence provided by the analysis of handwriting will depend on the amount of handwriting available, the number of distinctive features present, the degree of disguise and the suitability of the suspect samples obtained.

15.4 **Indented Impressions**

When a person writes on a piece of paper that forms part of a pad or note-book, for example, the indentations caused by the pressure of writing can be revealed from sheets several pages below the original. Such information can be used to link a series of malicious mailings or provide intelligence information.

The indentations caused by the pressure created by writing or by footwear when standing on paper, will not always be readily observed. A technique which is utilised in many in-force chemical development laboratories (or equivalent) to recover such impressions is the ESDA technique. This technique can potentially recover valuable information from apparently blank note-books or sheets of paper. ESDA is a simple and effective examination tech-nique and, as it is non-destructive to the sample, it can be undertaken prior to other examination techniques. The ESDA technique for recovery of indented impressions involves placing the piece of paper onto a porous bronze plate; a thin transparent film is then placed on the top of the paper. Air is drawn through the plate essentially pulling the paper and film flat. Following the application of an electrostatic charge to the film, a powdered toner is gently tipped onto the film. The indented areas will be fractionally lower than the surrounding area, so when the toner is applied to the statically-charged film, it will settle into the areas of indentations. Any indentations will be revealed by the toner on the film which is lifted from the paper and secured to a clear acetate sheet. Figure 15.1 shows an ESDA lift taken from a page of seemingly blank pad, which revealed writing that was linked to two malicious commu-nications. The technique can also reveal footwear marks and in some cases fingerprints.

This technique can also be useful to gather intelligence. For example, the pages of a map book from a recovered stolen vehicle which was believed to have been used in a series of burglaries were examined with ESDA. The examination revealed telephone numbers and other valuable information that was not vis-ible. The offender had probably leaned on the pages to write notes on pieces of paper. This provided investigators with information that opened up lines of enquiry.

Consideration of whether indented writing or footwear could be present and useful in a particular investigation is important, as crime scene investiga-tors (CSIs) (if they have recovered the item) and the chemical development laboratories (or equivalent) need to be made aware of this requirement.

POINT TO NOTE—INDENTED WRITING

ESDA may not be undertaken as a matter of course and if the document is treated with chemical techniques to recover potential fingerprints first it will render ESDA examination useless. If the item has been wet, this can dramatically reduce the presence of any indentations.

15.5 Other Document Examinations Available

15.5.1 Printed documents

A document examiner may be able to establish whether a photocopied or printed document has been produced on a particular machine, by examining defects that are reproduced by the different component parts of a particular machine. Computer printed documents can be examined in order to establish links between a document and the printer that produced it. Some printers will produce a mark on documents that is not visible to the naked eye, referred to as a bitmap or 'yellow dots'. These are embedded into the printer by the manufacturer and can identify the printer model and the dealership and country it was shipped to. Dealership records of sales can then lead to information that could be beneficial in an investigation. Another technique that may be embedded by the manufacturer is that of 'banding', whereby the printed document contains a series of bands, invisible to the naked eye, that could identify a particular printer. The technique of explicitly embedding traceable data in a printed document is referred to as 'passive' techniques of identification.

Active techniques are the examination of microscopic flaws that are created due to the unique wear and tear of a printer, scanner or copier, such as minute scratches on the glass of scanner beds and the wear and tear of the internal mechanics of a printer. These techniques can be used to compare a document to a particular printer but may not (unless passive data is present) be able to identify a specific machine.

Figure 15.1 Example of ESDA lift

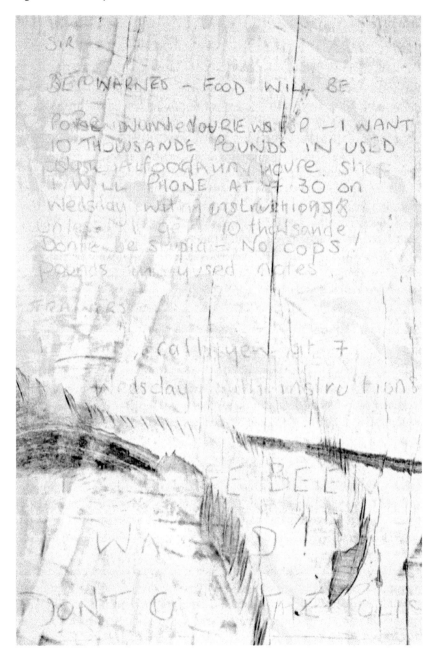

For guidance on samples required for such comparisons, seek advice from the forensic service provider who can offer guidance in line with the particular circumstances of each case.

15.5.2 **Analysis of inks**

A scientist can provide information on the type of ink and indicate the type of writing instrument used to create a questioned document. Ink analysis can provide information regarding the presence of any alterations on a document, such as when a cheque or vehicle excise license (tax disc), for example, has been altered. The video spectral comparator (VSC) technique may be provided by some in-force laboratories (or equivalent). This technique involves observing the fluorescent properties of the ink on the document. Different inks, although appearing to be the same colour in natural daylight, will react differently when fluoresced. This makes it possible to distinguish between ink used for the original document and ink used to alter the document.

The chemical composition of inks can be analysed to potentially provide links between written documents and a particular pen and can also be used for analysis of the inks/toners used in printers and photocopiers.

15.5.3 **Paper analysis**

The examination and analysis of paper can be undertaken to compare two or more pieces of paper to determine if they have a common origin. The manufacture of paper involves differing materials, pigments and bleaching agents. A document examiner can examine these variable properties of paper production to establish whether the pieces can have come from a common source.

15.5.4 **Physical fit**

It may be possible to determine whether two pieces of paper were originally part of a larger sheet by microscopically examining torn edges to potentially match pieces together. This type of examination may establish links between pieces of paper torn from a pad, or between a document that has been torn up or shredded.

Shredded documents can be examined and potentially reconstructed. It is important that where there is a possibility that this analysis may be required, that the 'layers' of shredded paper are *not* disturbed. Investigators should sieze the shredder unit in its entirety and transport it in a manner which does not disturb the shredded contents.

15.6 **Recovery and Preservation of Documents**

In order to maximise potential evidence available from documents, the considerations outlined in the following checklist should be made.

Checklist—Considerations for recovering/preserving documents

- Always wear gloves when handling items of potential forensic evidence.

- A photograph or photocopy of the original document should be made and exhibited, depending on the requirements of the case.

- To preserve a document for the examination of indented writing or footwear, the item must be placed in a cardboard box or card folder, the lids from photocopier paper boxes are ideal. These can then be placed into a paper or plastic evidence bag.

- Never lean on a document exhibit to complete the exhibit/continuity label, the writing will transfer onto the document to be revealed by the ESDA examination. This may jeopordise any useful indented evidence recovered.

- If indented impressions are not required, a paper or plastic evidence bag is suitable for exhibiting documents.

- Documents should be stored in cool dry conditions; dampness and heat can alter or destroy potential evidence.

- Do not stick, staple or clip anything to the document.

- Submit original documents for handwriting analysis and not photocopies.

- Chemical development techniques used for fingermark examination will prevent ESDA examinations being undertaken, the detection of alterations and ink or paper comparisons. Chemical fingermark development techniques should be undertaken last if other forensic examinations are required.

- If the development of fingerprints is required, it is vital to inform the laboratory if the document has been wet between the time of the offence and the time it was recovered as an exhibit. This is because the techniques utilised to examine such items will differ from those of a known dry exhibit.

- Where shredded document reconstruction may be required, the shredder unit and contents should be recovered and preserved in a manner that will not disturb the layer structure of shredded contents.

15.7 **Chapter Summary**

The examination of documents can provide investigators with intelligence information and/or forensic evidence.

Handwritten documents, such as malicious mail or forged cheques can provide evidence of authorship. The comparison of the handwriting from a crime scene sample with that produced by a suspect will be more reliable where investigators can supply the scientist with numerous samples of a suspect's handwriting. Ideally this should be in the form of unrequested samples, but where this is not feasible, requested samples produced under supervision of investigators are acceptable.

ESDA can recover indented impressions such as writing or footwear that may not be visible. It is important that the CSI or laboratory technician (or equivalent) is informed of the requirement for ESDA, as it may not be undertaken automatically. The use of chemical fingerprint development techniques will render any ESDA examination invalid, as will be the case where the document has been wet.

Printed documents can be linked to the printer or copier that produced them and the analysis of inks can determine where different writing implements have been used to alter documents. Physical fit examinations can determine if a piece of paper has originated from a certain pad, for example. It can also be possible for shredded documents or hand torn paper to be reconstructed.

The chemical fingerprint development techniques are the most destructive form of examination regarding documents; investigators should consider the potential evidence that may be available in the context of the particular investigation. Where other aspects of document examination may be beneficial, these should be undertaken before chemical development for fingerprint recovery.

KNOWLEDGE CHECK—DOCUMENTS

1. What can an ESDA examination provide to an investigator?

Electrostatic Document Apparatus (ESDA) is a technique that can potentially recover valuable information from notebooks or sheets of paper, even where they appear to be apparently blank.

It is a non-destructive technique that can reveal the indentations caused by the pressure created by writing, or by footwear when standing on paper. The impressions can be recovered from several sheets beneath the original surface and can reveal information that can be of intelligence value. Where impressions are recovered, this can provide a link to the original piece of paper bearing the writing, for example a piece of malicious mail recovered from a victim can potentially be linked to a writing pad recovered from the suspect.

---

2. How can indented impressions be best preserved for examination?

Any items bearing possible indented writing or footwear marks must be packaged in a manner that will prevent any further indentations occurring. A shallow bow, such as a lid from copier paper boxes, or a card folder sealed into a paper or plastic bag are suitable for this purpose.
The exhibit must not be leaned on to write notes or labels as this can be revealed by the ESDA and can destroy potential evidence.

3. What handwriting samples are required to compare a suspect's writing with that of a questioned (crime scene) document?

The minimum requirements will depend on the case. Typically the following are required:

- for signature comparison at least twelve samples, and
- for cheque fraud, at least twelve signature samples and a further six handwriting samples.

For handwritten document comparison such as in malicious mail cases, it is advisable to discuss the requirements with a document examiner who will offer guidance on the sampling process required for the particular case. The sample required will be dependent on the size of the handwriting sample that has been recovered from the crime scene.

4. State the considerations that should be made regarding the recovery of suspect samples.

- The sample should be representative of the person's usual handwriting and should contain enough writing to make an effective comparison with the scene samples.
- If the sample from the scene is written in capital letters, request that the suspect provide a sample in capital letters.
- Avoid directing suspects to produce a certain style of writing, for example cursive or disconnected writing.
- Where possible the same sort of pen used to produce the scene sample should be used to produce the suspect sample.
- Avoid using new pens for sample collection.
- Ensure the suspect has a suitable writing surface to produce the samples.
- Where possible, take samples from the suspect at different times.
- The suspect must never be shown the questioned (scene) sample.

- Dictate the words required at a reasonable pace in order to ensure the suspect produces their natural handwriting style.

- The suspect should sign and date each sample as it is completed.

- As each sample is completed, it must be removed from the sight of the suspect (to avoid any copying of characters or style).

- Each sample must be numbered sequentially as it is produced.

- The time of each sample must be recorded.

Recommended Reading

Criminalistics, 8th edn (2004) Saferstein, R.

Forensic Science, 3rd edn (2004) Jackson, ARW and Jackson, J.

Bibliography

Association of Chief Police Officers (ACPO) (2006) *Practitioner's Guide to Intelligence-Led Mass DNA Screening* [RESTRICTED].

—— (2008) *Evidential Drug Identification Testing in Police Stations*, <https://www.cps.gov.uk/legal/assets/uploads/files/NPIA%20Full%20EDIT%20Guidance.pdf>.

—— (2008) *Family Liaison Officer Guidance*.

—— (2011) *Guidance on Policing New Psychoactive Substances including Temporary Class Drugs*.

—— (2011) *Investigating Burglary: A Guide to Investigative Options and Good Practice*.

—— (2012) *Commercial Cultivation of Cannabis: Findings from the UK National Problem Profile*.

—— (2012) *Good Practice Guide for Digital Evidence*.

—— *Investigation of Volume Crime Manual*, <http://www.acpo.police.uk/asp/policies/Data/volume_crime_manual.doc>.

—— (2014) *eDiscovery in digital forensic investigations*, CAST Publication Number 32/14.

——/National Centre for Policing Excellence (NCPE) (2006) *Murder Investigation Manual*.

——/NPIA (2010) *Livescan Good Practice Guide*.

——/NPIA/College of Policing (2015) *The Prosecution Team Manual of Guidance for the preparation, processing and submission of prosecution files* (2011): Charging and case preparation, <https://www.app.college.police.uk/app-content/prosecution-and-case-management/charging-and-case-preparation/>.

Bevel, T and Gardner, RM (2008) *Bloodstain Pattern Analysis with an Introduction to Crime Scene Reconstruction* (3rd edn), CRC Press: London.

Bodziak, WJ (2000) *Footwear Impression Evidence, Detection, Recovery and Examination* (2nd edn), CRC Press: London.

Caddy, B (2001) *Forensic Examination of Glass and Paint: Analysis and Interpretation*, CRC Press: London.

Caddy, B, Taylor, G, and Linacre, A (2008) *A Review of the Science of Low Template DNA Analysis*. Home Office: London

College of Policing Authorised Professional Practice (APP) (2014) *Managing Investigations*, <http://www.app.college.police.uk/app/content/investigations/managing-investigations/>.

—— (2014) *Armed Policing*, <https://www.app.college.police.uk/app-content/armed-policing/>.

Cook, T, Hill, M and Hibbitt, S (2013) *Crime Investigators' Handbook*, Oxford University Press: Oxford.

Crown Prosecution Service (2015) *DNA-17 Profiling*, <http://www.cps.gov.uk/legal/d_to_g/dna-17_profiling/>.

Dix, J (2001) *Pathology for Death Investigators*, Academic Information Systems: USA.

Dix, J and Graham, M (1999) *Time of Death, Decomposition and identification—An Atlas*, Academic Information Systems: USA.

Forensic Science Regulator (2015) *The Control and Avoidance of Contamination In Crime Scene Examination involving DNA Evidence Recovery* (Draft).

——'Codes of Practice and Conduct *Guidance: Allele Frequency Databases and Reporting Guidance for the DNA (Short Tandem Repeat) Profiling*'.

—— *DNA Population Data to Support the Implementation of National DNA Database DNA-17 Profiling*.

——(2014) *Codes of Practice and Conduct. Appendix: Bloodstain Pattern Analysis*.

Royal College of Pathologists (2014) *The Use of Time of Death Estimates Based on Heat Loss From the Body*.

—— Home Office, Royal College of Pathologists, Home Office and Department of Justice (2014) *Legal Issues in Forensic Pathology and Tissue Retention*.

——(2014) *Code of Practice and Performance Standards for Forensic Pathology*.

Fortunato, SL (1998) 'Development of Latent Fingerprints from Skin' Journal of Forensic Identification 48 (6) pp 704–17.

Heard, BJ (1997) *Handbook of Firearms and Ballistics: Examining and Interpreting Forensic Evidence*, John Wiley and Sons Ltd: Sussex.

Home Office Circular No 30 (1999) *Post Mortem Examinations and the Early Release of Bodies*, London.

Home Office Centre for Applied Science (CAST) (2014) *Fingermark Visualisation Manual*, St Albans.

Home Office (2015) *Guidance on Firearms Licensing Law*.

——(2013) *Drying Exhibits: A Guide for Forces V.1*.

Home Office DNA Delivery Unit (NDU) (2014) *The NDNAD Strategy Board Policy for Access and Use of DNA Samples, Profiles and Associated Data*. Issue 5, London.

—— 'DNA Population Data to Support the Implementation of National DNA Database DNA-17 Profiling', <http://www.gov.uk/government/statistics/dna-population-data-to-support-the-implementation-of-national-dna-database-dna-17-profiling>.

Hutton, G and McKinnon, G (2014) *Blackstone's Police Manuals Vol. 4 General Police Duties*, Oxford University Press: Oxford.

Jackson, ARW and Jackson, J (2011) *Forensic Science* (3rd edn), Pearson Education Limited: Essex.

James, SH and Eckert, WG (1998) *Interpretation of Bloodstain Evidence at Crime Scenes* (2nd edn), CRC Press: London.

Johnston, D and Hutton, G (2014) *Blackstone's Police Manuals Vol. 2 Evidence & Procedure*, Oxford University Press: Oxford.

Lawton, D, Stacey, R and Dodd, G. Good Practice Guide for Managers of e-Crime investigation (2014) CAST Publication Number 32/14.

Lee, HC and Gaensslen, RE (2012) *Advances in Fingerprint Technology* (3rd edn), CRC Press: London.

Menzel, ER (1980) *Fingerprint Detection by Laser*, Marcel Dekker: New York.

National Policing Improvement Agency (NPIA) (2007) *Footwear Marks Recovery Manual*, London.

Ozin, P, Norton, H, and Spivey, P (2013) *PACE—A Practical Guide to the Police and Criminal Evidence Act* (3rd edn), Oxford University Press: Oxford.

Police National Legal Database (PNLD), Harfield, C and Sampson, F (eds) (2013) *Blackstone's Police Operational Handbook* (8th edn), Oxford University Press: Oxford.

Rinker, RA (2006) *Understanding Firearm Ballistics* (6th edn), Mulberry House Publishing: USA.

Saferstein, R (2014) *Criminalistics* (11th edn), Pearson Education Limited: Essex.

Zander, M (2013) *The Police and Criminal Evidence Act 1984*, Sweet & Maxwell: London.

Appeal Cases

R v Sean Hoey [2007] NICC 49 Ref: WEI7021.

R v Anthony Edward Martin [2001] EWCA Crim 2245.

R v Sion David Charles Jenkins [2004] EWCA Crim 2047, no 2003/02883/B4.

R v Broughton [2010] EWCA Crim 549.

R v Kuba Dlugosz, R v Pickering and R v MDS [2013] EWCA Crim 2.

R v Reed, Reed and Garmson [2009] EWCA Crim 2698

R v Bewley [2012] EWCA Crim 1457.

R v George (Barry) [2007] EWCA Crim 2722.

R v Dwaine George [2014] EWCA Crim 2507.

R v T [2010] EWCA Crim 2439.

Index

Lightning Source UK Ltd.
Milton Keynes UK
UKHW021436100920
369665UK00001B/1